Guide to Company Information in Great Britain

GUIDE TO COMPANY INFORMATION IN GREAT BRITAIN

Paul Norkett

Published by Longman Group Ltd in
association with ICC Information Group Ltd

Guide to Company Information in Great Britain

Published by Longman Group Limited, Longman House,
Burnt Mill, Harlow, Essex CM20 2JE, United Kingdom

in association with

ICC Information Group Limited, 28–42 Banner St,
London EC1Y 8QE, United Kingdom

British Library Cataloguing in Publication data

Norkett, P.T.C.
Guide to company information in Great Britian.
1. Corporations—Information services—
Great Britain
I. Title II. ICC Information Group
658.4′038′0941 HD2845

ISBN 0–582–97820–3

Printed in Great Britain by Butler and Tanner Ltd, Frome and London

Contents

Chapter 5 HOW TO USE A FINANCIAL DATABASE

ACKNOWLEDGEMENTS

A number of organisations have contributed to the development of this book. Much of the reference material, such as the finance glossary, has been extracted from the author's books *Accountancy for Non Accountants* volumes 1 and 2. These extracts have been used, with the kind permission of the publisher, Longman Group Ltd.

The summary of accounting standards given in Appendix 1 has been kindly provided by Matthew Patient and Leslie Campbell of Deloitte Haskins & Sells.

The accounts used as examples have been extracted from the STC Annual Report 1983 with the kind permission of STC. Permission to reproduce several documents published by the Companies Registration Office has been kindly granted by HMSO.

The databases and subsequent extracts were kindly made available by the main database providers; Datastream, and ICC.

Finally, there has been immense support from the staff at Inter Company Comparisons in providing reference material and proof reading the manuscript. Although every attempt has been made to minimise errors and omissions by the staff at ICC, any errors or important omissions are the responsibility of the author.

PREFACE

The purpose of this book is to provide a reference source for finding information about UK companies and how to interpret the results of the search.

To achieve this objective the book is divided into three main parts linked to reference appendices. The first part comprises two chapters about UK companies and sources of information. The second part a further two chapters on how to read accounts and how to assess company performance including a chapter on how to use a financial date base. The third part comprises for useful appendixes.

Chapter 1 provides an overview of the different legal forms of enterprise in the UK with an emphasis on companies. After explaining the types of enterprise the legal disclosure requirements are described and the role of the statutory auditor. There is also a summary of the markets for UK companies such as the Stock Exchange, Unlisted Securities Market (USM) and Over The Counter (OTC) market.

Chapter 2 focuses on the sources of information about UK companies and industry sectors. The chapter explains the increasing use of computer databases and summaries other sources of published information. This chapter is supported by Appendices 2, 3 and 4 which give extensive details of official and commercial sources of information, as well as details of the forms required by the Registrar of Companies that may be found when searching the public record.

Chapters 3 and 4 are provided for the non financial specialist and explain in considerable detail how to read accounts and how to assess corporate performance. Linked to these two chapters are two appendices. Appendix 1 briefly explains the different accounting standards that may be referred to in the accounts. Appendix 5 contains a large glossary of specialist financial terminology that the non financial specialist will find useful.

The final chapter explains, with many worked examples, how to use a financial database. Four financial datebases were used for the examples. Datastream to illustrate share price and related investor information, ICC Dialog file and ICC Viewdata file to illustrate accounting data that can be accessed for a variety of uses and Sharewatch for information about shareholdings in companies and different shareholders' portfolios.

1

UK COMPANIES

Introduction

Most UK businesses are incorporated (i.e. companies). This chapter will explain the different types of corporations found in the UK and their disclosure requirements.

In the UK there are some 1,000,000 incorporated businesses. Only about 2,200 of these companies are listed on the London Stock Exchange with a further 300 companies in the Unlisted Securities Market.

Before looking at the legal framework and information disclosure requirements of companies registered in the UK, this chapter will briefly review other types of enterprise.

Different forms of UK enterprise

Businesses in the UK can be broadly divided into the following categories:

Sole traders
Partnerships
Companies
Miscellaneous enterprises such as Associations, Societies and Clubs

Sole traders

These are people engaged in business on their own. Until recently they were required to register under the Business Names Act 1916 if they were not operating under their own name. The 1916 Act was repealed in the Companies Act 1981 and the Business Names Registry abolished.

Partnerships

This is where two or more people run a business where they are jointly and severally liable for the debts and liabilities of the firm. Partnerships are the most common form of enterprise for the professions in the UK such as accountants and solicitors because of the restrictions on them practising with limited liability. A partnership may have limited partners whose liability is limited to a specific amount, but not all the partners can be limited (Partnership Act 1880 and Limited Partnership Act 1907). The business names of partnerships are under the same legal restrictions as sole traders.

Neither sole traders nor partnerships are under any legal obligation to provide information about their business to the general public. The only disclosure requirements relate to business names.

Business names

The Registry of Business Names was abolished in 1981. Sole traders, partnerships and companies now have to display the owners, names and addresses at business premises, on business stationery and on request to any customer or supplier. Although a central registry of business names no longer exists, restrictions on the use of names apply to all forms of enterprise. The main restrictions are:

(i) Words which imply national or international pre-eminence, for example:

International	England	Wales
National	English	Welsh
European	Scotland	Ireland
Great Britain	Scottish	Irish
British		

(ii) Words which imply governmental patronage or sponsorship, for example:

Authority	Board	Council

(iii) Words which imply business pre-eminence or representative status, for example:

Association	Society	Institution
Federation	Institute	

(iv) Words which imply specific objects or functions, for example:

Assurance	Chamber of Commerce	Post Office	Building Society
Insurance	Chamber of Trade	Trust	Trade Union
Reinsurance	Chamber of Industry	Stock Exchange	Foundation
Insurer	Co-operative	Register	Fund
Reinsurer	Group	Friendly Society	Charter
Patent	Holdings	Industrial & Provident Society	

(v) There are also words and expressions that require the Secretary of State's consent. In seeking that approval the owner of the business must submit to the Secretary of State a statement that a written request has been made to the relevant body seeking its opinion as to the use of the word or expressions together with a copy of any response received.

These words and expressions include:

Royal,
Royalty
King
Queen
Prince
Princess
Windsor
Duke
His/Her Majesty
Police
Special School
Contact Lens
Dental
Dentistry
Nurse, Nursing
Midwife
Midwifery
Health Visitor
District Nurse
Health Centre
Health Service
Architect
Architectural
Credit Union
Veterinary Surgeon
Dentist
Dental Surgeon
Dental Practitioner
Chemist
Chemistry
Drug
Druggist
Pharmaceutical
Pharmacist
Pharmacy

Sole traders and partnerships are not legally required to provide financial information to the public.

Societies, Associations and Clubs

Building Societies In the UK the most common form of Society is the Building Society. These are governed by the Building Societies Act 1962. They are regulated by the Registrar of Friendly Societies and are required to send audited annual returns and accounts to the Registrar. These accounts are public documents and can be inspected at the Registry. The proforma accounts include the following details:

Number of staff (full and part-time)
Number of branch offices
Details of mortgages
Income and expenditure detail
Assets and liabilities detail
Total advances during the year analysed into size of advance
Salary details
Details of directors

It is best to let the Registry know what documents are required beforehand. There is a search fee and documents can be photocopied. Further information is available from: The Registry of Friendly Societies, 15/17 Great Marlborough Street, London W1N 2AY, telephone (01) 437 9992.

Trade Unions and Employers' Associations Registered trade unions and employers' associations are required to send annual returns and accounts to the Certification Officer. These are public documents and can be obtained by post, after paying the fee, or by visiting the Certification Office. Further information is available from The Certification Officer of Trade Unions & Employers' Association, Vincent House Annexe, Hide Place, London SW1P 4N6, telephone (01) 821 6144/6, or for Scotland, The Assistant Certification Officer for Scotland, 19 Heriot Row, Edinburgh EH3 6HT, telephone (031) 556 4371.

Clubs Clubs are often registered as companies limited by guarantee and annual returns and accounts are filed at Companies House as public documents. Alternatively, they may be registered as Friendly Societies and would then have to make annual returns and accounts to the Registrar of Friendly Societies where they would become public documents. If they are not registered at either of these places then the written constitution of clubs usually requires them to provide annual accounts for their members.

Charities UK registered charities are legally required to submit annual accounts and related information to the Charities Commission. These documents are held on public record. Further information is available from Charities Commission, 14 Ryder Street, London SW1Y 6AH, telephone (01) 214 6875/8773. Additional information is available from the Charities Aid Foundation (0732-356323).

Corporations in the UK

These are legal entities separate from the members and the agents which act on their behalf. A corporation created by law has perpetual existence and can only be destroyed by the law. The different types of corporation are shown in Figure 1:1 and the following notes are intended as a layman's guide through the legal maze.

Figure 1.1 Different types of UK corporation

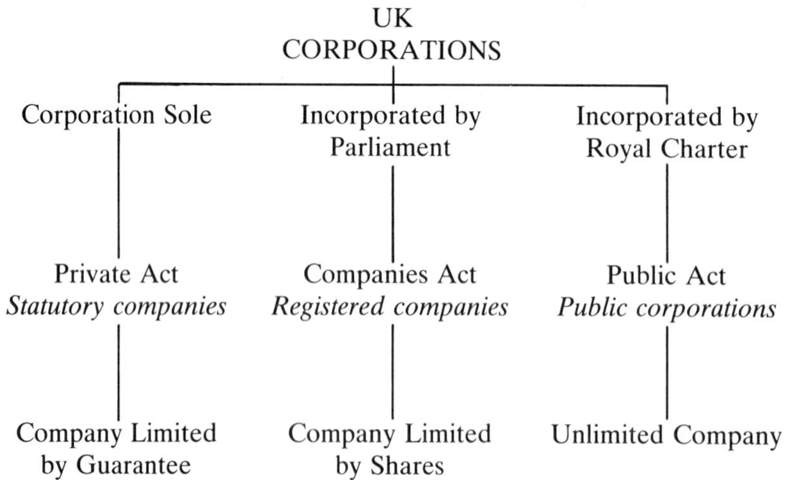

Corporations sole are of little general interest. They are meant to distinguish an important office from an individual, for example the Sovereign, a Bishop or Vicar, a Minister or Officer of the Crown such as the Public Trustee or Postmaster General. All other corporations are *Corporations Aggregate* where the legal entity has two or more members.

Corporations incorporated by Royal Charter date back to the seventeenth century when companies such as The East India Company and the Hudson Bay Company were granted charters of incorporation by the Crown. The Monarch may still grant a charter to groups of subjects who petition for that purpose. A royal charter was granted to the BBC in 1926. Some sections of company law apply to chartered companies unless the company is exempted by the Department of Trade.

Corporations incorporated by Parliament are created for specific purposes by the passing of an Act by Parliament. There are three main types of Act: private, public and general Acts referred to as Companies Acts. The three types are explained below.

(i) *Private Acts* of parliament were passed in the eighteenth century for the construction of large undertakings such as canals, harbours and railways. These corporations are referred to as *statutory companies* and their members and agents are subject to the provisions of a series of Acts known as 'Clauses Acts'. For example, The Harbours, Docks and Piers Clauses Act 1847 regulates statutory companies that were incorporated for these areas of enterprise.

(ii) *Public Acts* of parliament are passed when an industry is to be nationalised or promoted by the state because of its national importance. These are referred to as *Public Corporations*. This type of corporation does not have shareholders. It is responsible to government and major policy decisions are usually made by Parliament through the relevant Minister. Examples of public corporations are The National Coal Board by the Coal Industry Nationalisation Act 1946 or The British Railways Board under The Transport Act 1962.

(iii) *Companies Acts* which will allow companies to be incorporated by registration instead of special acts or royal charter began in 1844 with the Joint Stock Companies Act. Since then Companies Acts have been passed in 1855, 1856, 1862, 1900, 1907, 1908, 1929, 1947, 1948, 1967, 1976, 1980, 1981 and the consolidating legislation in 1985. Amongst all this legislation, the 1948 Act was a landmark in the UK company law. It was this Act that made registered companies accountable to the public, with some exceptions which were later removed by the 1967 Act.

The 1948 Act divided companies into broad categories: public and private. The private companies were further divided into 'private ordinary' and 'private exempt'. The major differences between public and private companies were that a private company had restrictions on share transfers and member limitation of 50, whilst the public company had no such restrictions. The distinction between the ordinary and exempt private company was not so simple. Essentially the exempt status was devised to save the small family business from publicly disclosing details about its operations. The exempt status was therefore not available to corporate subsidiaries. By the time the 1967 Companies Act abolished the exempt company status there were approximately 275,000 exempt private companies compared with only 12,400 ordinary private companies.

Companies limited by Guarantee do not need to obtain their initial capital from their members. Members only have to guarantee that funds will be available to the stated limit in the event of the company winding up. This type of enterprise is not generally considered suitable for business ventures. It is usually used by professional or trade associations or groups of individuals engaged in social or recreational activities. There are two types of guarantee company; a company limited by guarantee and having a share capital; or a company limited by guarantee and not having a share capital. The former is where the company required some initial capital and the latter where no initial capital was necessary.

Unlimited companies are included in the Companies Acts mainly because the formation of partnerships or other types of unincorporated businesses with more than twenty members is prohibited (Section 434 Companies Act 1948). This type of company is similar to a partnership because all the members of the company are liable to the company's creditors. The main differences between unlimited companies and partnerships are: the unlimited company has a separate legal existence, is subject to company law and is not restricted to a maximum of 20 members. The published name of the company does not need to incorporate the word 'Limited'.

Companies limited by shares are the most important classification of business unit in the UK Registered companies are divided into public and private. The main differences are that a public company can have more members and has no restrictions on the transfer of its shares.

(i) *Public companies* can openly invite the public to buy their shares and there is no maximum legal number of members. Under the 1980 Companies Act the company's name must be suffixed by the words 'public limited company' or 'p.l.c.' If the company is registered in Wales the suffix of 'cwmni cyfyngedig cyhoeddus' or c.c.c. is included. A public company is also required to have a minimum issued share capital of £50,000. The important distinction between a public and private company is the legal restriction on private companies' share issues, whereas the public company may issue shares to the public. Issue of shares is usually arranged by an issuing house. For shares to be issued to the public the company has to produce as 'prospectus' which contains the background to the foundation of the company and its current financial position.

Public companies are divided into quoted (listed) and unquoted (unlisted). Quoted means they have a stock exchange quotation for their shares to be bought and sold on the exchange and they are subject to stock exchange regulations. The main British stock exchange is in London. The British stock exchange system works under the principle of self regulation by the City. The two important regulators are The Council of the London Stock Exchange and The Panel on Takeovers and Mergers. One important form of investor protection is a regular supply of reliable and relevant information. This supply of information in the UK is through self regulation by the City. The disclosure requirements of the city regulators for listed companies are additional to the company law requirements.

(ii) *Private companies* have legal restrictions on the rights of members to transfer their shares. Basically, a shareholder in a private company cannot sell his/her shares on the open market. When the shares are to be sold a company valuation has to be made because there is no open market value. However there exists an 'over the counter' (OTC) market for the sale of unlisted company shares. Also the Stock Exchange is becoming more active in this area under their Rule 163 which allows jobbers to trade in unlisted securities if the Quotation Department gives specific permission for each deal.

The number of members of a private company is limited to 50 but this does not include employees and ex-employees holding shares.

The 1948 Companies Act divided private companies into private ordinary and private exempt. The exempt status was meant to protect the small family business and gave certain privileges such as not having to file annual accounts with the Registrar of Companies. The exempt status and privileges were abolished in the 1967 Companies Act. However the principle of exempting the small private company from part of the disclosure requirements of large public companies has been introduced into the EEC Fourth Directive. UK legislation to create a small private company, was introduced into the Companies Act 1981. This Act created for the first time, size categories of companies into small, medium and large designed to reduce the legal disclosure requirements for the small company. For instance, since June 1982, a small company does not have to provide a profit and loss account or directors' report.

A company is now classed as a small or medium size if it meets two or more of the following criteria:

	small	medium
Turnover not above	£1.4 mn	£5.75 mn
Gross assets not above	£0.7 mn	£2.8 mn
Average number of employees not above	50	250

Rights and responsibilities of auditors

The 1948 Companies Act was the auditor's licence. Section 161 of the Act gives authority to the Secretary of State for Trade to approve the qualifications of auditors. The recognised accountancy bodies for auditing are the institutions of Chartered Accountants in England, Wales, Scotland and Ireland and the Chartered Association of Certified Accountants. Some 4,000 individuals who are not members of these bodies have also been recognised and these are usually referred to as section 161 auditors. Not all members of the recognised accountancy bodies can sign the statutory audit report. The profession has its own strict set of rules for auditors. Only members who meet the profession's requirements can hold a *practising certificate* that authorises them to sign the statutory audit report.

The Act requires that every limited company at its Annual General Meeting shall appoint/reappoint the auditors. The appointed auditors have a legal right of access to the company's books of accounts. They are required to examine the accounts to be laid before the members of the AGM and report to the members if the accounts are a 'true and fair view' of the underlying records and the state of affairs of the business. This legal requirement of 'true and fair view' left the accountancy profession with a fairly wide are of discretion.

Therefore the profession has produced auditing and accounting standards in an attempt to limit the boundaries of discretion surrounding the 'true and fair view' concept. Accounting standards are explained in Appendix 1.

The legal rights of auditors can be divided into statutory and common law rights. Company law gives the statutory auditor the following rights:

(i) Access to all material information that is necessary for the normal conduct of an audit.

(ii) Explanations from officers of the company on matters necessary for the audit. The auditor does not have to explain why he is asking the questions. The legal responsibilities of officers of a company were increased in the 1976 Companies Act. It is now a legal offence if a director or company secretary gives misleading or false information to auditors. The auditor has no legal right to attend board meetings.

(iii) Attendance at general meetings of the company are a legal right as well as a responsibility. After the audit opinion is read out at the meeting, any shareholders' questions have to be made to the board of directors. The shareholders have no legal right to demand explanations directly from the auditor.

(iv) The auditor's appointment and fees are approved at each AGM. If a change of auditor is proposed notice must be given to the existing auditor, new auditor and the shareholders. The outgoing auditor has a right to present a written statement to the shareholders.

The auditor's Common Law rights are a right of lien over the books and documents of the company that the auditor has worked on and not received payment for, and rights under the law of contract. The document that outlines the auditor's contractual rights is the letter of engagement.

Auditors have onerous responsibilities to their clients, to third parties (in certain circumstances) and to their profession. They can be subject to criminal prosecution for fraud, civil actions in contract and tort, and disciplinary actions by their professional body for misconduct. The auditor client relationship is particularly difficult if the client does not appreciate the importance of the auditor's ethical code of conduct.

The auditor has a responsibility to report to the members of the AGM that the profit and loss account and balance sheet are a true and fair view of the state of the company's affairs. To make this statement the auditors have to be sure that proper books of account have been kept and there are adequate systems of internal administrative and financial controls. They also have to be certain that the audited financial statements reflect the underlying records and conform with the requirements of company law, accounting standards and stock exchange regulations where applicable.

The audited financial statements

The auditor has to be satisfied that the underlying records are reliable and accurate. Once the auditor is satisfied with the records and systems of internal control, he/she then has to be sure that the financial statements are a true and fair view of these records and the state of affairs of the business.

The statutory minimum financial statements are the profit and loss account and balance sheet. There are also accounting standards (see Appendix 1) requiring a funds flow statement for companies with a turnover above £25,000. The auditor is required to state in the audit report what financial statements have been audited.

The audit of a company's financial statements will include the following:-

(i) The statements are a true and fair view of the underlying records.
(ii) Full disclosure has been made of all material items.
(iii) The comparative figures for the previous year have been calculated and presented so that the valid comparisons between the two years' figures can be made.
(iv) The statements conform with company law requirements, accounting standards and stock exchange regulations where applicable.

Copies of the audited financial statements are made available to the company's shareholders and to the public through the Registrar of Companies.

UK companies' disclosure requirements

The first legal requirement for companies to disclose information about their activities was contained in the Companies Act 1970. This required public companies to produce an annual audited balance sheet for their shareholders. However, there were no specific requirements for the contents of the balance sheet and no conditions concerning the professional qualifications for auditors.

The 1948 Companies Act provides the foundations for UK company law even though amending Companies Acts have been passed since in 1967, 1976, 1980 and 1981.

The company law disclosure foundations laid down in the 1948 Companies Act were

(i) Public and private companies were required to present to their shareholders at an annual general meeting (AGM) the audited accounts.
(ii) The professional qualifications of auditors and their duty to present a true and fair view became law.
(iii) The minimum content of the accounts to be disclosed was defined.
(iv) Public and private companies were required to lodge a copy of their annual accounts and an annual return with the Registrar of Companies for public record.

Many of the points of detail attached to the disclosure provisions in the 1948 Companies Act have been amended subsequently such as the removal of the exempt private companies status in the 1967 Companies Act and the introduction of the small company reporting provisions in the 1981 Companies Act. But the fundmental requirement of providing audited annual accounts for shareholders and the public record is still intact.

Disclosure to shareholders

The disclosure requirements to shareholders are governed by company law, accounting standards and, in the case of companies quoted on the Stock Exchange, the Stock Exchange regulations.

Shareholders in quoted companies receive a copy of the annual report and accounts as explained in some detail in Chapter 2. A set of shareholders accounts will contain *Audited statements*: Balance sheet, Profit and loss account, Statement of funds flow, an

optional statement showing the effect of changing prices on balance sheet and profit and loss items, Report of the Directors, Notes to the accounts supporting the above statements, Report of the Auditors, Notice of Annual General Meeting (AGM).
Supplementary statements: There are many kinds of supplementary statements included in the shareholders' accounts that are generally not subject to the close scrutiny and true and fair view criteria of the auditor. These supplementary statements include statement by the chairman, added value statement and statements of future prospects. Chapter 2 explains these supplementary statements in detail.

Disclosure to employees

There is currently (1985) no legal obligation for companies to provide accounts or other corporate information for employees. The 1971 Industrial Relations Act introduced a reporting requirement for employees for any company with more than 350 employees but this Act was repealed in 1974 and subsequent labour law legislation did not re-introduce reporting for employees.

Some disclosure requirements were included in the Contracts of Employment Act 1963, Redundancy Payments Act 1965, Health & Safety at Work Act 1974, and the Social Security Pensions Act 1975. In the Employment Protection Act 1975 registered trade unions were given legal rights to demand information for collective bargaining.

Although there is no statutory requirement for companies to produce employee accounts, many companies produce them either as separate documents or included in the company's house journal. Details about employee accounts are given in chapter 2.

The public record

Company law requires companies to provide annual returns, accounts and certain other documents to the Registrar of Companies at the Companies Registration Office (Companies House), which is a part of the Department of Trade and Industry responsible for keeping on public record the annual returns and accounts of companies. Microfiche copies of company returns are held in London and there are separate Company Registration Offices in Edinburgh and Dublin. Companies are legally required to submit an annual return and accounts to the Registrar of Companies every year. However it was possible for companies to delay their AGM and delay sending in accounts. This practice was almost nullifying the system because accounts were often filed several years in arrears. The Companies Act 1976 sought to alter this practice and laid down tougher requirements. A private company must now submit accounts within ten months of the end of its accounting period and other companies have a seven month time allowance.

Figure 1.2 shows the information which companies are required to disclose for public record.

Figure 1.2 Summary of UK company disclosure requirements

	plc	Ltd
Directors Report and Accounts	7 months after financial year end	10 months after financial year end
Annual Return	42 days after Annual General Meeting	42 days after Annual General Meeting
Mortgage Register	21 days after creation of new mortgage	21 days after creation of new mortgage
Memorandum and Articles of Association	Upon Incorporation	Upon Incorporation
Change of Director	Within 14 days	Within 14 days
Increase in Share Capital	15 days after company passes resolution	15 days after company passes resolution

Directors' Report and Accounts:
a) Directors' Report – principal activities, business review, dividends declared, export figures, directors' interest in shares.
b) Auditors' Report
c) Profit and Loss Account
d) Balance Sheet
e) Notes to the Accounts

Annual Return:
a) Legal address of the company (registered office)
b) Issued Share Capital and class of shares issued
c) Shareholders' names and their shareholding
d) Names and home addresses of directors, together with other Directorships held
e) Total amount of indebtedness through debentures or mortgages.

Mortgage Register:
a) Date created and type of mortgage
b) Asset/s over which mortgage is charged
c) Company/bank extending the mortgage
d) Indication of whether paid off or still outstanding

Memorandum and Articles of Association:
a) The Memorandum governs the powers through which the company may trade
b) The Articles govern the internal structure of the company, i.e. the power of directors, rules governing meetings of shareholders

Changes

Apart from the changes shown above, a registered company will also be required to lodge with the Registrar of Companies any change in registered office or company name and, perhaps most importantly, any liquidation of winding-up proceedings. Changes have to be notified using the appropriate form. Appendix 4 provides a full list of the forms used by the Registrar of Companies.

The Stock Exchange

The Stock Exchange is an authoritative body which can exercise control without legal sanctions. The Council of the Stock Exchange is concerned about the information flow to existing and potential investors. The information flows may be divided into the following categories:

(i) Admission of a company for a stock exchange quotation.
(ii) The issue of shares and debentures
(iii) Regular provision of relevant information for investors.

For a company seeking a quotation the information requirements for the prospectus are contained in Schedule 11 Part A of the Council's rules 'Admission of Securities to Listing'. These rules are very detailed and exceed company law requirements. Once a company is accepted on the stock exchange it has to follow the rules of the stock exchange 'Listing Agreement'. These rules are closely aligned to company law and accounting standards but the listing emphasis is on investor needs.

Recent Companies Acts

The disclosure requirements explained so far in this chapter relate to the general legal conditions concerning reporting to shareholders, employees and the public through Companies House. The detailed financial statements sent to shareholders and to the Registrar of Companies are explained in chapter 2.

These legal disclosure requirements applied to all companies for accounts filed up to the 14 June 1982. After that date the 1981 Companies Act disclosure rules apply bringing UK company law closer into line with EEC company law.

The major disclosure provisions of this Act reduced the disclosure requirements for two new classes of companies defined as *small* and *medium-sized*, see page 9. These new classes of companies have been able to file accounts since June 1982 which contain less information than the full accounts previously required. However, all companies must still prepare full accounts for their shareholders.

The reduction in disclosure requirements is quite considerable. For a small company only a Balance Sheet with the main headings and a few notes is required plus a special audit report. A medium-sized company still has to provide a full set of accounts, but the content does not have to be so detailed. A key figure that does not have to be shown is turnover. Medium-sized companies also have a special audit report.

The 1981 Companies Act for the first time prescribed the form and content of accounts and laid down statutory rules which have codified some accounting standards. The prescribed formats are shown in the figure below. These were embodied in the Companies Consolidation Act 1985.

Figure 1.3 Balance Sheet Format 1 (Companies Act 1981)

Called up share capital not paid

Fixed assets

Intangible assets
1. Development costs
2. Concessions, patents, licences, trade marks and similar rights and assets
3. Goodwill
4. Payments on account

Tangible assets
1. Land and buildings
2. Plant and machinery
3. Fixtures, fittings, tools and equipment
4. Payments on account and assets in course of construction

Investments
1. Shares in group companies
2. Loans in group companies
3. Shares in related companies
4. Loans in related companies
5. Other investments other than loans
6. Other loans
7. Own shares

Current assets

Stocks
1. Raw materials and consumables
2. Work in progress
3. Finished goods and goods for resale
4. Payments on account

Debtors
1. Trade debtors
2. Amounts owed by group companies
3. Amounts owed by related companies
4. Other debtors
5. Called up share capital not paid
6. Prepayments and accrued income

Investments
1. Shares in group companies
2. Own shares
3. Other investments

Cash at bank and in hand

Prepayments and accrued income

Creditors: amounts falling due within one year

1. Debenture loans
2. Bank loans and overdrafts
3. Payments received on account
4. Trade creditors
5. Bills of exchange payable
6. Amounts owed to group companies
7. Amounts owed to related companies
8. Other creditors including taxation and social security
9. Accruals and deferred income

Net current assets (liabilities)

Total assets less current liabilities

Creditors: amounts falling due after more than one year

1. Debenture loans
2. Bank loans and overdrafts
3. Payments received on account
4. Trade creditors
5. Bills of exchange payable
6. Amounts owed to group companies
7. Amounts owed to related companies
8. Other creditors including taxation and social security
9. Accruals and deferred income

Provisions for liabilities and charges

1. Pensions and similar obligations
2. Taxation, including deferred taxation
3. Other provisions

Accruals and deferred income

Capital and reserves

Called up share capital

Share premium account

Revaluation reserve

Other reserves

1. Capital redemption reserve
2. Reserve for own shares
3. Reserves provided for by the articles of association
4. Other reserves

Profit and loss account

Figure 1.4 Balance Sheet Format 2 (Companies Act 1981)

ASSETS

Called up share capital not paid

Fixed assets

Intangible assets
1. Development costs
2. Concessions, patents, licences, trade marks and similar rights and assets
3. Goodwill
4. Payments on account

Tangible assets
1. Land and buildings
2. Plant and machinery
3. Fixtures, fittings, tools and equipment
4. Payments on account and assets in course of construction

Investments
1. Shares in group companies
2. Loans to group companies
3. Shares in related companies
4. Loans to related companies
5. Other investments other than loans
6. Other loans
7. Own shares

Current assets

Stocks
1. Raw materials and consumables
2. Work in progress
3. Finished goods and goods for resale
4. Payments on account

Debtors
1. Trade debtors
2. Amounts owed by group companies
3. Amounts owed by related companies
4. Other debtors
5. Called up share capital not paid
6. Prepayments and accrued income

Investments
1. Shares in group companies
2. Own shares
3. Other investments

Cash at bank and in hand

Prepayments and accrued income

LIABILITIES

Capital and reserves

Called up share capital

Share premium account

Revaluation reserve

Other reserves
1. Capital redemption reserve
2. Reserve for own shares
3. Reserves provided for by the articles of association
4. Other reserves

Profit and loss account

Provisions for liabilities and charges
1. Pensions and similar obligations
2. Taxation including deferred taxation
3. Other provisions

Creditors
1. Debenture loans
2. Bank loans and overdrafts
3. Payments received on account
4. Trade creditors
5. Bills of exchange payable
6. Amounts owed to group companies
7. Amounts owed to related companies
8. Other creditors including taxation and social security
9. Accruals and deferred income

Accruals and deferred income

Figure 1.5 Profit and Loss Account Format 1 (Companies Act 1981)

1. Turnover
2. Cost of sales
3. Gross profit and loss
4. Distribution costs
5. Administrative expenses
6. Other operating income
7. Income from shares in group companies
8. Income from shares in related companies
9. Income from other fixed asset investments
10. Other interest receivable and similar income
11. Amounts written off investments
12. Interest payable and similar charges
13. Tax on profit or loss on ordinary activities
14. Profit or loss on ordinary activities after taxation
15. Extraordinary income
16. Extraordinary charges
17. Extraordinary profit or loss
18. Tax on extraordinary profit or loss
19. Other taxes not shown under the above items
20. Profit or loss for the financial year

Figure 1.6 Profit and Loss Account Format 2 (Companies Act 1981)

1. Turnover
2. Change in stocks of finished goods and in work progress
3. Own work capitalised
4. Other operating income
5. *(a)* Raw materials and consumables
   (b) other external charges
6. Staff costs:
   (a) wages and salaries
   (b) social security costs
   (c) other pension costs
7. *(a)* Depreciation and other amounts written off tangible and intangible fixed assets
   (b) Exceptional amounts written off current assets
8. Other operating charges
9. Income from shares in group companies
10. Income from shares in related companies
11. Income from other fixed asset investments
12. Other interest receivable and similar income
13. Amounts written off investments
14. Interest payable and similar charges
15. Tax on profit or loss on ordinary activities
16. Profit or loss on ordinary activities after taxation

17. Extraordinary income
18. Extraordinary charges
19. Extraordinary profit or loss
20. Tax on extraordinary profit or loss
21. Other taxes not shown under the above items
22. Profit or loss for the financial year

Figure 1.7 Profit and Loss Account Format 3 (Companies Act 1981)

Charges
1. Cost of sales
2. Distribution costs
3. Administrative expenses
4. Amounts written off investments
5. Interest payable and similar charges
6. Tax on profit or loss on ordinary activities
7. Profit or loss on ordinary activities after taxation
8. Extraordinary charges
9. Tax on extraordinary profit or loss
10. Other taxes not shown under the above items
11. Profit or loss for the financial year

Income
1. Turnover
2. Other operating income
3. Income from shares in group companies
4. Income from shares in related companies
5. Income from other fixed asset investments
6. Other interest receivable and similar income
7. Profit or loss on ordinary activities after taxation
8. Extraordinary income
9. Profit or loss for the financial year

Figure 1.8 Profit and Loss Account Format 4 (Companies Act 1981)

Charges
1. Reduction in stocks of finished goods and in work in progress
2. *(a)* Raw materials and consumables
   (b) Other external charges
3. Staff costs:
   (a) wages and salaries
   (b) social security costs
   (c) other pension costs
4. *(a)* Depreciation and other amounts written off tangible and intangible fixed assets
   (b) Exceptional amounts written off current assets
5. Other operating charges
6. Amounts written off investments
7. Interest payable and similar charges
8. Tax on profit or loss on ordinary activities
9. Profit or loss on ordinary activities after taxation
10. Extraordinary charges
11. Tax on extraordinary profit or loss
12. Other taxes not shown under the above items
13. Profit or loss for the financial year

Income
1. Turnover
2. Increase in stocks of finished goods and in work in progress
3. Own work capitalised
4. Other operating income
5. Income from shares in group companies
6. Income from shares in related companies
7. Income from other fixed asset investments
8. Other interest receivable and similar income
9. Profit or loss on ordinary activities after taxation
10. Extraordinary income
11. Profit or loss for the financial year

Markets for companies

In the UK there are three markets where the public can buy shares in companies. They are: the Stock Exchange, the Unlisted Securities Market (USM) and Over the Counter (OTC) Market.

Stock Exchange

The Stock Exchange is a market place where shares in companies and fixed interest stocks issued by government, local authorities and companies are bought and sold. For a company's shares to be sold on the Stock Exchange it must be a public company and be approved by the Stock Exchange for 'listing'. Once on the list the company's quoted price is determined by market forces. Public companies wanting to be quoted on the Stock Exchange have to meet extensive disclosure requirements as stated in the Stock Exchange rules on 'Admission of Securities for Listing'. The dislcosure document that provides all the information for prospective and existing shareholders is called the 'prospectus'.

Thus unlisted or unquoted companies are those whose shares are not bought and sold on a Stock Exchange, except for those trading under rule 163, see **USM** below.

Over the Counter Market (OTC)

Some companies which do not want to go through the lengthy and costly procedure of obtaining a listing on the Stock Exchange can still have their shares bought and sold in the so-called 'over the counter' (OTC) market. The OTC market was well established in the USA but did not start developing in the UK until the 1970's. The shares in these unlisted companies were being bought and sold by licensed dealers who were in effect creating their own market place. The real boost to the UK OTC market came with the introduction of the Business Expansion Scheme (BES). The scheme started in 1981 as the Business Start Up Scheme and was then improved in 1982 and renamed the Business Expansion Scheme. This scheme offered handsome tax relief to equity investors in certain unlisted companies. As a result the OTC market boomed with many licensed dealers acting as market makers between investors looking for BES tax approved companies and unlisted companies looking for equity funding.

Unlisted Securities Market (USM)

Under the Stock Exchange rule 163 dealings in unlisted securities were allowed on the Stock Exchange subject to certain constraints. In 1980 the Stock Exchange relaxed its 163 rule and the USM began to develop. Now companies who do not want or do not qualify for a full listing on the Stock Exchange can apply for a '163 quotation' which is less expensive and does not have so many regulations attached to the prospectus as a full listing. It is possible for a company to progress through the markets from OTC to USM and then for a full listing on the Stock Exchange.

Market changes

Legislation is to be introduced to reform financial services in the UK. The White Paper on Financial Services in the UK has proposed a new framework for investor protection and opening up the closed environment of the London Stock Exchange. As part of the new framework, the 4,500 members of the London Stock Exchange have voted on a range of changes such as allowing 'outsiders' to own member firms, the removal of single capacity that is the separation of the jobber (market maker) from the broker (investor's agent) and the abolition of fixed commissions.

The move to dual capacity and removal of fixed commissions are due to take place in October 1986. 'Outsiders' such as the UK clearing banks and other financial institutions have been buying stakes in London Stock Exchange firms in preparation for deregulation. Markets in UK securities are being developed through Authorised Depositary Receipts (ADR's) by traders in New York and other leading Stock Exchanges. There are also off-Exchange markets being developed by financial institutions. With the growth of electronic transaction systems (see databases, Chapter 2) additional markets for UK securities will come into existence to compete with existing markets.

2

SOURCES OF BUSINESS INFORMATION

The provision of business related information and the means of communicating it are high growth industry sectors. A decade ago a large part of business information was published in the form of of directories, surveys, fact books and specialist magazines. This traditional hard copy form of storing and communicating information is still a main-stream publishing activity. But the real growth industry sector is the database where information is stored in digital form.

There are now thousands of databases and the number is growing daily. Even the most traditional of hard copy publishers are moving into what is generally called electronic publishing. Thus most areas of business information are, or soon will be, available in electronic form.

Once a publisher has created a database in digital form there are three main publishing options:

(i) Hard copy publications in the form of regularly updated directories or fact books.

(ii) Off line arrangements where subscribers can buy updated magnetic tape, hard or floppy disks that can be run on their own computer.

(iii) On line arrangements where subscribers can connect directly into the publisher's data base for interrogating the file and analysing the data.

The UK information industry is still in the transition phase from hard copy to electronic publishing and so both forms of business information are readily available. This chapter describes the main sources of business related information in both hard copy and electronic format. Details of major data bases are given in Appendix 2 and official information sources in Appendix 3.

This book is primarily concerned with sources of information relating to UK companies. However, from an investor's viewpoint, markets are becoming more international and information may be required on foreign companies. Therefore, Figure 2.1 lists sources of company information for American, European and UK companies with cross references to sub sections in this chapter.

Figure 2.1 Sources of Company Information

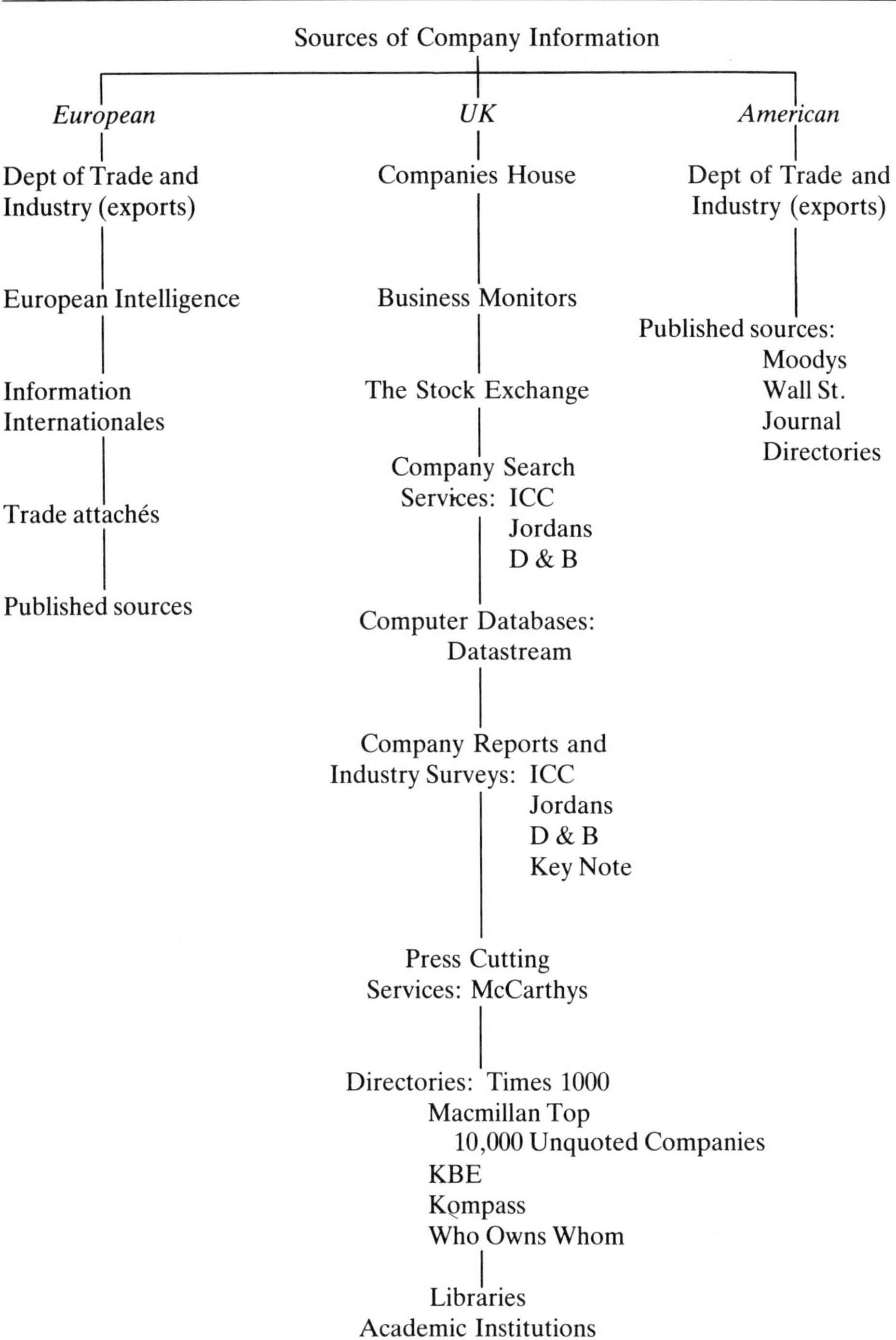

Companies House

The original data source for the accounts of UK registered companies is at Companies House. The addresses and telephone numbers of Companies House are given below. From this basic data source a wide variety of commercial information services have developed. The services take the form of publications such as directories, year books and surveys, search services and computer database services.

Anyone can purchase microfiche of a company's returns and accounts from Companies House at the following locations:
England Companies House, 55 City Rd, London EC1, telephone (01) 253 9393
Wales Companies House, Crown Way, Maindy, Cardiff CF4 3U2, telephone (0222) 388588
Scotland Companies House, Exchequer Chambers, 102 George St, Edinburgh EH2 3DJ, telephone (031) 225 5774
Ireland Companies Office, Dublin Castle, Dublin, telephone (0001) 713511

Business Monitors

Business monitors are an important part of government statistics about UK industry and commerce. The main categories of government industry statistics are:

Category	**Source**
Output	Production census and Business Monitors
Labour	Production census, British Labour Statistics Yearbook and New Earnings Survey
Material costs	Wholesale price indices and Price Index Numbers for Current Cost Accounting (PINCCA)
Finance	Business Monitor on Company Finance and financial statistics
Trade	Business Monitors and Trade statistics

A detailed guide is available from HMSO called *A Guide to Official Statistics*.

The main categories of Business Monitors are:
PM Series – Monthly Production Monitors
PQ Series – Quarterly Production Monitors
PA Series – Annual Census of Production Reports
SDM Series – Monthly Service & Distribution Monitors
SDQ Series – Quarterly Service & Distribution Monitors and
SDO Series – Annual Census of Distribution and Other Services
M Series – Miscellaneous Monitors
Business Monitors may be purchased from the Library, Business Statistics Office, Cardiff Road, Newport, Gwent NPT 1XG, Telephone (0633) 56111 ext. 2973, or

subscription arranged through HMSO, PO Box 276, London SW8 5DT. A full list of Business Monitors is given in Appendix 3.

Other government sources

The Government Statistical Service (GSS) comprises the statistics divisions of all major departments plus the two big collecting agencies – Business Statistics Office and the Office of Population Censuses and Surveys – and the Central Statistical Office (CSO), which co-ordinates the system.

The GSS produces a range of free booklets. The most useful to businessmen are *Government Statistics – a brief guide to sources* and *Profit from Facts*. These can be obtained from the Central Statistical Office, Great George Street, London SW1P 3AQ.

A more comprehensive guide is published in *Guide to Official Statistics*.

Companies can use government statistics to compare their own and their competitors' performance in the following areas

Marketing

Business Monitor, Ministry of Agriculture Information Notice or *Housing and Construction Statistics* can be used to compare company performance against general sales trends. In consumer lines, trends in expenditure are available from the *National Food Survey* and the *Family Expenditure Survey*. For test marketing, the *Census of Population* and *Census of Distribution* can provide very localised data on numbers of consumers and retail outlets.

Many statistics are available on a regional or area basis and can assist in determining quotas for area salesmen.

Foreign competition can be monitored through the import figures available from the Customs and Excise Bill of Entry Service.

Contracts

Many contracts contain escalation clauses. The Property Services Agency's *Monthly Bulletin of Construction Indices*, gives the most appropriate materials and labour indices to use.

Buying

Sales trends of materials inputs can be checked through *Business Monitors*, and their prices with the appropriate wholesale prices indices from the Department of Industry.

Personnel

The Department of Employment Gazette and other DE publications provide trends in earnings, wage rates, overtime, unemployment, vacancies, hours of work, work stoppages due to industrial disputes and retail prices.

Management efficiency and finance

Company costs and operating ratios with the relevant industry can be compared, for example,

net output per head, stocks as a percentage of sales, wages per £ of total sales, from the annual *Census of Production*;

return on capital, dividends and interest as a percentage of assets, profits as a percentage of turnover, from *Business Monitor MA3 (Company Finance)*.

Investment

Major investment decisions are made against the background of trends and prospects in the economy. Regular press notices on output, demand, earnings, prices, unemployment, trade, are released by government departments. *Economic Trends* collects them all together once a month.

Each government department prepares and publishes its own statistics via Her Majesty's Stationery Office and may be purchased from government bookshops.

London

49 High Holborn, London WC1 6HB (callers only)	(01) 928 6977
PO Box 569, London SE1 9NH (telephone and mail orders only)	(01) 928 1321

Outside London (callers or mail order)

13A Castle Street, Edinburgh EH2 3AR	(031) 225 6333
80 Chichester Street, Belfast BT1 4JY	(0232) 34488
41 The Hayes, Cardiff CF1 1JW	(0222) 23654
258 Broad Street, Birmingham B1 2HE	(021) 643 3740
Southey House, Wine Street, Bristol BS1 2BQ	(0272) 24306
Brazenose Street, Manchester M60 8AS	(061) 834 7201

There are a number of booksellers who act as HMSO agents.

Department of Trade and Industry (Exports)

The Export Data Branch of the Department of Trade and Industry contains some 50,000 status reports on overseas companies. They are mainly intended for use as guides for UK companies seeking an overseas agent or outlet for their products. The reports do not include credit ratings. (See Appendix 3 for address)

The Stock Exchange

The London Stock Exchange provides continuous broadcasting of securities and commodities prices, economic indicators, and company news on-line for subscribers. The SE Economics Department maintains an extensive coverage of FT-SE index statistics on its TOPIC service, for subscribers.

The service covers the latest information backed by graphs, including options and details of London International Financial Futures Exchange (LIFFE) contracts.

The Stock Exchange also publishes a range of publications available separately or through subscription to the Stock Exchange Fact Service.

Stock Exchange Fact Book

The Stock Exchange Fact Book is produced quarterly and is a reference work containing statistical information about The Stock Exchange and securities industry. The material is produced mainly by the work of The Stock Exchange Statistics Unit.

Stock Exchange Fact Sheet

The Stock Exchange Fact Sheet is produced monthly as a statistical and analytical backup to the Fact Book, but is also a free-standing service in its own right. The tables show the latest information on new companies, share issues, the USM and shares traded.

Shareholder Survey

The Shareholder Survey is an in-depth study of the pattern of equity share ownership.

Stock Exchange Companies

Published quarterly, The Stock Exchange Companies replaces the '1000 Largest Listed United Kingdom Companies', and also incorporates the 'Classification of Equity Securities by Institute of Actuary Groups'. Its contents include the 1000 largest listed UK companies, tabling performance over the last five years and a classification of listed equities by actuary groups providing information for every company on turnover (both UK and overseas), market value, capital employed, pre-tax profit (loss), the number of shareholders and employees, dividends and the chairmen's names.

Also published in this book is information on the Unlisted Securities Market providing details on every USM Company including their activities, the 100 largest Overseas Companies, the 25 largest Irish Companies and an international stock market comparison.

The Stock Exchange also participates in the production of the FT-SE 100 share index.

In general terms the index includes the largest 100 companies, measured by their Stock Exchange valuation. For various reasons however, some companies with large market values are not suitable for inclusion in the 100 Share Index and are thus omitted. The Stock Exchange's leading 100 Companies account for nearly 70% of the total market value of UK equities. Therefore the 100 Share Index represents a substantial part of the market.

The FT-SE 100 Share Index is a weighted arithmetic index. This means that a change in the price is weighted by the issued share capital of the company, so that a 5% change in the smallest constituent has less 'weight' than a 5% price movement in the largest. The capitalisations were summed and given the base figure of 1000.

The base value is recalculated at the beginning of each quarter to reflect changes in the constituents and their market valuations. The issued share capital of most of the constituents should remain constant throughout the quarter, although adjustments are made in the case of rights issues, capitalisations, consolidations or reductions in share capital.

See Appendix 2 for address.

Company Search Services

Because of the cost and time involved in making a search at Companies House a number of companies have developed a search service. They all provide basically the same service and charge for the search and photocopies of one set of accounts. The addresses of the companies are given in Appendix 2. The three main search companies are

Extel Statistical Services Ltd.
ICC Company Information Services Ltd.
Jordan and Sons Ltd.

See page 33 for further information.

Computer Databases

There exists a wide variety of databases that can be distinguished by their subject matter, time frame, format, indexing, accessing and operation. A database can be:

Numeric

A common form of numeric database contains financial data. The financial databases can be divided into *database services* and *real time services*. The financial database usually contains accounting data extracted from Companies House fiche and analysed in a variety of ways such as the ICC database or Jordans. Alternatively price information on securities and commodities is available, usually analysed in time series and various ratios, percentages and graphed such as the Datastream database. These databases collect, store and analyse information and make it readily available for financial analysts and other users. The real time services are growing very rapidly in providing money markets with exchange rates and interest rates information. These price information networks are capable of being used for dealing as well as providing data. Similar real time services exist for commodities and securities. The London Stock Exchange has established its own international electronic stock market through a real time system called 'TOPIC'. A competing real time system for electronic dealing in UK securities is being established by Reuters which already has a firm hold in international currency and commodity markets.

Bibliographic

These databases include name and address listings with sort facilities, various indexes with powerful cross indexing sort facilities and journal/news abstracts or full texts, also with sort facilities. They are used extensively by libraries and research organisations, and are often derived from an existing hard copy product.

Representational

The representational database stores graphic information and is mainly used by the scientific community who may wish to see for instance, pictures of a cell structure as well as the related text. These kinds of databases can also have powerful sort and analysis facilities enabling a researcher to undertake substantial literature searches in a fraction of the time it would have taken using hard copy records.

A distinction needs to be drawn between database producers, database suppliers, database retailers and communication networks.

Database producers

These are publishers and information service companies. They may be working exclusively in electronic form, or converting or supplementing their hard copy operations with electronic publishing. There are two types of producers; non-integrated and integrated. The non-integrated producer compiles and maintains the database but does not get involved in the marketing side of the operation. The integrated producer maintains computer systems for communicating to end users and markets their product both on and off line.

Database distributors (hosts)

Distributors or hosts use their computer systems for creating 'packages' from producers' databases that they can sell to selected markets. The distributors design software to work on producers' data so that it is presented in a saleable format for different markets. Many distributors develop their own databases and thus become integrated producers as well as distributors. Appendix 2 lists distributors and the databases they provide.

Database retailers

These are institutions or private firms which provide information, generally offline, for people and companies that do not have access to databases and do not have the skills to use a database. Some UK libraries such as the Science Reference Library of the British Library (see page 39) are accessing data bases and can offer the public a very comprehensive computer search service. Most library database searches are used to provide a print out of reading references and abstracts on a clearly defined scientific, technical and/or commercial topic.

Communication networks

The two main communication channels are through telephone lines and/or unused lines on television signals. The main television systems are CEEFAX (BBC) and ORACLE (IBA). These teletext systems provide continuous broadcasting of statistics, news and miscellaneous data. The telephone lines provide the main networks. A major network supplier is the Post Office Viewdata system which can connect a subscriber to a wide range of databases to be viewed on a television set and selected data printed out as required. There are also private networks using dedicated terminals connected direct to the host computer with the database using a closed circuit system or renting telephone lines. To reduce telephone line costs, especially for smaller users located a long way from the host computer, packet switched networks are being established through leased telephone lines. A conventional telephone circuit creates a direct link between the user and the database, whereas packet switching can send packets of information through a combination of network routes to link the user and host computer. The eventual outcome of communication network developments will be a universal terminal where a user can access any commercially available database through a single terminal.

Costs and equipment

The equipment needed to use a database can range from the simple Teletext services CEEFAX and ORACLE using an adapted television set to a dedicated terminal. To use an interactive database the equipment will be a telephone, a means of connecting the telephone to the user's computer or dedicated terminal (a modem or acoustic coupler), a computer with a compatible operating system complete with VDU and printer. Assuming the user owns a compatible micro/mini computer system, then the modem or acoustic coupler can be bought or rented to complete the hardware requirements. The database usage costs will depend upon the supplier's charging methods and database usage. Charging methods can include a subscription fee, rental, time usage charges, printing charges and the telephone costs. The telephone costs will include the time/distance charge and additional rental costs such as the charge for British Telecom's Packet Switching Service.

It is the cost and lack of expertise that currently prohibit the wider use of databases. These factors are likely to exclude a wide range of users for a long time and therefore the markets for traditional hard copy publishing in the form of offline services and books, will still be substantial.

Datastream

One of the major commercial computer databases available in the UK is Datastream which provides computer-based information and computation services – both online and in printed form – including investment research, investment accounting and portfolio valuations, together with analysis and graphics capabilities. These services are supported by databases giving international coverage of securities, companies, interest rates, exchange rates, financial futures, commodities and economic series. The databases are continually updated and cater for the financial research information needs of stockbrokers and jobbers, bankers, investment analysts, fund managers, as well as experts in insurance, industry and many other disciplines. These databases cover

(i) Equity stocks – major companies in Australia, Belgium, Canada, France, Germany, Hong Kong, Ireland, Italy, Japan, Netherlands, Scandinavia, Singapore, South Africa, Switzerland, UK, USA. London quoted foreign equities are also covered.

(ii) Fixed Interest Instruments in the UK, Benelux, Canada, France, Germany, Japan, Netherlands, Switzerland and USA including 5,000 International and Eurobonds.

(iii) Company Accounts – all UK quoted and USM companies and 500 of the largest unquoted UK companies and non-UK owned subsidiaries. Data is also collected on selected quoted companies in USA, Canada, France, Germany, Netherlands, Hong Kong and Ireland.

Other databases cover International market indices, interest and exchange rates, commodities, main indicators direct from the OECD, financial and commodity futures and a range of other services. Contact Datastream, Monmouth House, 58–64 City Rd, London EC1Y 2AL, telephone (01) 250 3000.

Company Reports and Industry Surveys

A few informative services specialise in providing in-depth data and analysis on selected companies. The main companies offering this kind of service are:

Extel Statistical Services Ltd
ICC Information Group Ltd
Jordan and Sons Ltd.

Extel Statistical Services Ltd

Extel provides a range of information services on UK companies including:
British Company Card Service Covers about 3400 quoted companies and 2400 unquoted companies. The service cards include details of company activities, Chairman's statement, balance sheets, dividend record, Board members, profit and loss accounts, yields, earnings and capital history. Similar detail is given in the *Fact Sheet Service* which covers a further 1200 companies.
Overseas Company Service Similar to the Annual Card Service for large European, Australian and North American companies.
Shareholding Service. A phone-in service with access to a record of directors' interests and of all other holdings over 5% for every listed company.
New Issues Books A number of publications relating to new issues of share made during the year.
Analysts Service covering about 1500 quoted companies with Trustee status. The service is similar to the British Company Service and provides an analysed and adjusted record of accounting data and share prices that is updated weekly with an average of 30 replacement cards.
Unquoted Company Service covering about 2400 leading unquoted companies with data similar to the British Company Service. Revised cards are sent out weekly.

Company Fact Sheet About 1200 selected companies not covered by other services, providing similar data to the Unquoted Company Service, updated annually.

Extel also provides an offline database service, *Exstat*, which contains the accounts of British quoted and unquoted companies, European companies and Australian companies. Contact Extel Statistical Services Ltd, 37 Paul St, London EC2, telephone (01) 353 3400.

ICC Information Group (ICC)

ICC produce a series of publications covering all areas of company information including:
Business Ratio Reports Covering 60–100 of the leading companies in an industry or sector of industry operating in the UK. The companies are chosen to reflect the actual manufacture or distribution or service of a particular group of products. Industry sectors covered include construction food, drink, chemicals and plastics, electrical and electronics equipment and services, transport equipment and services, metals, engineering, textiles and footwear, paper, printing and publishing, timber and furniture, and miscellaneous categories including glass, jewellery, opticals and defence industries as well as new titles covering agrochemicals, catering, employment agencies, oil and petroleum processors and printed circuit manufacturers.

Data for the *Business Ratio Reports* is extracted from company accounts for a three year period. The reports also show a list of directors, the name of the company secretary and other background information taken from the most recent accounts.
Financial Survey and Company Directories A series of 196 publications covering 100–500 companies and showing comparative figures for turnover, profits before tax, payments to directors, total assets and current liabilities as well as business address, principal activity and holding company details.
Industrial Performance Analysis Published annually, *IPA* is a review of British industry based on an analysis of over 12,000 public and private company accounts and represents a comprehensive survey of the profitability efficiency and growth of British industry over a three year period. The report covers 25 major industrial groupings ranked under 16 headings. A profit and loss account and a balance sheet is constructed for each sector together with performance ratios.
Credit Rating Reports These reports compare the subject company's financial results with those of its own industry sector, arriving at a credit score giving an indication of potential company failure.
Sharewatch ICC's *Sharewatch* service available both on and offline provides the names of all investors who hold ¼% or more issued equity in UK quoted companies.
Datacards The Service covers all limited companies in the UK and can supply a single A4 size report on a company's financial position over a period of up to four years. The cards give details of profit and loss accounts, balance sheet and key ratios calculated from this information, together with information on location, activity and directors.
ICC database Financial information database covering over 70,000 companies available via the Viewdata or Dialog systems.
ICC Services are available from the following addresses:
Business Ratio Reports and *Financial Survey and Company Directories*:
28–42 Banner St, London EC1Y 8QE, telephone (01) 253 3906

Credit Ratings and *Sharewatch*:
51 City Rd, London EC1Y 1AU, telephone (01) 251 6675/4941
ICC Database:
81 City Rd, London EC1Y 1BD, telephone (01) 250 3922

Jordan and Sons Ltd

Jordan publications cover private and foreign-owned companies and rank the major companies in the following industry sectors, electronics, motor distributors, plant hire, printing, road haulage and stationery.
Industrial Surveys Additional industry surveys are available for airlines, animal foods, brewing, publishers, catering, computers (general and software), defence, DIY, food processing, freight forwarders, grocery retailers, hotels, mail order companies, newspapers, pharmaceuticals, security companies, soft drinks and tour operators and travel agents.
Jordanwatch Jordans have recently (1984) launched a computerised service which claims to allow online access to information on 950,000 British companies. Details include date of last filed accounts or return, name changes, share capital, directors and receivership or liquidation documents. For the 35,000 most frequently requested companies further information is available to include profit and loss summaries, balance sheet information, SIC codes and names and addresses of directors. Further information available from Jordan & Sons Ltd, Jordan House, Brunswick Place, London N1 6EE, telephone (01) 253 3030

Dun & Bradstreet

Dun & Bradstreet is one of the largest international business information companies.

The company mainly provides data on business credit and company accounts. In 1984 D&B added to their services by acquiring Datastream (see page 32). Other services include:
Market Identification Service Data on active UK companies and sectors by market and geographic divisions.
Dun & Bradstreet Register Condensed credit rating reports on UK companies (available on subscription only).
Credit Reporting Services based on credit data from the D&B database. Includes overseas credit reports.
Stubbs Tax Services Taxation services for accountants and solicitors.
Key British Enterprises Directory covering 20,000 top UK companies giving details of location, directors, line of business, turnover and number of employees. Also available online.
Who Owns Whom Four volume series of directories covering companies worldwide identifying parent companies, subsidiaries and associates. Also available online.
Dun & Bradstreet Ltd, 28–32 Clifton St, London EC2P 2LY, telephone (01) 377 4377.

Key Note Publications Ltd

The Key Note series of reports encompass a wide range of industrial and commercial market sectors, and contain details of industry structure, market size and trends, recent developments, future prospects and a financial appraisal with brief financial data on a sample of companies. Key Note Publications Ltd, 28–42 Banner St, London EC1Y 8QE, telephone (01) 253 3006.

Press Cuttings Services

There are a number of press cuttings bureaux in the UK each providing a similar service, that is, monitoring a prescribed selection of the daily/weekly national and international press on a subscription basis.

One of the most well-known services is McCarthy Information Ltd which offers a range of services covering UK quoted companies, European, Australian and North American companies, companies by industry, (including special services for property and energy) and an International Banking Service.

Directories

A large and varied number of directories are available covering UK and overseas companies. Many specialise on a single industry while others concentrate on a particular geographical area (*Europe's 15,000 Largest Companies*) or type of information (*Who Owns Whom*).

Trade Directories

The following summary gives the names of the most useful and easily available trade directories. Most trade directories are funded by advertisements or paid entries promoting companies' productions and services.

Yellow Pages and the classified sections of some telephone directories provide a quick indicator of the level of trade and competition for trades and services in local areas. The main detail is address and telephone numbers and advertisements sometimes explain the products and services.

Kelly's Manufacturers and Merchants Directory published by Information Services Ltd, contains an alphabetical listing of over 130,000 businesses with their address and telephone number, tele: and a brief trade description. There are also regional editions of Kelly's directories that have similar business detail and an alphabetical listing of private residents.

Kemps Directory is produced in three volumes covering most of the UK. They contain classified and alphabetical listings of businesses stating their addresses, telephone numbers, telex and brief details of products and services.

Chambers of Trade and Commerce Directories are produced independently by Chambers

covering their own areas. They usually contain alphabetical and classified listings of business in the Chamber's area but are not normally comprehensive because only members and paid insertions are included.
Trade Associations' Directories can be very useful reference sources for a specific industry or industry sector. For example *The Building Societies Association Year Book* provides a lot of detail about individual Building Societies and their finances. Some trade association directories however are simply a vehicle for members and paying subscribers' advertisements. They are not comprehensive and provide little useful information.

General Reference

There are a number of independently compiled directories where the information is systematically collected and is usually of a high standard. They are primarily reference directories and the content is not influenced by advertising.

The Times 1000

A ranking of the 1,000 largest UK companies with brief financial detail. Listings of 500 leading European companies, 100 American companies, 50 Japanese companies, 30 Canadian companies, 20 Australian companies, 20 South African companies and 20 companies from the Republic of Ireland. Brief financial detail is given for each company. There is also some coverage of clearing banks, finance houses, accepting houses, discount houses, property companies, building societies, unit trusts, investment trusts and insurance companies. Published by Times Books Ltd, 16 Golden Sq, London W1, telephone (01) 434 3767.

Top 10,000 Unquoted Companies

Published by Macmillan in association with ICC, this directory lists the top 10,000 private companies in the UK with a turnover of more than £3 million. Financial details are given for the last three years.

Key British Enterprises

A list of the top 20,000 companies in the UK. Details are given of location, directors, line of business, turnover and number of employees. Published by Dun & Bradstreet.

Who Owns Whom

Also available from Dun & Bradstreet. Four volumes covering in detail the pattern of ownership between parent companies, subsidiaries and associates in the UK, Continental Europe, North America and Australasia and the Far East. Detailed indexes cross refer subsidiaries and associates with their parent companies.

Financial Times International Year Books

A series of four annual directories covering international companies in the following industry sectors, oil and gas, mining, insurance and industrials. Published by the Longman Group Ltd.

Europe's 15000 Largest Companies

Ranking of major companies in 16 European Countries with brief financial details. Indexed by country and by industry.

Kompass

Details on products and services as well as directors, address and turnover of the major companies in the UK. Separate volumes cover most European countries as well as the Far East. Published by Information Services Ltd, Windsor Court, East Grinstead House, East Grinstead, W. Sussex RH19 1XA.

Biographical Directories

Sometimes it is necessary to find out about the directors of companies, especially directorships held in other companies. This information is available in the *Directory of Directors* (Information Services Ltd) that provides an alphabetical listing of over 44,000 directors of UK public and private companies. A list of board appointments is entered below each director's name.

Personal details may be available if the director is a public figure and included in one of the *Who's Who* Directories (A &C Black). There are a number of these directories covering political, social academic and industrial leaders and important people. The information usually contains a brief biography including career, publications and honours.

Company information from overseas

There is a variety of sources of information covering companies registered overseas, ranging from the simple ranking in *Europe's 15,000 Largest Companies* to the more detailed information compiled in the relevant country. The most useful sources are:
European Intelligence A weekly service providing reports on European companies. Cumulative issues are published regularly.
Information Internationales An eight volume work produced in France containing details of over 1,000 European companies and their subsidiaries. The volumes are arranged by subject group and country with a quick alphabetical reference index. The company detail includes products, services, management, company background, subsidiaries and a little financial data.

Trade Attachés of relevant Embassies

Some embassies have trade enquiry sections which provide information on request. The request should be in writing and would probably be redirected to the company concerned. If the country has a chamber of commerce office in the UK, details of a company may be available through the chamber.

United States of America

The following sources are useful starting points for information on US-registered companies.
Standard and Poor's *Register of Corporations, Directors and Executives*
Contains information on 37,000 large American and Canadian companies with brief financial data, notes on company structures and biographical details of directors.
Moody's Investors' Services A two card system where a large card contains details of the annual report and a small card has brief details of recent published events. There is a UK and American quoted company service. An American service consists of a series of manuals covering broad subject groups such as industrial or banking. These manuals contain information on companies structures, products and accounts.
Wall Street Journal Index A monthly publication containing up to date references to reports on American companies and major companies outside the USA. Cumulative annual publications are available.
Funk and Scott *Index of Corporations and Industries* A fortnightly index based on reports from over 750 publications. A cumulative index is included regularly and corporations have a separate index.
Standard Directory of Advertisers A directory of over 17,000 major US corporations containing brief company data including detail about personnel.

Libraries

Most libraries carry a range of reference books. Some of the annual publications referred to in this chapter are expensive and therefore only held by the larger public libraries.

In London a major source of business information is at the City Business Library, Gillet House, Basinghall St, London EC2V 5BX (01) 638 8215/6. This library stocks a wide range of current directories, company reports, Extel cards, news abstracting service, statistics, official publications and over 850 periodicals and 100 newspapers are filed and available on request. The advisory staff have a good knowledge of sources of business information and photocopying facilities are available.

The Science Reference Library of the British Library, is the national reference library for science and technology, business and commerce and for patents, trade marks and designs. The Library is freely available for reference by any member of the public without making prior arrangements.

The library has reading rooms at two main sites, Holborn and Aldwych, with literature grouped by subject.

The Holborn Reading Rooms are at 25 Southampton Buildings, Chancery Lane, London WC2A 1AW (01) 405 8721 ext 3345). The literature of physics, chemistry, engineering, technology and commerce is housed here together with all patents and trade mark publications. Most recent publications are on open shelves for immediate consultation. Older items are in reserve store, normally available within 90 minutes.

The Aldwych Reading Room is at 9 Kean Street, Drury Lane, London WC2B 4AT (01) 636 1544 ext 229). The collection here contains the literature of the life sciences and technologies, including biotechnology medicine, earth sciences, astronomy and pure mathematics. Books and recent issues of periodicals are on open shelves or available within minutes. Earlier volumes of periodicals are in reserve store, normally available for consultation within 90 minutes.

The Science Reference Library and City Business Library hold a range of government publications and official statistics. But for a wider selection the *Statistics and Market Intelligence Library* at 1 Victoria Street, London SW1H 0ET should be visited. This library is part of the Department of Trade and Industry but it is open to the general public. Collections include general statistical compilations and statistics of trade, production, distribution, population and other economic topics for all countries of the world.

Official publications are also available at the *Official Publications Library* The British Library at Great Russell Street, London WC1B 3DG.

This library houses permanent files of statistical material including all UK and intergovernmental organisations' publications and the main statistical serials of overseas countries. A reader's ticket is required and it is advisable to telephone first (01) 636 1544 Ext 234/5 to ensure that the items required will be readily available.

The Science Reference Library provides a computer search service by using major online databases. The sources available through the service include the computerised versions of well-known journals such as *Biological Abstracts, Chemical Abstracts, Physical Abstracts, Engineering Index* and many others, giving a total of over 80 files. Computer terminals situated at the Holborn and Aldwych reading rooms can be linked to online information retrieval systems as far apart as Rome and California.

Searches may be requested in person at the library, by telephone, telex or by letter.

Academic Institutions

Some academic institutions with business and management schools offer business information services on a commercial basis, for example, the London Business School (LBS) runs a financial service for investors called the 'Risk Measurement Service' and 'Portfolio Analysis' service. The LBS provides quarterly publications that analyse UK public companies in terms of risk profiles, containing alphabetical and industry company listings with key investor data. LBS Financial Services, London Business School, Sussex Place, London NW1 4SA (01) 262 5050.

Summary

This chapter has reviewed a wide range of sources of corporate and related industrial and commercial information. Most of the information is freely available to the public from reference libraries. There is also a substantial amount of commercial information provided to meet specific user needs.

There are many companies operating in the UK information industry providing data on UK companies and industry sectors. The publications range from the Financial Times and the city pages in the quality press providing company information on a daily basis to the directories and one-off specialised publications on specific aspects of an industry. But by far the most significant development in the information industry has been the increasing use of online data bases.

Some newspapers and magazines are a valuable source of commercial and industrial information. Details about UK companies and industry sectors published in newspapers and the trade press are analysed and published in the Research Index. Cumulative indices for magazines are available, such as Anbar and some magazines such as *The Economist* produce their own cumulative subject index. These indices together with back copies of the main newspapers and magazines are held in many libraries and thus provide a useful free information service.

However, using subject indexes and working through back copies of journals can be time consuming. For businesses wishing to monitor press coverage of a company or companies (including their own) there are several commercial press cutting services that work through a large number of UK and overseas publications.

News and featurer extracting services are also available online (see Appendix 2).

Some institutions provide useful information in their publications. The main institutional data sources in the UK are from trade associations and professional bodies. Although there are over 400 trade associations in the UK, some do not provide original data and their publications tend to be public relations documents for their association and its members. However, many trade associations employ full time research officials who monitor their industry and thus provide a useful service. (See Appendix 2)

The confederation of British Industry (CBI) undertakes some careful research and its publications are worthwhile reading. The CBI produces monthly, quarterly and annual industry surveys based mainly on returns from their members plus occasional publications. Available from Confederation of British Industry, Centre Point, New Oxford St. London WC1, telephone (01) 379 7400.

The British Institute of Management (BIM) also provides occasional publications relating to industries and established the Centre for Interfirm Comparison. The Centre provides a confidential service to its member companies enabling them to compare their performance by the use of ratios. Details about the Centre's work are occasionally published by the BIM.

Parts of this chapter explained about government sources of information. The British government provides much of the data on companies and industries that is subsequently refined and sold by commercial organisations as specialised information. A comprehensive listing of government and other official information sources is given in Appendix 3.

3

HOW TO READ THE ACCOUNTS

The purpose of this chapter is to provide a quick reference guide to UK published accounts for the layman. It will concentrate on explaining specialist terms and layouts of financial documents. All extracts are taken from the STC Shareholders' Accounts (1983). The assessment of company performance using the accounts, is explained in the following chapter.

The accounts sent to shareholders will generally have more supplementary statements than the statutory accounts sent to Companies House. Many companies provide accounts for their employees even though there is no statutory requirement to do so. These accounts are generally simplified.

Chapter 2 explained that the contents of a microfilm record at Companies House contained many legal documents and three years' accounts. Each year's accounts will contain figures for the current and the previous year. The accounts sent to shareholders will have current and prior year figures plus a variety of supplementary statements.

This chapter will explain each of these statements in the following order:

1. Balance sheet
2. Profit & loss account (also called income statement)
3. Notes to the accounts
4. Consolidated accounts
5. Statement of sources and applications of funds
6. Report of the directors
7. Report of the auditors
8. Notice of annual general meeting (AGM)

and supplementary statements that may not be audited:

9. Statement by the chairman
10. Added value statement
11. Report for employees
12. Highlights of the year statement
13. Historical summary
14. Statement of future prospects
15. Disaggregation statement

Balance Sheet

A balance sheet is a statement of a company's assets (what it owns) and liabilities (what it owes) at a point in time. There are two main types of layout. The traditional layout has assets on the left and liabilities on the right. In some other countries for example, the USA, the liabilities are on the left and assets on the right. The other main layout is called a 'vertical balance sheet'.

These two main types of balance sheet are illustrated in figures 3.1 and 3.2 showing the main categories of assets and liabilities.

Figure 3.1 Balance Sheet – traditional layout

	£		£
Capital	80,000	Fixed assets	50,000
Current liabilities	20,000	Current assets	50,000
	100,000		100,000

Figure 3.2 Balance Sheet – vertical layout

	£	£
Fixed assets		50,000
Current assets	50,000	
less current liabilities	20,000	
Net current assets		30,000
Net assets		80,000
Financed by:		
Capital		80,000
Capital employed		80,000

The four segments shown in these simplified balance sheets will be present in all balance sheets and in most instances be referred to by the names given in this example.

The example will now be extended by taking each of these segments and explaining what it represents and its constituent parts. At the end of the example the full balance sheet will be constructed.

Fixed assets

Examples of fixed assets are property, plant and machinery, fixtures and fittings. Details of these fixed assets will be entered in the notes to the accounts cross referenced to 'notes numbers' in the balance sheet. There are two main terms to look for in the fixed assets' notes depreciation and leased/hired or rented assets.

Depreciation is an accounting technique for writing down the value of an asset over its useful working life. In its simplest form, if a car costing £10,000 is kept for four years and then expected to be sold for £2,000 then the depreciation would be £2,000 per annum. The cost of the asset less depreciation is entered in the balance sheet as shown in Figure 3.3.

Figure 3.3 Balance Sheet – depreciation

Fixed Assets	£	£
Motor vehicle	10,000	
less depreciation*	6,000	4,000

* Assume three years @ £2,000 p.a.

The book values of fixed assets in the balance sheets rarely represent their market values. They only represent the cost less an arbitrary amount. Accordingly, they should only be viewed as guides to value. With properties, a note to the accounts will generally give an estimated market value.

There are many ways a company can acquire the use of fixed assets. Some of the main ways are listed below.

(i) *Cash purchase* – Title passes with contract of sale and new owner has unrestricted use of the asset.
(ii) *Loan purchase* – Similar to cash purchase except loan arranged. If loan is secured on the asset there may be some restriction on its use.
(iii) *Hire purchase* – Similar to loan purchase except title to the asset does not pass until the option to purchase is exercised.
(iv) *Hiring* – This may be short term, such as hiring a car for a weekend, or longer term, often called contract hire, such as hiring a car for say 12 months. Hiring is a form of bailment, not a contract of sale, where the bailee is permitted to take possession of goods belonging to the bailor for a stated period. Title does not pass and there are often restrictions on the use of the assets.
(v) *Renting* – Basically the same principles as hiring.
(vi) *Lending* – The same as hiring but there is no payment.
(vii) *Leasing* – Title remains with the lessor but in most cases the lessee has almost unrestricted use of the asset.

With alternatives (i) (ii) and (iii) the assets are owned by the business but with (iv) (v) (vi) and (vii) the business has the use of the assets but does not own them. As the assets are not owned they will probably not be entered in the balance sheet. This is often referred to as 'off balance sheet finance' because a company can have the income earning capacity of assets that are not included as part of their total assets.

The entries in the published accounts will also vary according to the nature of the lease. There are many types of lease but the two broad categories are:

Operating leases – This is when the lease period is far shorter than the asset life and the lessor bases the lease payments on the assumption that the asset will be re-leased or sold at the end of the lease period.

Finance leases – Generally arranged to last for the whole useful life of the asset. The reality of this type of lease is that the lessee has effectively purchased the asset and it should therefore be shown in the lessee's balance sheet.

Within the fixed asset category there may be an 'intangible asset'. Tangible assets are those that can be seen and touched such as machinery or buildings. Intangible assets cannot be seen, but they can be the most valuable assets of a business, for example the good reputation of a company's product or service. An intangible asset usually gets into the balance sheet under the heading of goodwill. Goodwill is an intangible asset which is meant to represent the difference between the asset value of a business and its going concern value. For example if a business had net assets valued at £100,000 and was sold for £150,000 the extra £50,000 would be described in the accounts as goodwill. Goodwill usually appears in the balance sheet when a business is sold. Once it is in the balance sheet it is usually written off as quickly as possible.

Investments are assets that are generally included in the fixed asset category of the balance sheet. Sometimes, short term investments are included in the current assets category. A breakdown of the investments, with their cost and current market value will be given in the notes to the accounts. Points to note are if the investments are in quoted companies where the investment can be converted into cash if needed. Or, if they are investments in subsidiary or associate companies where the investment is more difficult to realise.

Extracts of fixed assets and their notes to the accounts from the STC Shareholders' Accounts (1983) are shown in figures 3.4 and 3.5.

Figure 3.4 Balance Sheet – Fixed Assets

	Note	1983	Group 1982
		£m	£m
Fixed assets			
Intangible assets	10	—	5.2
Tangible assets	11	165.8	103.6
Investments	12	10.3	3.0
		176.1	111.8

Figure 3.5 Notes to the Accounts – Fixed Assets

Note 10	**Intangible assets**	1983	Group 1982
		£m	£m
	Goodwill:		
	At beginning of year	5.2	5.2
	Additions	36.3	—
	Written off (see note 20)	(41.5)	—
		—	5.2

Note 11 **Tangible fixed assets**

Group

	Land and buildings			
	Freehold	Long lease	Short lease	Plant and machinery
Cost:				
Beginning of year	21.7	13.5	6.4	132.7
Businesses acquired	7.3	3.2	1.4	27.9
Additions	1.8	1.4	0.4	41.8
Disposals	(0.8)	(0.1)	(0.5)	(8.5)
Transfers and reclassifications	0.7	(0.9)	0.3	(0.1)
End of year	30.7	17.1	8.0	193.8
Depreciation:				
Beginning of year	8.7	4.5	2.2	72.5
Businesses acquired	0.2	1.1	0.5	15.2
Charge for year	1.0	0.9	0.6	20.1
Disposals	(0.5)	(0.1)	(0.4)	(7.4)
Transfers and reclassifications	0.7	(0.9)	0.3	(0.1)
End of year	10.1	5.5	3.2	100.3
Net book value	**20.6**	**11.6**	**4.8**	**93.5**
Land included in cost and not depreciated	1.2			

Note 12 **Investments**

Group £m

	Related companies	Other investments	Total
Cost of shares:			
Beginning of year	0.5	—	0.5
Businesses acquired	1.2	2.7	3.9
End of year	1.7	2.7	4.4
Loans and long term advances, net:			
Beginning of year	—	—	—
Businesses acquired	0.6	—	0.6
Other additions, net	—	—	—
End of year	0.6	—	0.6
Revaluation (see note 20):			
Share of post-acquisition retained profit –			
Beginning of year	2.5	—	2.5
Businesses acquired	2.1	—	2.1
Retained for year	0.7	—	0.7
Revaluation deficit on businesses acquired	—	—	—
End of year	5.3	—	5.3
Net book value	**7.6**	**2.7**	**10.3**

Current assets

This section of the balance sheet is divided into three main categories, stock, debtors and cash.

Stocks will sometimes include an amount for work in progress. Stock in the balance sheet is valued at the lower of cost and net realiseable value. For instance, if an item of stock cost £5.00 but could only be realised for £3.00 then the value of £3.00 would be in the balance sheet stock value. Because of the difficulty of valuing large and varied stock holdings, the stock value in the balance sheet is not necessarily as precise as the figure implies.

Debtors are customers who owe the company money for goods and/or services received. This figure sometimes includes prepayments which are amounts paid in advance by the company, such as rent and rates.

The cash figure in the balance sheet is the amount held in current accounts and short term deposit accounts. Short term investments are normally separated from the cash figure. Some balance sheets will show a cash figure on the assets side and a bank overdraft on the liabilities side. This can easily occur with group accounts where some of the group companies may have overdrafts and others cash balances.

An extract of current assets and their notes to the accounts are given in Figures 3.6 and 3.7.

Figure 3.6 Balance Sheet – Current Assets

	Note	1983	Group 1982
		£m	£m
Current assets			
Stocks	13	193.0	151.9
Debtors	14, 15	242.5	184.5
Cash at bank and in hand		24.2	30.7
		459.7	367.1

Figure 3.7 Notes to the Accounts – Current Assets

Note 13 **Stocks**

	1983	Group 1982
	£m	£m
Raw materials and consumables	53.5	44.8
Work in progress	68.9	45.0
Finished goods and goods for resale	85.0	62.6
Payments on account	(14.4)	(0.5)
	193.0	**151.9**
Estimated replacement cost of stocks in excess of balance sheet value	1.5	2.2

Note 14 **Debtors**

	1983	Group 1982
	£m	£m
Amounts falling due within one year:		
Trade debtors	188.2	145.8
Amounts owed by subsidiaries	—	—
Amounts owed by related companies	2.8	—
Prepayments and accrued income	20.0	14.8
Deferred tax asset (see note 15)	10.2	7.6
Other debtors	3.0	—
	224.2	168.2
Amounts falling due after more than one year		
Trade debtors	11.7	11.2
ACT recoverable	6.6	5.1
	18.3	16.3
	242.5	**184.5**

Note 15 **Deferred taxation**

	1983	Group 1982
	£m	£m
Deferred tax asset at 52% provided in the accounts and included in debtors:		
Restructuring and rationalisation provisions	10.2	7.4
Accrued pension expense	0.6	0.7
Other	(0.6)	(0.5)
	10.2	**7.6**
Deferred tax liability at 52% not provided in the accounts (also see note 23):		
Excess of tax allowances over book depreciation of tangible fixed assets	70.2	46.6
Other	(5.5)	(4.7)
	64.7	41.9

Current liabilities

This part of the balance sheet lists the company's short term debt. The main items found in this list are: trade creditors, bank overdraft, declared but unpaid dividends and short term tax liabilities.

Trade creditors are suppliers to whom the company owes money. This figure may also include accrued expenses (often called 'accruals') which are amounts due for payment but are not trade creditors such as royalties.

Bank overdraft may be combined with short term loans. Details will be given in notes to the accounts.

At the balance sheet date dividends may have been declared by the directors but not paid. The amount due to be paid would be entered in the current liabilities.

With taxation there are three entries that can arise in the balance sheet:

(i) Tax payable on the previous year's profits entered as a current liability.

(ii) Tax payable on the current year's profits entered as a reserve.

(iii) A deferred tax adjustment mainly due to capital allowance and stock relief calculations that may be payable at a later date. Stock relief was introduced in FA. 75, changed in FA. 81 and abolished in FA. 85.

Figures 3.8 and 3.9 show how the STC accounts have separated the short term and medium term debt into payments due within one year and payments due in more than one year. There are also some accounting adjustments to the short/medium term liabilities that are recorded in a section of the balance sheet.

Figure 3.8 Balance Sheet – Current Liabilities

	Note	1983	Group 1982
		£m	£m
Creditors: amounts falling due within one year			
Loans and overdrafts	16	32.5	0.7
Other	17	280.6	196.0
		313.1	196.7
Net current assets		146.6	170.4
Total assets less current liabilities		322.7	282.2
Creditors: amounts falling due after more than one year			
Loans and overdrafts	16	9.1	24.9
Other	17	29.4	35.7
		38.5	60.6
Provisions for liabilities and charges	18	19.8	13.8
Net assets		**264.4**	207.8

Figure 3.9 Notes to the Accounts – Current Liabilities

Note 16 **Loans and overdrafts**

	1983	Group 1982
	£m	£m
Amounts falling due within one year:		
Bank loans and overdrafts	32.0	0.7
Other loans	0.5	—
	32.5	0.7

	Amounts falling due after more than one year:		
	Debentures	0.7	0.8
	Bank loans and overdrafts	7.5	24.0
	Other loans	0.9	0.1
		9.1	24.9
	Total borrowings	**41.6**	**25.6**

	Analysis of borrowings:		Group
		1983	1982
		£m	£m
	Borrowings are repayable as follows:		
(a)	Due within five years:		
	Within 1 year – bank	32.0	0.7
	other	0.5	—
	Within 2 years – bank	3.4	18.0
	other	0.1	—
	Within 3–5 years – bank	3.8	6.0
	other	0.3	—
		40.1	24.7
(b)	Due wholly or in part by instalments after more than five years:		
	Debentures		
	7% Debenture stock 1989–1994	0.1	0.2
	7.25% Debenture stock 1990–1995	0.3	0.3
	8.5% Debenture stock 1990–1995	0.3	0.3
		0.7	0.8
	Other loans	0.1	0.1
		0.8	0.9
(c)	Due otherwise than by instalment after more than five years:		
	Bank loans	0.3	—
	Other loans	0.4	—
		0.7	—
	Total borrowings	**41.6**	25.6
	The total of instalments due after more than five years included in (b) above:		
	Debentures	0.6	0.7
	Other	—	0.1
		0.6	0.8

Note 17 **Other creditors**

	1983	Group 1982
	£m	£m
Amounts falling due within one year:		
Payments received on account	28.6	15.6
Trade creditors	98.7	84.4
Amounts owed to subsidiaries	—	—
Proposed dividend	15.4	12.0
Taxation on profit	31.5	5.3
ACT on proposed dividend	6.6	5.1
Social security and other taxes	20.0	19.8
Accruals and deferred income	75.8	50.3
Deferred credit on sale of rental assets	2.4	2.8
Deferred government grants	1.6	0.7
	280.6	**196.0**
Amounts falling due after more than one year:		
Trade creditors	0.2	—
Taxation on profit	19.8	20.6
Accruals and deferred income	2.9	7.0
Deferred credit on sale of rental assets	3.7	5.9
Deferred government grants	2.8	2.2
	29.4	35.7

Note 18 **Provisions for liabilities and charges**

	1983	Group 1982
	£m	£m
Movement on provisions:		
Beginning of year	13.8	6.3
(Expended) arising during the year	(4.7)	1.1
Charged to profit and loss account	10.7	6.4
End of year	**19.8**	13.8

The provisions are in respect of site restructuring and business rationalisation programmes.

Capital

This section of the balance sheet lists the long term liabilities of the business. These long term liabilities are divided into categories – equity and debt. Equity is the owners' capital and comprises different classes of shares. The main classes are ordinary shares and preference shares.

Ordinary shares The ordinary share capital of a company is divided into authorised and issued. Authorised is simply the amount the shareholders will allow to be issued and the completion of a legal process. The important part is issued share capital. This may be issued in many different ways and the notes to the accounts will give details of the type of shares, the number issued and the value. The balance sheet value of shares is often called the 'nominal value' or 'par value'. This value rarely represents the market value of shares. For example if a company issued in 1960 100,000 ordinary shares at £1.00 each, then the balance sheet value will remain £100,000 and this nominal value will not be the same as the market value of the shares.

The main thing to look for is the voting power. The ultimate voting power of the company can be used at an Annual General Meeting (AGM) or at an extraordinary general meeting. Details of shareholdings are contained in the Annual Return to the Registrar of Companies.

Preference shares There are a number of different types. The common types are

Cumulative When profits are too low to pay the preference dividends the entitlement is carried forward and paid out of figure profits. With *non-cumulative* preference shares the dividend entitlement is lost when profits fall below a certain level.

Redeemable This means the preference shareholders are paid an agreed sum at a stated date for redemption of the shares. The redemption date is usually shown as follows:

10% Cumulative Preference Shares (1999)

If no redemption date is stated then the shares would be *irredeemable.*

Convertible Instead of being redeemed the preference shares may be converted to ordinary shares. Usually the preference shareholder is given a choice of cash or ordinary shares at a stated date.

Participating When profits are high the participating preference shareholders will have a right to a limited share of the profits.

Whatever the type of preference share the legal position is basically the same. Preference shareholders only have class voting rights. That means they have no rights at annual general meetings except when a decision is likely to directly affect their class rights, i.e. a vote to alter the preference share redemption date or dividend payments. Preference shareholders have a prior claim over ordinary shareholders for dividends and for capital repayment if the company is wound up. The main disadvantage of preference shares is that they do not increase in capital value as the company expands. This is especially relevant when there is a take over bid and the ordinary shareholders make large capital gains.

Employee shares A wide range of companies now operate employees share ownership schemes. Recent finance acts have encouraged employee shareholdings by allowing tax concessions for employees on their share issues providing they hold the shares for more than five years. Generally employee shareholdings do not constitute a significant amount of a company's total shares.

Reserves

These are basically profits retained by the business. The profits may arise from trading and are referred to as realised profits, or they may arise from revaluations of for example, freehold property and are called unrealised profits. Realised profits not distributed are classed as revenue reserves and unrealised profits as capital reserves. There are often secret reserves that do not appear on the balance sheet. The Companies Act 1948 required reserves to be stated in the balance sheet under separate headings of capital reserves and revenue reserves. This requirement was removed in the Companies Act 1967, but many balance sheets still divide reserves into these categories. The main legal problems relating to reserves are if they can be distributed to the shareholders. Generally speaking, there are legal restrictions on distributing capital reserves and no restrictions on distributing revenue reserves. For example, if a company issued £1.00 shares at say £1.50, the £0.50 premium on each share would be recorded in a capital reserve often called a Share Premium Account. This would ensure that this amount was retained by the company and not subsequently distributed. Apart from a few technical reserves such as the Share Premium Account, most other reserves are provisions set aside to meet specific or general contingencies. For example a reserve may be created to provide additional funds for the replacement of an asset. The depreciation provision, explained earlier, based on the historic cost of the asset will probably retain insufficient funds in the business for the asset's replacement. Therefore an asset replacement reserve will be created. A distinction can be drawn between a provision and a reserve. A provision such as depreciation or bad debts can be fairly accurately estimated whereas a reserve is more of a general fund for a particular contingency. The main points about reserves are summarised in the following notes:-

Capital reserves: Generally arise out of capital transaction such as issue of shares at a premium and profits from revaluation or sale of fixed assets.
Revenue reserves: Usually arise from trading profits where provisions are made to meet contingencies such as: losses on foreign exchange transactions or simply a transfer to a general reserve to reduce a large profit balance being carried forward.
Secret reserves: A balance sheet may understate the value of its assets because of excessive depreciation, undervaluation or omission of assets. For example, the balance sheets of some football clubs do not include their players even though the transfer fee for just one player can be over £100,000.

Capital or revenue reserves will always be represented on the other side of the balance sheet by assets. However, it is unlikely that the reserves will be represented by cash. Even a company with large reserves can still be in financial difficulty.

Loan Capital

The long and medium term debt of a company is normally divided in the 'Notes on the Accounts' into loans repayable within five years and repayable after five years. Sometimes the division may be three of four years. The main type of company debt is a debenture. The detail lists the redemption date and the interest rate i.e.

9% Debenture Stock 1990
11% Debenture Stock 1995

Figure 3.10 Balance Sheet – Capital

	Note	1983	Group 1982
		£m	£m
Capital and reserves			
Called-up share capital	19	81.3	75.0
Revaluation reserve	20	—	—
Other reserve	20	6.5	—
Profit and loss account	20	173.9	132.8
Shareholders' funds		**261.7**	**207.8**
Minority interests		2.7	—
Total capital employed		**264.4**	207.8

Figure 3.11 Notes to the Accounts – Capital

Note 19 **Called-up share capital**

	1983	Group 1982
	£m	£m
Authorised: 354,000,000 (1982 – 330,000,000) Ordinary shares of 25p each	88.5	82.5
Allotted, called up and fully paid: 325,000,000 (1982 – 300,000,000) Ordinary shares of 25p each	**81.3**	75.0

During the year the company allotted 25,000,000 ordinary shares with a nominal value of £6,250,000 and at a premium of £48,828,609 in part payment for 98.9% of International Aeradio plc, and in full payment for STC Industries Limited acquired from ITT Corporation.

At 31st December 1983 options granted during the year under share option schemes were outstanding as follows:

	Number of shares	Subscription price
Savings-related share option scheme for employees	3,225,070	257p
Share option scheme for executives	920,000	286p

		1983	Group 1982
		£m	£m
Note 20	**Reserves**		
	Arising on acquisitions	48.0	—
	Goodwill written off	(41.5)	—
	End of year	**6.5**	—

The reserve arising on acquisitions, net of related expenses, represents the excess of fair value over nominal value of shares issued in connection with acquisitions.

	1983	Group 1982
	£m	£m
Profit and loss account:		
Beginning of year	132.8	155.2
Capitalisation	—	(44.6)
Retained profit for year	41.1	22.2
End of year	**173.9**	132.8

The notes usually include any special details about the loans that the shareholder should be aware of, such as if the debt is secured on property or fixed assets, called a fixed charge. Or, on all the assets of the company not otherwise mortgaged, called a floating charge. The relationship of loan capital to shareholder's interest is referred to as the 'gearing' of a company and is explained in the following chapter.

Figures 3.10 and 3.11 show the equity part of capital. The debt part was built into the net asset calculation. This is an illustration of how the generally accepted format of a balance sheet can be adjusted to meet the individual requirements of a company. The minority interests shown in the STC example are explained in the notes covering the profit and loss account.

This section on the balance sheet has explained how this important financial statement is constructed and what the terms mean. For analysis purposes the important terms to look for are:

Capital employed – the same figure as net assets
Net Current Assets – also called working capital
Current assets and current liabilities – used for liquidity ratios explained in the next chapter
Capital divided into debt and equity – used in gearing ratios explained in the next chapter

All of these terms can be seen on the STC Balance Sheet in Figure 3.12. Note that the debt part of the capital has been deducted from the assets instead of the normal practice of being added to the liabilities.

Figure 3.12 STC Balance Sheet

	Note	1983	Group 1982
		£m	£m
Fixed assets			
Intangible assets	10	—	5.2
Tangible assets	11	165.8	103.6
Investments	12	10.3	3.0
		176.1	111.8
Current assets			
Stocks	13	193.0	151.9
Debtors	14, 15	242.5	184.5
Cash at bank and in hand		24.2	30.7
		459.7	367.1
Creditors: amounts falling due within one year			
Loans and overdrafts	16	32.5	0.7
Other	17	280.6	196.0
		313.1	196.7
Net current assets		146.6	170.4
Total assets less current liabilities		322.7	282.2
Creditors: amounts falling due after more than one year			
Loans and overdrafts	16	9.1	24.9
Other	17	29.4	35.7
		38.5	60.6
Provisions for liabilities and charges	18	19.8	13.8
Net assets		**264.4**	207.8
Capital and reserves			
Called-up share capital	19	81.3	75.0
Revaluation reserve	20	—	—
Other reserve	20	6.5	—
Profit and loss account	20	173.9	132.8
Shareholders' funds		**261.7**	207.8
Minority interests		2.7	—
Total capital employed		**264.4**	207.8

Profit and Loss Account

This financial statement (often called the Income Statement) is a calculation of profit or loss made by a company over an accounting period. The accounting period is usually 52 weeks, but can cover longer or shorter periods when accounting years are being changed. This makes comparison of results more difficult.

The main classifications of profit which may be encountered in published statements are:

Manufacturing profit -	A notional profit that can be varied according to the 'value' of finished or partly finished goods leaving the factory. Refer to the Manufacturing Account.
Gross Profit -	Sometimes called trading profit. This is an important classification. It is the sales less direct cost of sales. Refer to the Trading Account.
Net profit before tax -	The most important classification for assessing business performance. It is gross profit less expenses. Refer to the Profit and Loss Account.
Net profit after tax -	The tax deducted in the Profit and Loss Account is not necessarily the tax that is paid. Although this is an important classification for shareholders.
Retained profit -	The after tax profit less appropriations plus the previous year's retained profit or loss. Refer to the Profit and Loss Appropriation Account.

There is no legal standardised layout and terminology with UK accounting. Whilst the lack of standardisation allows flexibility, it does create difficulties. Numerous terms are substituted for the above basic terms, such as net revenue, net surplus, net income, operating income. With inflation accounting more terms have been introduced such as current cost profit, holding gains, operating gains, realised and unrealised gains and monetary gains. Consequently, it is important to understand how the main categories of profit are calculated to be able to identify the abuses of standard terminology.

The Calculation of Profit

Manufacturing Account This account is rarely published because there is no legal obligation to provide detail of manufacturing expenses for shareholders. However, employee accounts often include manufacturing expenses giving details of raw material and labour costs. Whilst some of the Manufacturing Account does appear in Employee Accounts the method of presentation is usually left to labour relations, public relations or personnel departments. The result is often a pretty but meaningless document. For the accountant a Manufacturing Account has the following detail:

Manufacturing Account for the period ending . . . . . .

£	£
Example of manufacturing costs:- Raw materials used Partly finished goods used Direct labour Factory overheads such as: factory rent, rates, heating, lighting, etc. Total costs transferred to Trading Account	Some accounting systems have a notional stock value for finished goods. The total costs are deducted from this value to derive a manufacturing profit or loss.

Trading Account The Trading Account is where the gross profit is calculated. Sales are entered on the credit side and the cost of sales on the debit side. The difference is the gross profit. Cost of sales is an important term and is calculated by taking :

Opening stock + purchases and/or manufacturing costs use = closing stock

This calculation is more easily understood by using a simple example.

		£
Opening stock	100 units @ £1 each =	100
add Purchases	900 units @ £1 each =	900
Goods available for sale	1,000 units @ £1 each	1,000
less Closing stock	300 units @ £1 each	300
Unit sales	700 Cost of sales	£700

Stock Valuation In most circumstances stocks of many different priced products are held and the costs are not constant over time. Therefore it can be appreciated that if closing stock value is overstated cost of sales will be understated and gross profit will be over stated. This can be very critical with large stock holdings, for example,

Closing Stock value	1 million
Gross Profit	£100,000

A 10% error in closing stock value could mean nil or £200,000 gross profit.

With a manufacturing company stocks and work in progress are, added together when calculating the cost of sales. Some manufacturing processes are very complicated and to value work in progress accurately is almost impossible.

The Profit and Loss Account The net profit (or loss) is calculated in this account. The gross profit is entered on the credit side and expenses listed on the debit side. A traditional layout for a profit and loss account would be as follows:

Profit and Loss Account for the period ending . . . . . .

	£		£
Salaries		Gross profit	
General expenses		Discounts received	
Insurance		Other income not related to the trading base of the business	
Rent, rates			
Depreciation			
Bad Debt Provision			
Selling expenses			
Administrative expenses			
Heating and lighting			
Interest			
Postage and stationery			
Net Profit before Tax			
Tax			
Net Profit after tax			

Published accounts rarely provide more than the statutory minimum expense items in the profit and loss account. The usual presentation is to list the main figures and then provide the statutory detail in the notes on the accounts. For example

	Notes	19	19 . . . .
Sales (often called Turnover)	1		
Profit before taxation	2		
Profit after taxation etc.	3		

Notes

1. Sales should be divided into the major categories of the business and by major geographical location. For instance, a common division for a computer equipment supplier is goods sold and leased. This could also be divided into UK sales and overseas sales by major market categories.

2. The note on profit is generally written as follows :

'The profit is stated after charging the following :

	£
Hire of plant and equipment	x
Interest charges	x
Depreciation of fixed assets	x
Auditors remuneration	x
Directors fees and/or emoluments	x
Loss/profits on sales of fixed assets	

(*This is not a comprehensive list*).

3. Details of the tax charges and provisions will be given such as U.K. tax. overseas and deferred tax.

The accountants' calculations of net profit before tax using manufacturing, trading and profit and loss accounts are not usually published. All that is published are the profit figures and selected expense items.

The Profit and Loss Appropriation Account In this account the retained profit is calculated. The traditional layout is as follows :-

Profit and Loss Appropriation Account for the period ending . . . . . .

Dividends paid or proposed interim and final	Retained profit brought forward from the previous year
Transfers to reserves	Profit after tax for the current year
Retained profit carried forward (This is the profit figures that appears in the balance sheet)	Profit on the sale of investments or fixed assets

When looking at published accounts it is important that the key figure of net profit before tax is not confused with the retained profit. Because of the lack of standardised layout in accounts the reader should know what figures he/she is looking for before attempting to interpret the accounts. What to look for will be covered in the next chapter.

The Income Statement

The traditional accounts that have been explained are often amalgamated into one statement called the 'Income Statement'. The following Income Statement has explanatory notes for each heading.

Income Statement for the period ending . . . . . .

Notes	£000	£000
1. Sales		
2. less: cost of sales	______	______
3. **Gross Profit**	______	______
4. less: Depreciation		
5. Auditors remuneration		
6. Interest charges		
7. Directors remuneration		
8. etc.	______	______
9. **Net Profit before tax**	______	______
10. less: taxation	______	______
11. **Net Profit after tax**	______	______
12. add: retained profit B/Fwd		
13. extraordinary items		
14. less: dividends paid or proposed interim and final		
15. transfers to reserves	______	______
16. **Retained Profit**	______	______

Other headings that may appear on the income statement:-
17. Consolidated Accounts
18. Minority interests
19. Earnings per share (E.P.S.)

Notes on the Income Statement

1. Sales The total sales figure excludes VAT and any discounts or allowances. The sales figure can be misleading if the company operates a generous discount policy. For example, some business machine companies allow up to 50% discounts on their list prices. Aggregate sales may be analysed by major product category and geographical location.

2. Cost of sales Refer to earlier notes on the Trading Account.

3. Gross Profit Refer to earlier notes on the Trading Account.

4. Depreciation Refer to earlier notes on the Balance Sheet which explain the principles of depreciation.

5. Auditors' remuneration The fees payable to the statutory auditors. This does not include fees for other accountancy services such as tax advice that may be provided by the auditor.

6. Interest charges This is an important figure because it provides an indication of how dependent the company is on loans. The balance sheet only shows the loans at the balance sheet date. The company may have been borrowing heavily during the year. There is a legal requirement to show these figures separately.

7. Directors' remuneration There is a legal requirement to show directors fees and other emoluments. Amounts paid to individual directors do not have to be shown. Examples of possible detail are :-

Fees
Pension to former director
Compensation for loss of office
Chairman's emoluments
Highest paid director
Other directors

8. Other expense items may be shown such as rents and hire of equipment. The full list of expenditure does not need to be published.

9. Net Profit before tax Refer to earlier notes on Profit and Loss Account.

10. Taxation A company calculates its tax liability on the current year's profits and makes a provision in the accounts. The Inland Revenue may not agree with the company's calculations and when the tax becomes payable it may be different from the provision. These adjustments sometimes appear in published accounts under the heading 'under/over provison'. Also, there are tax adjustments for stock relief and capital allowances.

11. Net Profit after tax Refer to earlier notes on the Profit and Loss Account. This heading is of interest to investors.

12. Retained Profit B/Fwd This is the accumulated profit brought forward (B/Fwd) from previous years. Refer to Profit and Loss Appropriation Account notes.

13. Extraordinary items Profits or losses arising from transactions that are outside the normal business activities of a company are referred to as extraordinary items. For example, it a manufacturer sold a freehold part of his factory making a substantial profit, it would be treated separately from the business profits.

14. Dividends Usually a quoted company declares two dividend payments during the year. The interim dividend based on the half year results and the final dividend based on the annual accounts. The accounts may contain dividends paid from the previous year and dividends proposed in the current year. The proposed dividends are also entered in the balance sheet as a liability.

15. Transfers to reserves The notes in the Balance Sheet section describe the different types of reserves.

16. Retained Profit Refer to notes on Profit and Loss Appropriation Account. This is the most 'adjusted' of all the profit figures and is of little use for analysis purposes.

17. Consolidated accounts Company law requires holding companies to produce group accounts by consolidating the accounts of the company and all its subsidiaries. The holding company is under no legal obligation to show separately the profits of its subsidiaries. The consolidated income statement summarises an immense volume of accounting data and only provides a very broad picture of the company's activities.

18. Minority interests Refer to notes on subsidiary companies in the Balance Sheet section. A subsidiary may not be wholly owned. For example, if the holding company had 80% of the voting shares the remaining 20% represent a 'minority interest'. When the profit from the subsidiary is added in to the holding company's profit in the consolidated income statement the minority interest in the subsidiary's profit is deducted under the heading 'less minority interests.' (See Consolidated Accounts page 69)

19. Earnings Per Share (E.P.S.) This is derived after a fairly complicated calculation and basically represents the profit in pence attributable to each equity share. The formula for calculating E.P.S. is : Profit after tax, preference dividends and minority interests and before extraordinary items divided by the number of equity shares in issue, e.g.

Profit after tax and minority interests	600,000
less preference dividend payment	100,000
	500,000

(No extraordinary items)
Number of equity shares in issue 5,000,000

$$\text{E.P.S.} = \frac{500{,}000 \times 100}{5{,}000{,}000} = \text{10p per share (see Appendix 1 SSAP 3)}$$

The STC example of a profit and loss account in Figure 3.13 is particularly good because the company discloses more information than is legally required. The supporting notes in Figure 3.14 for the STC profit and loss account provide more detail than is usually found in shareholders' accounts.

Notes to the accounts

The notes contain detail relating to the main financial statements. The notes from the STC accounts show how much supporting detail is given for the balance sheet and profit and loss account. The notes should always be read in conjunction with the accounts.

Accounting Policies

The notes usually begin with a statement of accounting policy on such items as:

depreciation of fixed assets
treatment and amortisation on intangibles such as research and development expenditure, patents and trademarks
stock and work in progress
long-term contracts
deferred taxation
hire-purchase or instalment transactions
leasing and rental transactions
conversion of foreign currencies
repairs and renewals
consolidation policies
property development transactions
warranties for products or services

This list is not exhaustive, and may vary according to the industry involved.

Figure 3.13 STC Consolidated Profit and Loss Account

	Note	1983	1982
		£m	£m
Turnover	1	920.6	628.5
Cost of sales		668.2	453.1
Gross profit		252.4	175.4
Marketing, selling and distribution expenses		60.6	43.3
Administrative expenses		45.4	26.1
Research and development expenses	2	53.3	37.5
Operating profit		93.1	68.5
Investment income	3	4.8	1.9
Interest payable	4	5.7	6.1
Profit on ordinary activities before taxation	1, 5	92.2	64.3
Tax on profit on ordinary activities	7	26.5	24.1
Profit on ordinary activities after taxation		65.7	40.2
Minority interests		0.2	—
Profit for the financial year		65.5	40.2
Dividends paid and proposed	8	24.4	18.0
Retained profit for the year		**41.1**	22.2
Attributable to:			
The company		25.6	10.6
Group companies		14.8	11.4
Related companies		0.7	0.2
		41.1	22.2
Earnings per share	9	**20.6p**	13.4p

Figure 3.14 Notes to the Accounts – Profit and Loss Account

1 **Turnover**

	Turnover		Profit on ordinary activities before taxation	
	1983	1982	1983	1982
	£m	£m	£m	£m
Turnover and profit on ordinary activities before taxation by activity:				
Telecommunications	406.5	322.0	52.9	49.6
International communications and services	245.3	112.9	23.8	5.8
Components and distributors	251.9	193.6	15.1	8.9
Residential electronics	16.9	—	0.4	—
	920.6	**628.5**	**92.2**	**64.3**
Acquired companies included in above	163.5	—	7.5	—
Turnover by geographical market:				
United Kingdom	647.4	485.2		
Continental Europe	39.0	41.9		
The Americas	38.2	41.0		
Asia and Australasia	99.1	53.8		
Africa and Middle East	96.9	6.6		
	920.6	**628.5**		

Sales to British Telecom, the principal customer of the group, amounted to £305.4 million (1982 – £239.0 million).

2 **Research and development expenses**
Included in research and development expenses are payments to ITT for access to technology, under an agreement effective from 1st October 1982. Payments in respect of 1983 were £7,905,000 (1982 final quarter – £2,000,000).

3 **Investment income**

	1983	1982
	£m	£m
Income from shares in related companies – unlisted	2.2	1.1
Profit on sale of investment	0.1	—
Income from other fixed asset investments	0.2	—
Other interest receivable	2.3	0.8
	4.8	**1.9**

Dividends received by the group from related companies in the year totalled £857,000 (1982 – £537,000).

		1983	1982
4	**Interest payable**	£m	£m
	On bank loans, overdrafts and other loans:		
	Repayable within five years, by instalments	1.2	1.7
	Repayable within five years, not by instalment	4.3	4.3
		5.5	6.0
	On all other loans	0.2	0.1
		5.7	**6.1**

		1983	1982
5	**Profit on ordinary activities before taxation**	£m	£m
	Profit on ordinary activities before taxation is stated after the following charges (credits):		
	Depreciation	28.5	18.5
	Hire of plant and machinery	15.7	11.4
	Auditors' remuneration	0.6	0.3
	Staff costs (see note 6)	302.5	208.4
	Currency (gains) losses	(0.3)	0.3
	Exceptional items	—	(3.0)

		1983	1982
6	**Staff costs**	Number	Number
	Average weekly number of persons employed by the group:		
	Telecommunications	12,694	12,999
	International communications and services	5,963	2,095
	Components and distributors	7,496	6,681
	Residential electronics	698	—
	Technology	1,380	1,107
		28,231	**22,882**

Employee costs:	1983	1982
	£m	£m
Wages and salaries	264.3	178.0
Social security costs	18.8	16.2
Other pension costs	19.4	14.2
	302.5	**208.4**

A significant part of the increase in the number of persons employed and in employee costs is attributable to businesses acquired.

The number of employees in the United Kingdom (other than directors of the company) receiving more than £30,000 per annum, excluding pension contributions:	1983	1982
	Number	Number
£30,001 – £35,000	40	24
£35,001 – £40,000	24	14
£40,001 – £45,000	12	4
£45,001 – £50,000	7	4
£50,001 – £55,000	1	—
£55,001 – £60,000	2	3
£60,001 – £65,000	2	—
£65,001 – £70,000	1	—
£75,001 – £80,000	1	—

Loans to three senior employees amounting in total to £30,000 were outstanding at 31st December 1983.

Directors' emoluments:	1983	Company 1982
	£000	£000
Fees as directors	108	97
Other emoluments	926	743
Payment on termination of executive office	87	—
Pensions to former directors	24	43

The emoluments, excluding pension contributions, of the directors were:

	1983	1982
Chairman (fees waived 1983 – nil; 1982 – £24,000)	201	137

	1983	1982
	Number	Number
Other directors:		
£ 0 – £ 5,000	1	2
£ 5,001 – £10,000	3	4
£10,001 – £15,000	—	1
£15,001 – £20,000	3	1
£35,001 – £40,000	1	—
£50,001 – £55,000	—	1
£60,001 – £65,000	—	2
£70,001 – £75,000	—	3
£75,001 – £80,000	1	—
£85,001 – £90,000	3	—
£90,001 – £95,000	2	1

7 **Tax on profit on ordinary activities**

		Group
	1983	1982
	£m	£m
Taxation on profit for the year (also see note 23)		
Group companies:		
U.K. corporation tax, at 52%	27.6	26.4
Deferred taxation	(1.9)	(2.0)
Double taxation relief	(6.1)	(1.1)
Prior year adjustments	(0.6)	(0.9)
Overseas taxation	6.4	1 1
	25.4	23.5
Related companies:		
U.K. corporation tax, at 52%	0.3	0.1
Deferred taxation	0.1	0.1
Overseas taxation	0.7	0.4
	1.1	0.6
Total taxation	**26.5**	**24.1**

Had the group been providing the full amount of potential deferred taxation there would have been a further charge to taxation of £17,410,000 (1982 – £6,031,000).

The corporation tax charge for the year has been reduced by £4,942,000 (1982 – £3,570,000) as a result of stock relief.

8 **Dividends paid and proposed**

	1983	1982
	£m	£m
Interim dividend 2.75p per share (1982 equivalent – 2.0p per share)	9.0	6.0
Proposed final dividend 4.75p per share (1982 – 4.0p per share)	15.4	12.0
	24.4	**18.0**

9 **Earnings per share**

Earnings per share have been calculated by dividing the profit for the financial year by 318.0 million, being the average number of shares in issue during the year weighted on a time basis (1982 – 300.0 million). The potential dilution arising from options granted under share option schemes is not material.

Consolidated Accounts

Company law requires holding companies to include the details of their subsidiaries in the accounts. Basically the balance sheet of the holding company and its subsidiaries are added together to produce a consolidated balance sheet.

Subsidiary companies A company becomes a subsidiary of another when the holding company owns over half the issued share capital and controls the composition of the subsidiary's board of directors.

Associated companies When a company makes an investment of not less than 20% of the voting rights and can exercise influence over the company it will be considered as an 'associate company'.

Over the last thirty years there has been a growing trend of company amalgamations. Usually the companies are engaged in related business activities and economists refer to these amalgamations as vertical and/or horizontal integration. For example, a publishing company may amalgamate vertically by acquiring interests in printing and bookselling, or horizontally by acquiring other publishers. There are other kinds of amalgamations that seek to diversify the group interests instead of integrating them. The common term for this kind of company grouping is 'conglomerate', but they prefer to be called industrial or general holding companies.

Whatever the purpose or structure of grouped companies, as soon as two or more companies are in a relationship of holding and subsidiary then there is a legal requirement for group accounts to be produced. Although amalgamations and consolidated accounts are complicated technical areas of accountancy it is useful to understand the principles of consolidation and some of the terminology.

Figure 3.15 Illustration of consolidated accounts

Assume two companies wish to amalgamate, there are a number of ways this could be undertaken. The main options are as follows:-

Method 1 *C takes over A and B then A and B are wound up.*
Setting up a new company, C, into which all the assets and liabilities of A and B are transferred. Then A and B are wound up.

Method 2 *Set up holding company H.*
Setting up a holding company, H, which will purchase the shares of A and B for cash. Alternatively, H will issue its own shares in exchange for shares in A and B. The two companies will continue trading but the shares will be held by the holding company.

Method 3 *A purchases controlling interest in B.*
A controlling interest is when the holding company, A owns over half the issued voting share capital of the subsidiary B and controls the composition of the subsidiary's board of directors. This is often called a take over bid.

Method 4 *A completely absorbs B.*
A purchases all the assets and liabilities of B by giving B's shareholders cash or shares in A. Then B is wound up.

With amalgamation methods 1 and 4 there are no subsidiaries or holding companies and consequently group accounts are not required. With methods 2 and 3 there are subsidiaries and group accounts are required. To show the effect of amalgamations on balance sheets the following basic data will be used for companies A and B with each amalgamation method. The examples are only meant to illustrate the principles of a consolidated balance sheet and its relationship to the subsidiaries' balance sheets and are simplified.

Figure 3.16 Basic Balance Sheets

Method 1 – C takes over A and B then A and B are wound up

	Company A		*Company B*	
	(£000)	*(£000)*	*(£000)*	*(£000)*
Fixed assets		20		10
Current assets	10		5	
less current liabilities	5		3	
Net current assets		5		2
Net assets		25		12
Financed by:				
Share capital and reserves		25		12
Capital employed		25		12

	Company C	
	(£000)	*(£000)*
Fixed assets		30
Current assets	15	
less current liabilities	8	
Net current assets		7
Net assets		37
Financed by:-		
Share capital and reserves		37
Capital employed		37

Method 2– Set up holding company H

	Subsidiary A (£000)	*Subsidiary B (£000)*	*Holding H (£000)*
Fixed assets	20	10	30
Current assets	10	5	15
less current liabilities	5	3	8
Net current assets	5	2	7
Net assets	25	12	37
Financed by:-			
Share capital and reserves	25	12	37
Capital employed	25	12	37

Method 3 – A purchases an 80% interest in B

	Company A (£000)	*Subsidiary B (£000)*	*Group A (£000)*
Fixed assets	20	10	30
Investment in subsidiary	9.6	—	—
Current assets	10	5	15
less current liabilities	5	3	8
Net current assets	5	2	7
Net assets	34.6	12	37
Financed by:			
Share capital and reserves	34.6	12	34.6
Minority interest *(Note 1)*	—	—	2.4
Capital employed	34.6	12	37

Note 1 – The minority interest liability in the consolidated balance sheet of 'Group A' represents the 20% interest held by subsidiary B's shareholders.

Method 4 – A completely absorbs B

Balance Sheet – Company A

	(£000)	*(£000)*
Fixed assets		30
Current assets	15	
less current liabilities	8	
Net current assets		7
Net assets		37
Financed by:-		
Share capital and reserves		37
Capital employed		37

The difference between a wholly owned subsidiary, a subsidiary that has a minority interest, an associated company and investments in other companies is the way the profits of these different inter-company 'arrangements' are consolidated. i.e.

Wholly owned subsidiary If the subsidiaries are 100% owned and there are no inter-company dividends or other complications then all the profit and loss accounts are added together to form the consolidated profit and loss account.

Partly owned subsidiary When a subsidiary has a minority interest, then the holding company will include all the subsidiary's profit in the consolidated profit and loss account, deduct all the corporation tax and from the after tax profit, deduct the subsidiary company's minority interest share of the profits. The example in figure 3.17 will help to illustrate the consolidated profit calculation,

Figure 3.17 Principles of a consolidated profit calculation

A
Holding Co.

B — *80% subsidiary*
C — *100% subsidiary*

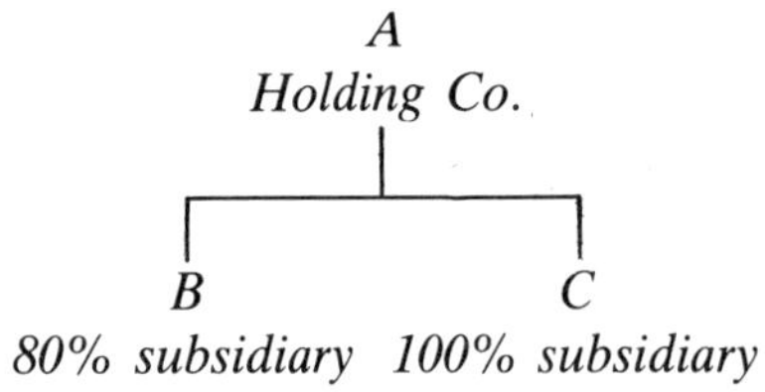

Company	Profit before tax *(£000's)*
A	3,000
B	1,000
C	1,000

Company A — Consolidated Profit and Loss Account

	(£000)
Profit before tax	5,000
less corporation tax	2,500
Profit after tax	2,500
less minority interest (Note 1)	100
Group profit after tax	2,400

Notes:

(1) The minority interest shareholders in company B are entitled to 20% of the after tax profit of company B, (i.e. £1,000,000 × 20%) 50% = £100,000. This minority interest is then deducted from the consolidated profit to give the profit belonging to the group.

(2) All of company C's profits have been consolidated because it is a 100% owned subsidiary.

Statement of Sources and Applications of Funds

A statement of sources and application of funds, also described as a funds flow statement or sources and uses of funds is not a legal requirement. However the accounting profession has produced an accounting standard that requires any company with a turnover of more than £25,000 per annum to include a funds statement with its annual accounts.

The purpose of the funds statement is to show the movements of assets, liabilities and capital during the year and the effect on net liquid funds. The balance sheet lists values of assets and liabilities at a point in time and the income statement calculates profit over a period of time. Neither statement clearly shows where the company funds came from and how they were used over a specific period of time. Each of the three statements have an information role in the annual report yet the funds flow statement tends to receive the least attention.

Content of a funds statement

A simple funds flow statement would list the sources of funds, such as retained profit and external finance, then deduct the uses of funds, say increase in working capital and purchases of assets. The resultant figure would be the movement in net liquid funds. In most instances this is simply if the bank balance has gone up or down. A *detailed* listing of the movement of funds would be a useful disclosure function. However many accounts employ the principle of 'netting off' even though SSAP 10 recommends this type of adjustment should be kept to a minimum. For example if some assets have been sold and some purchased the detail may be netted off as 'movement in fixed assets'. If a company has reported for example £50 million profit before tax, then the funds flow statement should give an explanation of where the funds have been used. But because of netting off and broad groupings of funds flow categories it is sometimes not very clear what has happened during the year. The use of funds can fall into the following categories:

Increased fixed assets such as the purchase of new plant and equipment.
Increased current assets of stock, debtors, cash balances and short term investments.
Decrease of current liabilities like reducing the bank overdraft or paying back short term loans.
Decrease in long term debt by redeeming debentures or paying off long term loans.
Financing trading losses because the income from sales was less than the costs.
Paying tax ACT and/or MCT.
Distributions of profit by way of dividend payments.

Conversely, the sources of funds will come from the following categories:

Profit before tax and depreciation As depreciation is a book-keeping entry and not a movement of funds it is added back to the calculated profit.
Sale of assets are usually shown if the amount is material. Small receipts from the sale of assets may be netted off against purchase of assets.

Issue of shares to employees, institutions or the public.
Increase in trade creditors may be netted off against increases in current assets and called 'changes in working capital'.
Sale of investments – mainly long term. Sale of short term investments would probably be netted into the movement in net liquid funds.
Increase in short term finance would normally be shown as a decrease in net liquid funds.
Increase in long term finance such as issuing a debenture.

These movements in funds will ultimately affect the cash balance. At the bottom of funds flow statements the difference between sources and uses of funds is described in net liquid funds.

The principles of funds flow are illustrated in the examples given in Figures 3.18, 3.19 and 3.20.

Figure 3:18 Purchase of an Asset

A company made £5,000 profit before tax and depreciation and had an opening cash balance of £10,000. During the year a machine was bought costing £15,000. Assume all other assets and liabilites remained constant. The funds flow would show the detail as follows:-

	£
Sources of funds	
Profit before tax and depreciation	5,000
deduct: Application of funds	
Purchase of asset	15,000
Movement in net liquid funds	(10,000)

Figure 3:19 Increase in working capital

A company made £5,000 profit before tax and depreciation and during the year increased stocks by £6,000, debtors by £5,000 and trade creditors by £7,000. Assume all other assets and liabilities remained constant. The funds flow would show the details as follows:-

	£	£
Sources of funds		
Profit before tax and depreciation		5,000
Increase in trade creditors		7,000
		12,000
deduct: Application of funds		
Increase in stocks	6,000	
Increase in debtors	5,000	11,000
Movement in net liquid funds		1,000

Figure 3.20 General movements of funds

Assume a company has made a profit of £10,000 before tax after charging depreciation of £5,000. During the year an asset was sold for £7,000 and further property bought for £40,000. Ordinary shares to the value of £20,000 were issued and a mortgage debenture of £10,000 was secured on the property. Stocks increased by £12,000, debtors increased by £8,000 and trade creditors increased by £11,000. £5,000 tax was paid and £10,000 was paid out in dividends. The funds statement would show this detail as follows:-

	£	£
Sources of funds		
Profit before tax	10,000	
add back depreciation	5,000	
Sale of asset	7,000	
Issue of ordinary shares	20,000	
Issue of debenture	10,000	52,000
Less: Application of funds		
Purchase of property	40,000	
Payment of tax	5,000	
Payment of dividends	10,000	55,000
		(3,000)
Changes in working capital		
Increase in stocks	12,000	
Increase in debtors	8,000	
	20,000	
less: Increase in trade creditors	11,000	(9,000)
Movement in net liquid funds		(12,000)

The funds flow statement in the STC shareholders' accounts (Figure 3.21) shows that a major source of funds during the year was from a share issue.

Figure 3.21 STC Consolidated Source and Application of Funds.

	1983			1982
	Businesses acquired £m	Funds flow £m	Total movement £m	£m
Source of funds				
From operations:				
Profit for the financial year	—	65.5	65.5	40.2
Depreciation	—	28.5	28.5	18.5
	—	94.0	94.0	58.7
From other sources:				
Minority interests	2.5	0.2	2.7	—
Issue of shares, less expenses	—	54.3	54.3	—
	2.5	148.5	151.0	58.7
Application of funds				
Working capital:				
Stocks	27.6	13.5	41.1	27.4
Debtors	60.0	(2.0)	58.0	12.0
Other creditors and provisions	(63.9)	(17.0)	(80.9)	(64.2)
	23.7	(5.5)	18.2	(24.8)
Other applications:				
Businesses acquired	(64.4)	100.7	36.3	—
Fixed asset investments	6.6	0.7	7.3	0.1
Tangible fixed assets	36.6	54.1	90.7	30.9
Dividends paid	—	21.0	21.0	15.0
	2.5	171.0	173.5	21.2
Funds required (released)	—	**22.5**	**22.5**	(37.5)
Represented by				
Increase (decrease) in net borrowings:				
Loans and overdrafts	13.2	2.8	16.0	(7.8)
Cash at bank and in hand	(13.2)	19.7	6.5	(29.7)
	—	22.5	22.5	(37.5)

Report of the directors

Company law requires that a report by the directors must be attached to the final accounts presented at the Annual General Meeting (AGM). The report is an integral part of the annual accounts and may include any information that is required by law to be in the published accounts.

The legal requirements

(i) The state of the company's affairs.
(ii) The amount, if any, which the directors recommend should be paid by way of dividend.
(iii) The amount, if any, which the directors propose to transfer to reserves.
(iv) The names of the directors, and of any persons who were directors at any time during the financial year of the company.
(v) The principal activities of the company and of its subsidiaries during the year, and of any significant changes.
(vi) Any significant changes in the amount of the fixed assets of the company and of its subsidiaries during the year.
(vi) Where the market value of any land or buildings is materially different from the book value at the end of the year, the difference must be stated as precisely as possible. This need only be mentioned if the directors are of the opinion that the difference is of such significance that members' attention should be drawn to it.
(vii) The number and amount of all shares and debentures issued during the year, the consideration received and the reasons for the issue(s). Each class must be shown separately.
(viii) Details of any material interests of directors in contracts with the company, where the contracts are material to the company's business.
(ix) The directors' rights to acquire any shares or debentures in the company.
(x) The interests of the directors in shares or debentures of the company, or any other company in the group, as at the beginning and at the end of the year.
(xi) Any matters not required by law to be disclosed, but which are necessary for a clear understanding of the accounts. This does not apply if disclosure would be harmful to the company or its subsidiaries.
(xii) An analysis showing how the turnover and profit or loss before taxation is divided between the various classes of business of the company. A holding company must include its subsidiaries. If the company is neither a holding company nor a subsidiary, turnover need not be disclosed if it is £50,000 or less.
(xiii) Average number of employees per week, if 100 or more, of the company (unless a wholly owned subsidiary of a UK holding company) or the group. Employees working overseas are excluded.
(xiv) Aggregate remuneration paid or payable to employees for the year, including bonuses. This information is only given in cases where the average number of employees per week is given.
(xv) Political and charitable contributions made by the company or the group during the year, unless the company is a wholly-owned subsidiary of a UK company.
(xvi) If the total turnover of the company or the group is £50,000 or more, the value of the exports, or the fact that no goods were exported. This only applies if the company or a subsidiary is engaged in the business of supplying goods, other than

as agent for another person, and need not be given if turnover need not be disclosed, or if the Department of Trade and Industry agree that disclosure would be harmful to the national interest.

Some of this information such as changes in fixed assets is often given in the notes on the accounts. In addition to the statutory requirements the directors report often contains useful information relating to the company's future prospects. The directors report is an important part of the annual accounts and in most instances not difficult to understand. Accordingly, it is useful to read the report before looking at the accounts and make brief notes of any salient points.

Report of the auditors

This report is for the shareholders and is available to the general public with the annual return and accounts filed at Companies House. There are basically two types of audit reports: qualified and unqualified.

For the audit report to be qualified the matters at issue must be material. The circumstances when qualification is necessary include:-

(i) If the auditors have not been able to obtain all the information and explanations necessary for the purpose of their audit.
(ii) If proper books of account have not been kept or proper returns not received from branches not visited by the auditors.
(iii) The financial accounts are not in agreement with the underlying records.
(iv) The financial accounts do not give a true and fair view of the state of affairs of the business.
(v) Inadequate internal control.
(vi) Uncertainties on material issues such as a significant contingent liability.

A qualified report need not necessarily be a cause for concern. Technical qualifications are quite common where accounting policies do not conform with accounting standards. But the most serious type of qualification is when the auditor states he/she has been unable to form an opinion that the accounts give a true and fair view of the business.

Notice of Annual General Meeting (AGM)

A company is legally required to hold an AGM each year at an interval of not more than 15 months after the preceeding AGM. The ordinary business at the AGM is:

(i) to declare a dividend
(ii) to consider the accounts and the reports of the directors and auditors
(iii) to elect, re-elect directors
(iv) to appoint, re-appoint auditors and fix their remuneration. Auditors are automatically re-appointed unless there is a resolution to change them or they wish to resign.

Any other business is referred to as 'special business'.

At least 21 days notice of the AGM must be given to the members (shareholders) and the auditors. The notice must specify the date, time and place. Normally the reports and accounts are sent with the Notice of an AGM.

Supplementary statements

The statements explained so far are required by law or by accounting practice. The following supplementary statements are not legally required, but are produced by many companies and often contain useful information.

Statement by the chairman

This statement often provides some useful insights into a company which would not normally be available elsewhere in the accounts. The chairman is not constrained by law, and some chairman make surprisingly candid statements in their reports to shareholders.

Added value statement

At present there is no legal requirement to include an Added Value Statement with the published accounts. However the accounting profession in 1975 recommended that a statement of added value should be included in the corporate report of listed companies. The recommendations were that the minimum information should be:

(i) Turnover
(ii) Bought materials and services
(iii) Employees' wages and benefits
(iv) Dividends and interest payable
(v) Tax payable
(vi) Amount retained for reinvestment

However, few companies include an added value statement in their accounts for shareholders.

Principles of Value Added The basic idea of a value added statement is to show the wealth that a business has created and how the wealth was used. This may be illustrated as follows:-

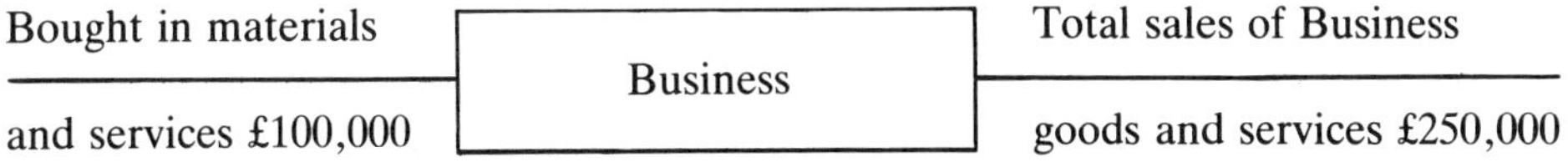

Bought in materials		Total sales of Business
	Business	
and services £100,000		goods and services £250,000

The value added of £150,000 is due to the efforts of the company's workforce and the use of its physical and financial assets. Calculated as sales less bought in materials and services. The value added might be applied as follows:-

	£
Payment of wages, pensions and other benefits	75,000
Interest on loans	25,000
Dividends	10,000
Taxation	15,000
Retained in the company to replace assets and pay for the growth of the business	25,000
	£150,000

Difference between Value Added Tax and Value Added Statement The underlying concept of added value provides the basis for value added tax calculations. The basic calculation is to tax outputs (sales) and deduct tax paid on inputs (purchases of goods and services). In its simples form a value added tax calculation would be as follows:-

Total outputs for the period	£20,000 @ 10%	=	Output tax of £2,000
Total inputs for the period	£15,000 @ 10%	=	Input tax of £1,500

Value added tax payment due is output tax less input tax, i.e. £500.

The VAT calculation is complicated by inputs and outputs being exempt from VAT or charged at different rates. Therefore the value added statement could not be used as a basis for calculating a businesses VAT liability. Moreover VAT calculations are made quarterly and the value added statement will usually be annually: Whilst both statements are based on the same principles they are quite different in purpose and method of calculation and presentation.

Types of Value Added Statement The published accounting statements such as balance sheets, income statements and flow of funds statements all have regulated content and recommended formats. Even so, there is still a wide variety of presentation. With value added statements there is no regulated content and no formally recommended content. Consequently there are many, many types of value added statements. The greatest variety is in employee accounts. Popular presentations include a pound note or pile of coins to represent total sales and percentage divisions representing the way the sales revenue was applied.

Report for employees

There is no statutory obligation to produce accounts for employees. The Industrial Relations Act 1971 Section 57 required firms with more than 350 employees to provide an annual statement but this section was not re-enacted in any of the subsequent legislation.

Consequently any employee accounts produced by management are on a voluntary basis. Moreover employee accounts are not a recent reporting innovation. During the 1950's the British Institute of Management identified 73 large companies providing information direct to employees. Therefore this voluntary reporting practice has been developing for over thirty years.

Content of Employee Accounts The content of Employee Accounts may be divided into the following categories:

General information about the company
Accounting information
Personnel information

General Information Many companies use house journals to convey general information about the company. However, once a year it is a useful exercise to summarise the principal activities of the company together with plans and future prospects. General information that may be of interest to employees would include products and product development, sales, structure, plans for the future and information regarding the ownership and directors. Most of this information is not secret. It may be in the directors report or be general knowledge in certain parts of the company. Some advantages of a general information section are that it provides management with an opportunity to explain to employees the achievements of the company and the plans for the future. It also gives all employees some idea of what is happening to the company and may increase their interest in the company's future.

A useful starting point for determining employee accounts content is the published accounts. Decisions then have to be made concerning what information to exclude because of difficulties in interpretation and the possibility of creating discontent and feelings of job insecurity, and what to include to best help the employee to understand the accounts.

The Corporate Report produced by the accounting profession, showed some useful ways of presenting personnel information, the content being analysis of numbers employed, full/part time male and female, employment location, age distributions, hours worked, sick leave, accident, disputes and layoffs, pension details, education and training analysis and costs, details about trade unions and an extensive range of employment ratios.

Highlights of the year statement

Highlights statements are often placed at the beginning of the shareholders' accounts to save the reader looking through the accounts for key figures. These statements are also the ones used in corporate advertising when the company publishes its accounts.

There are no regulations for the content or presentation of highlights statements. Generally, they contain this year and last year figures for: sales, profit before tax, profit after tax, earnings per share and dividends per share.

Historical summary

The history usually covers between 5 to 10 years and summarises data such as total sales, exports, before tax profit, capital employed, earnings per share and dividends. It is a useful quick reference but care is needed not to jump to conclusions. For example a rapid growth in sales and profits may be due to an acquisition policy lasting several years and not increased company efficiency. If two companies with declining sales and profits

Figure 3.22 Example of historical summary

	1979 £m	1980 £m	1981 £m	1982 £m	1983 £m
Results					
Turnover	436.8	537.7	567.5	628.5	920.6
Operating profit	43.0	55.0	59.0	68.5	93.1
Interest less investment income	9.6	10.9	8.4	4.2	0.9
Profit before taxation	33.4	44.1	50.6	64.3	92.2
Taxation	5.9	15.4	14.1	24.1	26.5
Profit after taxation	27.5	28.7	36.5	40.2	65.7
Minority interests	—	—	—	—	0.2
Profit for the financial year	27.5	28.7	36.5	40.2	65.5
Dividends	8.0	10.0	13.5	18.0	24.4
Retained profit for the year	**19.5**	**18.7**	**23.0**	**22.2**	**41.1**
Earnings per share	9.2p†	9.5p†	12.2p†	13.4p	20.6p
†Restated for the 2 for 1 issue of 5th November 1982					
Net assets employed					
Fixed assets	70.4	79.0	94.1	111.8	176.1
Other assets (net)	112.3	114.7	119.5	120.9	97.4
	182.7	**193.7**	**213.6**	**232.7**	**273.5**
Financed by:					
Shareholders' funds	144.0	162.7	185.6	207.8	261.7
Minority interests	—	—	—	—	2.7
Long-term loans	38.7	31.0	28.0	24.9	9.1
	182.7	**193.7**	**213.6**	**232.7**	**273.5**
Other data					
Plant additions	18.4	21.4	29.6	33.4	58.2
Depreciation	10.9	12.4	14.4	18.5	28.5
Overseas sales	77.3	94.7	125.7	143.3	273.2
Average number of employees (000)	28.0	27.3	25.0	22.9	28.2
Dividends – per share as paid					
Interim dividend	2.0p	4.0p	4.5p	6.0p	2.75p*
Final dividend	6.0p	6.0p	9.0p	4.0p*	4.75p*

*After 2 for 1 issue of 5th November 1982

Shareholdings at 31st December 1983

	Number of holders		Total holdings	
1–1,000	11,258	60%	5.46 million	2%
1,001–10,000	6,271	34%	15.52 million	5%
10,001–100,000	711	6%	24.34 million	7%
100,001–500,000	248		58.20 million	18%
above 500,000	77		106.48 million	33%
ITT	1		115.00 million	35%
	18,566	100%	325.00 million	100%

amalgamate, then the consolidated accounts for the year will show a substantial growth in sales and profits.

Statement of future prospects

Shareholders, employees and creditors are interested in a company's future. The accounts however, only show what has happened in the past and there are limits to the relevance of historical information when assessing a company's future prospects. It is therefore important to search the accounts for any statements on future prospects. Such statements sometimes appear in the chairman's report and/or disaggregation reports. Generally directors of listed companies are cautious with statements relating to their company's future prospects. Even when financial forecasts are made there is the possibility of them being optimistic and misleading. Useful statements that you need to look for would include:

(i) Orders in hand are especially important for capital goods industries such as shipbuilding, aircraft, heavy construction and expensive machinery. If the company has enough *firm* orders in hand to last for say, three years then this would be significant if the trading results are being compared with a similar company with an empty order book.

(ii) New investment projects where expenditure has been committed are very important. Unfortunately, little financial detail is given about investment programmes but the points to look for are:
How much will it cost?
How will it be financed?
Have the lavour force accepted the project?
When will the cash benefits from the project start to flow?

(iii) Research and development is speculative expenditure. Successful R & D can transform the fortunes of a company, but with some justification, companies do not disclose details. However, if the accounts show that the company has been gradually increasing its R & D expenditure and the chairman hints that a new project is being developed this is important information.

(iv) Crisis policies are usually forced onto companies. A common crisis is shortage of cash. There are several main alternative policy actions:

Trade out of debt This means increasing sales usually through expensive marketing programmes. A risky policy that can worsen the company's cash position.

Debt restructuring Basically converting short term to long term debt and if possible issuing more equity to improve the gearing.

Cuts programme Cutting back expenditure through cuts in the labour force, pruning output of marginal products, halting investment programmes, imposing tight cost budgets, selling off some assets to improve the cash flow and de-stocking.

These types of crisis polices are not disclosed in any great detail in the annual accounts but often the financial press obtains a substantial amount of detailed disclosure.

Summary

This chapter has explained the content of the statements found in the shareholder's accounts. The first eight of these statements are legally required, and will also be found in the accounts of companies (subject to exceptions explained in Chapter 2) lodged at Companies House. The remaining supplementary statements may be found in the published accounts sent to shareholders.

The purpose of this chapter has been to provide a quick reference guide to all these different statements. The three most important however are: balance sheet, profit and loss account and the report of the directors. These three statements provide the major source of data for the financial data bases that are explained in chapter 5. The data from these statements is also used for the calculation of ratios that enable comparisons to be made between companies and industries. Business ratios and the interpretation of accounts is explained in the next chapter.

4

HOW TO ASSESS COMPANY PERFORMANCE

Introduction

Any performance assessment is based upon some form of comparison. The quality of the assessment will depend upon:

(i) Quality and quantity of information being used.
(ii) The relevance of the basis of comparison.
(iii) The knowledge and experience of the person making the assessment.

The majority of assessments made by people in their everyday lives are subjective, where the comparative base is a personal storehouse of experiences and prejudice. These so-called value judgements are inappropriate for assessing a company's performance. The assessment has to be far more objective.

When assessing a company, facts need reliable and relevant comparative bases. This chapter explains how to assess a company's performance using appropriate comparative measures.

For example, to say a company has sales of £100,000 and before tax profits of £10,000 is just a statement of facts. These figures have to be compared with something to assess the company's trading performance.

Comparison with figures from earlier years' accounts

If the previous year's sales and pre-tax profits were £80,000 and £20,000 respectively then the assessment would be that sales have increased at the expense of profits. A profit margin calculation enables the comparison to be made more easily for example,

	This year		Last year	
Before tax profit	$\frac{10,000}{100,000}$	% = 10%	$\frac{20,000}{80,000}$	% = 25%

If in earlier year the profit margins were 30% then the falling trend in profit margins shown by this ratio over a period of time is an important part of the assessment of this company.

Comparison with figures from comparable companies

To compare one company with another it is necessary to convert the data to a comparable base. The best comparable base is a ratio. For example a company with a turnover of £20 million and pre-tax profits of £1 million can be compared with the company given in the above example by calculating their profit margins. i.e.

$$\text{Profit margin} = \frac{\text{Pre-tax profits}}{\text{Sales}} \qquad \frac{1{,}000{,}000}{20{,}000{,}000} \times 100 = 5\%$$

Thus an inter-company comparison can be made using business ratios.

Comparison with figures based on industry averages

The ratios that are used for inter-company comparisons can also be used for industry averages. For instance, the government produces average returns on capital for different industries. The largest database in the UK for industry averages using business ratios has been compiled by the ICC Information Group Ltd. The ICC database representing over 80,000 UK companies' accounts has been summarised in industry sector ratios annually for over 10 years in the publication *Industrial Performance Analysis*.

Using the example of a company with a 10% profit margin a quick assessment could be made to see if this was above or below average by referring to the relevant industry sector profit margin. The comparison could also be made over time comparing a company with its relevant industry sector.

This chapter will explain how to assess a company's performance using business ratios and how to value a company.

Business Ratios

A ratio simply expresses the relationship of two (or more) figures. The calculation can put the relationship as a straight ratio, for example, 4:1 or as a percentage 25%, in value terms or in terms of time. All these types of calculations arise in business ratios. There are six main categories of business ratios:-

Performance ratios	Assessments of business performance using such ratios as Return on Capital Employed and Profit on Sales.
Value added ratios	A set of ratios that use added value relationships with other variables.
Efficiency ratios	Ratios that use alternative variables such as ton/miles in transport or sales per sq ft in retailing.
Employee ratios	A form of productivity measure using employees number/ remuneration with other variables.

Financial ratios	Ratios which are mainly concerned with business liquidity. It is important to look at these ratios in conjunction with performance ratios because a profitable business can go into liquidation through lack of cash.
Investment ratios	Concerned with shareholders interests. Areas such as earnings per share, dividend yield and return on equity are attempts at measuring investment performance.

Performance Ratios

The most widely used business ratio is Return on Capital Employed (ROCE). The formula is:

$$\frac{\text{Profit before tax, interest and extraordinary items}}{\text{Capital employed*}}$$

* Refer to the notes on the Balance Sheet for a definition of Capital Employed.

This is the basic measure for business performance. For example, Company 'A' made a profit of £1 million whilst Company 'B' only made £½ million profit. Therefore 'A' is more efficient.'

The statement could be incorrect because nothing is known about the two companies. If Company 'A' had £20 million capital employed and Company 'B' had £2 million then Company 'B' has made better utilisation of its resources. The ROCEs would be:-

Company 'A' $\frac{1}{20}\% = 5\%$ Company 'B' $\frac{0.5}{2}\% = 25\%$

In most business circumstances the ROCE is the best general measure of business performance. For some businesses such as banks, building societies and insurance companies it is less useful because of the nature of the business that requires them to hold substantial reserves. If a company has a low ROCE when compared with its competitors it will be due to either insufficient profits or too many assets.

To find out why ROCE is low, profit/cost ratios and asset/turnover ratios should be calculated.

(i) If profit is low it can be due to the following reasons:
  (1) Low turnover
  (2) Small profit margins due to:
    (2.1) Costs too high
    (2.2) Selling prices too low

There are dozens of ratios that analyse costs and profit margins, this section will cover the major categories.

(ii) If there are too many assets this may be due to:
  (1) Excess stocks and work in progress in relation to sales
  (2) Excess fixed assets in relation to sales
  (3) Poor credit control

There are also many ratios that analyse assets in relation to sales, this section will cover the major categories.

Pyramid of ratios
There is a logical structure to all these ratios, usually referred to as the pyramid of ratios. Some of these ratios cannot be calculated from the published accounts because there is insufficient disclosure. For example cost of sales is rarely given in published accounts.

Figure 4.1 ROCE Pyramid

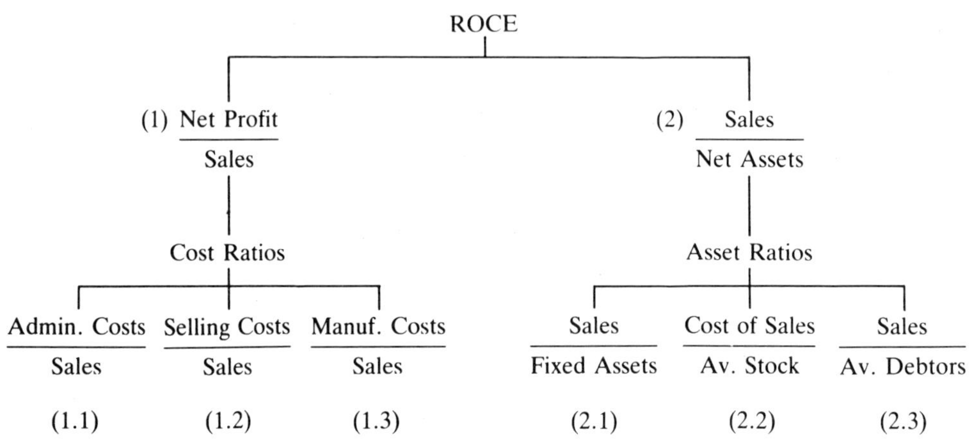

1. Net Profit/Sales Often called the net margin. If the gross profit figures are available gross margins could also be calculated. If the margin is low when compared with competitors, look at the cost ratios.

Cost Ratios

1.1 *Administrative costs/Sales* Administration often tends to grow disproportionately creating an increasing volume of superfluous internal paperwork. As sales rise there should not be a proportionate rise in administration costs. If this ratio is rising rapidly look at management salaries or if there has been a recent computer installation.

1.2 *Selling costs/Sales* Should be fairly constant because of standard discount and commission policies, could possibly rise if advertising budget was substantially increased. If the ratio is rising and the sales are falling then either the product/service is wrong or there are difficult market conditions.

1.3 *Manufacturing costs/Sales* Pricing policy should keep this ratio steady to allow for increased material and labour costs. If this ratio is rising and margins are constant or rising then some costs may be getting out of control.

There are many other cost ratios but they all basically follow the same principle of taking a specific cost in relation to sales over several accounting periods.

2. Sales/Net Assets Often called asset turnover. The ratio indicates whether the total value of sales justifies the value of assets. For example, if a business had £1 million of assets and an annual turnover of £10,000 then clearly it either has to sell off some assets or increase turnover. In most instances the asset turnover is determined by the nature of the industry. There are some industries that are capital intensive and have a low turnover, whilst other companies only need a rented office and a little office equipment and they are in business. The secret is to compare like with like when using business ratios.

Asset Ratios

2.1 *Sales/Fixed Assets* The assets are taken at book value after depreciation therefore this ratio is only useful as a general guide (Refer to Balance Sheet notes on assets and depreciation).

2.2 *Cost of Sales/Average Stock* Often called stock turnover. The cost of sales are used instead of the sales because the value is more closely related to stock values. This ratio is usually calculated in weeks. Therefore it is often referred to as say an eight week stock turnover. The nature of the industry will determine the stock turnover. For grocery retailing, stock turnover would be measured in days whereas for say, antiques the measurement would probably be months. If stock turnover is rising and sales in volume terms are falling then the business should be increasing sales and/or decreasing/switching production.

2.3 *Sales/Average debtors* Often called debtor turnover. The normal credit period is 30 days and average debtor turnover for these trading terms would be between 30 and 40 days. If it was say 60 days then the company may be carrying bad debts and/or have weak credit control.

There are other asset ratios that follow the same principle of relating asset value to sales.

Using Performance Ratios

When using performance ratios the starting point is to compare the ROCE with other ROCEs in the industry and if it is significantly different use the ratio pyramid to locate the problem areas before looking at the accounts. Figure 4:2 provides an illustration of using the ratio pyramid.

Figure 4.2 Using the ROCE Pyramid

ROCE	'Company A'	Industry Average
ROCE	5%	14%
Net Profit/Sales	17%	16%
Sales/Net Assets	8.1	11.1
Administrative costs/Sales	20%	28%
Selling costs/Sales	30%	20%
Manufacturing costs/Sales	30%	28%
Sales/fixed Assets	4.1	4.1
Cost of Sales/Average Stock	14 weeks	9 weeks
Sales/Average Debtors	45 days	34 days

From these figures it can be seen that Company 'A' has a low ROCE. The net margin is good and this seems due to low administrative costs. Selling costs are high possibly indicating a market orientated company. Therefore there is little to worry about on the cost ratio side of the pyramid. On the assets side utilisation of fixed assets is the same as the industry average. But working capital items such as stock and debtors seem to be getting out of control and this is causing the low ROCE. Thus the ratios have highlighted a business performance fault with Company 'A'. A detailed study of the accounts will help to complete the picture.

Figure 4.3 Quick Reference Table – Performance Ratios

ROCE Structure

$$\text{ROCE} = \frac{\text{Profit before tax, interest, extraordinary items and minority interests}}{\text{Average Capital Employed}}$$

$$\text{Profit margin} = \frac{\text{Profit before tax, interest, extraordinary items and minority interests}}{\text{Turnover}}$$

$$\text{Asset turnover} = \frac{\text{Turnover}}{\text{Average Net Assets}} \text{(times)}$$

$$\text{Expense ratios} = \frac{\text{Specific expense}}{\text{Turnover}} \%$$

Added Value Ratios

The main reason for using an added value ratio structure in preference to an ROCE structure is that the input/output aspect of added value makes it a better base for efficiency measurement. See page 80 for a full definition of added value.

Figure 4.4 Added Value Ratio Structure

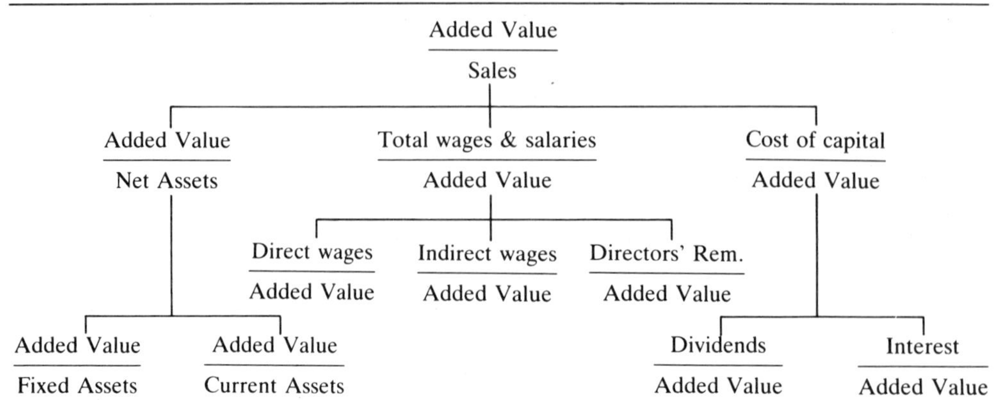

1 *Added Value/Sales* This ratio must be calculated first because this is a primary relationship. For example if a company decided to sub-contract some of its production instead of increasing its productive capacity, this could cause a significant change in the primary added value ratio that would affect all added value based ratios. Similarly when making inter-company comparisons with added value base ratios they will be invalid if there are large differences in the primary relationships between the companies. For instance if two companies produced an identical product but one bought in sub assemblies whereas the other made the sub assemblies, the added value/sales relationship would be significantly different. In these circumstances the ROCE structure would provide a better basis for comparative performance measurement.
2 *Expense categories/added value* For an external analyst using the published accounts the expense categories are fairly limited, being mainly labour and capital as shown in the published added value statement. The main use for added value expense ratios is for internal purposes, because added value is becoming a widely used measure for productivity agreements.
3 *Asset utilisation/added value* If a company really wants to use added value as a base for performance measurement then the ratio structure should include asset utilisation measures as well as expense measures. The ratios are similar to the ROCE pyramid asset ratios except added value is used instead of sales or cost of sales. Providing the primary added value ratio is fairly constant the added value base would probably be more appropriate than the sales base especially if there are seasonal sales fluctuations.

Figure 4.5 Quick Reference Table – Value Added Ratios

$$\text{Added value/Sales} = \frac{\text{Added value}}{\text{Sales}}\ \%$$

$$\text{Expense/Added value} = \frac{\text{Expenditure category}}{\text{Added value}}\ \%$$

$$\text{Asset utilisation/Added value} = \frac{\text{Added value}}{\text{Asset category}}\ \text{(times)}$$

Efficiency Ratios

An efficiency ratio structure must be tailormade for an organisation. The ratios are mainly used as internal monitoring devices and can be incorporated into control systems. The bespoke aspect of efficiency ratio structures is in the selection of the appropriate measurement base. Profit is rarely suitable and is best left in the ROCE pyramid. For example a common efficiency measure for retailers is sales per square foot of retail floor space. Alternatively, a road haulier may use cost ton/mile as a primary efficiency measure. These types of efficiency measures complement profit based ratios, they are not a substitute.

Figure 4.6 Efficiency Ratio Structure

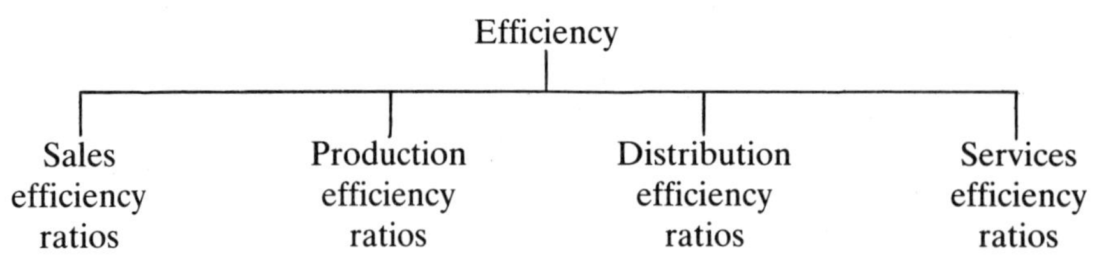

1 **Sales efficiency** This can be divided into two broad categories, direct and indirect, where direct represents retailing and indirect all other types of selling.

The efficiency of a direct selling operation can be measured in terms of:

Product Value $\dfrac{\text{Total sales value of products within stated price ranges}}{\text{Total sales value}}$ %

Retail Space $\dfrac{\text{Total sales value}}{\text{Square feet of retail floor space}}$

Sales Assistant $\dfrac{\text{Total sales value}}{\text{Number of sales assistants}}$

Large retail organisations have developed quite a wide range of efficiency ratios for comparative measurements of individual retail outlet efficiency.

With indirect selling efficiency measures may be based on the salesman, the geographical location, the product or by branch agency or department, for example,

By Salesman $\dfrac{\text{Total sales value by individual salesman}}{\text{Total sales value}}$ %

By Area $\dfrac{\text{Total sales value in clearly defined areas}}{\text{Total sales value}}$ %

By Product $\dfrac{\text{Total sales value by product category}}{\text{Total sales value}}$ %

2. **Production efficiency** Many production efficiency ratios are linked to standard costing. If the company does not have a standard costing system then output is often used as a general measurement base. There are hundreds of ratios that fit into the category of production efficiency and it would be inappropriate to explain just a few of them. Any company wishing to introduce production control ratios into their administrative systems could benefit from discussions with 'Interfirm Comparison', through the British Institute of Management.

3. **Distribution efficiency** The measurement base for most distribution efficiency ratios is distance. Costs are broken down into main categories such as fuel, tyres, repairs and wages, then measured against miles, ton/miles or passenger/miles, for example,

Total Costs per ton/mile $\dfrac{\text{Total costs}}{\text{Miles travelled} \times \text{tonnage hauled}}$

Tyre Costs $\dfrac{\text{Replacement cost of tyres}}{\text{Miles travelled between tyre changes}}$

Fuel Costs $\dfrac{\text{Total fuel costs per vehicle}}{\text{Miles travelled per vehicle}}$

Repair Costs $\dfrac{\text{Total repair costs per vehicle}}{\text{Miles travelled per vehicle}}$

Cost ratios per vehicle are particularly useful, because they provide a quick guide for management on high cost vehicles. The same principles could be applied to identify drivers that use more fuel and cause vehicles to be repaired more frequently.

4. **Services efficiency** It is difficult to select a suitable base for service efficiency. Service departments in companies such as personnel, general administration, data processing and accounting cannot be reliably measured in terms of output. There are specific measurement bases that departmental heads may use but they are usually for support rather than illumination. The one common factor that all service departments have is that they all spend money. As expenditure has to be paid for, it is suggested that the best measurement base is either sales or added value. If the primary added value ratio is constant then added value is a better base. If the added value ratio is irregular then it is preferable to use sales as the base.

Indirect Labour Costs:

$$\frac{\text{Personnel department labour costs}}{\text{Sales (or added value)}} \%$$

$$\frac{\text{Data processing department labour costs}}{\text{Sales (or added value)}} \%$$

The main function of these cost ratios is to highlight areas that may require corrective action.

Figure 4.7 Quick Reference Table – Efficiency Ratios

Manufacturing efficiency = Standard cost categories/Sales value or volume

Sales efficiency = Product, retail space or salesman/sales value

Distribution efficiency = Cost categories/miles

Service efficiency = Cost categories/Sales value

Employee Ratios

If employees are to be used as a base for ratio calculations then the first decision is whether to use number of employees or employee remuneration. If remuneration is to be used, then should it be gross, net or somewhere between, that excludes say pensions or employer's contributions? To avoid the remuneration problem the following ratios are based on number of employees.

Figure 4.8 Employee Ratio Structure

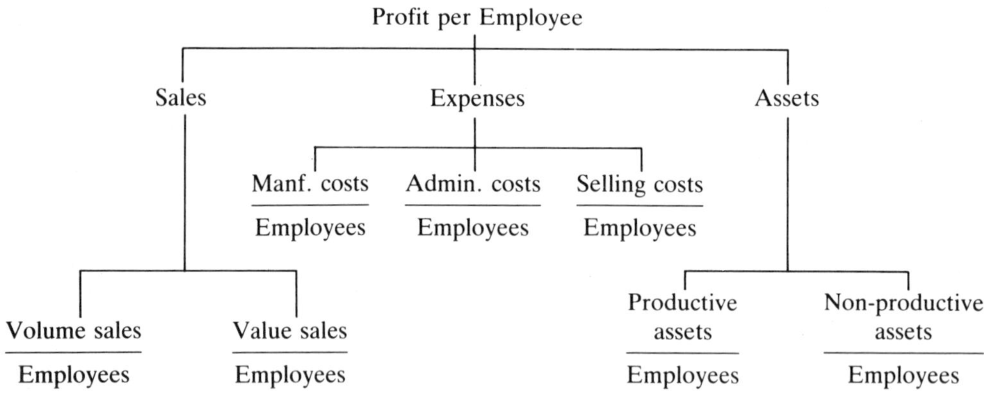

1. **Profit per employee** For companies with a profit maximisation objective this is the primary ratio. If the overiding corporate objective was increasing market share, then sales per employee would be the primary ratio. Profit will be defined in the same way as in the ROCE calculation and the number of employees will be the average number for the period under review.

Profit per employee $= \dfrac{\text{Profit before tax, interest, extraordinary items and minority interests}}{\text{Average number of employees}}$

A fall in the ratio could be due to:
(i) Reduction in output/sales. Refer to sales per employee ratios.
(ii) Inefficient production. Refer to assets per employee ratios.
(iii) Rising costs. Refer to expense per employee ratios.

2. **Sales per employee** This may be calculated in volume and/or value terms. For a homogeneous output a volume base can be used, but when there is a variety of products and revenue sources, a value base has to be used. The turnover calculation should exclude interest received, extraordinary items and minority interests.

Volume sales per employee $= \dfrac{\text{Volume sales}}{\text{Average number of employees}}$

Value Sales per employee $= \dfrac{\text{Turnover} - \text{(Interest received, extraordinary items and minority interests)}}{\text{Average number of employees}}$

3. **Assets per employee** If the company is working at normal capacity and fixed assets per employee increase, then output per employee should increase. However if the company is operating below capacity, due to a fall in demand, and has reduced the labour force, then this ratio would increase, without a related increase in output per employee. However, fixed assets need to be divided into two categories: productive and non productive. For example if £10,000 was spent on power tools to speed up a production process this is clearly productive investment. Whereas if £10,000 was spent on luxury fittings for a director's office, this would tend to distort the assets per employee ratio. Thus, for internal analysis the company's asset register needs to be divided into productive and non productive assets.

Productive assets per employee $= \dfrac{\text{Productive assets}}{\text{Average number of employees}}$

Non-productive assets per employee $= \dfrac{\text{Non-productive assets}}{\text{Average number of employees}}$

For the external analyst using published accounts, it is preferable not to use net assets or total assets, because the inclusion of current assets in this ratio may distort the analysis. It is suggested that you use the written down book values of fixed assets as shown in the historic cost balance sheet. If you have confidence in the current cost balance sheet, then these figures may be used providing they have been consistently calculated over the periods under review.

$$\text{Fixed assets per employee} \quad \frac{\text{Fixed assets written down value}}{\text{Average number of employees}}$$

4. **Expenses per employee** The function of this grouping of ratios is to identify cost trends in relation to employees. However for this type of ratio the number of employees needs to be fairly constant. For instance expense per employee could be improved by simply employing more people. Alternatively if cost savings were made by reducing the number of employees expense per employee would increase.
   Accordingly, some caution is necessary when interpreting expense per employee ratios. The information needed to calculate the expense ratios may not be available to the external analyst. The use of these ratios would be mainly as internal control measures.

$$\text{Manufacturing expenses per employee} \quad \frac{\text{Total manufacturing costs}}{\text{Average number of employees in manufacturing}}$$

$$\text{Administrative expenses per employee} \quad \frac{\text{Total administration costs}}{\text{Average number of employees in administration}}$$

$$\text{Selling expenses per employee} \quad \frac{\text{Total marketing costs}}{\text{Average number of employees in marketing}}$$

If this type of ratio is being included in a control systems package the systems analyst will have to be careful to avoid double counting. For example an employee may be included in both the sales and administration ratios.

Figure 4.9 Quick Reference Table – Employee Ratios

$$\text{Profit per employee} = \frac{\text{Profit before tax, interest, extraordinary items and minority interests}}{\text{Average number of employees}}$$

$$\text{Assets per employee} = \frac{\text{Productive or non-productive assets}}{\text{Average number of employees}}$$

$$\text{Sales per employee} = \frac{\text{Volume or value sales}}{\text{Average number of employees}}$$

Financial Ratios

Businesses go into liquidation through lack of cash not necessarily through lack of profits. One of the biggest dangers of fast business growth is running out of cash. Most bank managers have witnessed this problem, especially with the small under-capitalised fast growing business. As a basic rule, if a business is not financing its sales growth working capital needs from retained funds, then it is overtrading. It is not uncommon for fast growing businesses to finance their growth from trade credit and bank overdraft. Thus one of the first figures to look at in the balance sheet is the net current assets (working capital) and its composition. An assessment is needed on the ability of the company to meet its short term debt. This is often referred to as liquidity which should be distinguished from solvency. Solvency refers to the underlying financial strength of a business such as its financial structure. Figure 4.10 broadly divides the financial ratios into liquidity (short term) and solvency (long term).

Figure 4.10 Financial Ratio Structure

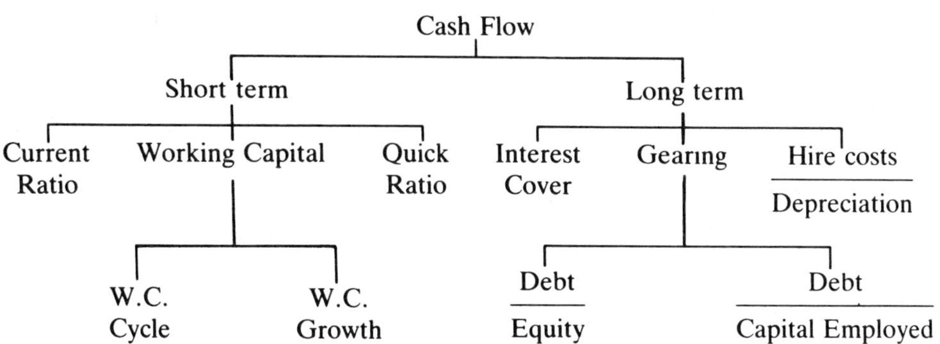

1. **Liquidity** The two main liquidity ratios are

   (i) The Current ratio
   (ii) The Quick ratio (sometimes called the acid test).

   Current Ratio This is calculated as follows:

$$\frac{\text{Current Assets}}{\text{Current Liabilities}}$$

   Generally speaking this should be greater than 1, that is, current assets should be greater than current liabilities.

   Quick Ratio This ratio indicates whether the business can meet its short term debt. It is calculated as follows:

$$\frac{\text{(Current Assets} - \text{Stock)}}{\text{Current Liabilities}}$$

   It is unwise to lay down general guidelines on liquidity ratios by saying quick ratios should be above 1 and liquidity ratios above 1.5 because safe liquidity depends on the nature of the business. Some businesses have front loaded cash flows. With most retailing businesses customers pay cash on delivery and with mail order they sometimes pay more than 30 days in advance. This type of up front cash business can have a very low quick ratio compared with a manufacturer with a working capital cycle of over six months. Therefore when looking at liquidity it is necessary to consider the timing of working capital movement.

2. **Working Capital Cycle** The principle of the working capital cycle is a basic circular flow from cash to stock, to debtors and back to cash. The balance sheet only provides a static picture of the flow by saying at this point in time cash, debtors, creditors, stock etc. had these values. What is needed, is to get a feel for the working capital. How fast does it move? How long does it take for cash to pass through the flow and back into cash? For some companies, cash can be locked up for months and for others only weeks. There are two main ways of making the liquidity assessment a little more dynamic: the working capital cycle approach and the cash flow approach. Figure 4:11 and the following notes and examples illustrate the working capital cycle calculations.

Figure 4.11 Illustration of average Working Capital Cycle

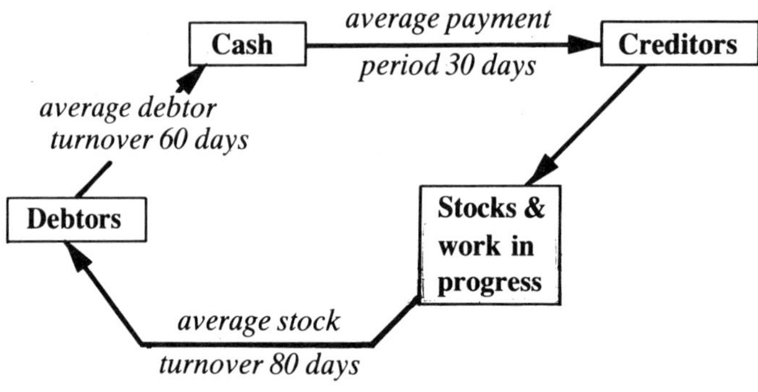

(Working Capital Cycle = 80 + 60 − 30 = 110 days)

The timing of working capital movement can be measured by activity ratios. These ratios use time as a base. The time base may be daily, weekly or monthly. The following example uses a daily time base and measures the timing of stock, debtors and creditors. The formulae are as follows:

$$\text{Average stock turnover in days} = \frac{\text{Average stock}}{\text{Cost of Sales}} \times 365$$

$$\text{Calculation of average stock} = \frac{\text{Opening stock} + \text{Closing stock}}{2}$$

If cost of sales is not available then an approximate cost of sales should be calculated by deducting the estimated gross margin from sales – i.e. if estimated gross margin is 35% then multiply sales by 0.65. Although this is a crude measure it will probably be more accurate than using sales. If sales are used then stock turnover will always be understated. For example if 100 units costing £1,000 were sold for £2,000 and the average stock over the period was ten units, then the stock turnover calculations would be as follows:

	Units	Cost of Sales	Sales
Stock turnover	$\frac{10}{100} \times 365$	$\frac{100}{1,000} \times 365$	$\frac{100}{2,000} \times 365$
	= 36.5 days	= 36.5 days	= 18.25 days

If it is necessary to estimate a gross margin then the figure must be applied consistently over every accounting period examined.

$$\text{Average collection period in days} = \frac{\text{Average debtors}}{\text{Sales}} \times 365$$

$$\text{Calculation of average debtors} = \frac{\text{Opening debtors} + \text{Closing debtors}}{2}$$

This calculation is similar to the stock turnover calculation except sales are used instead of cost of sales. Often balance sheets include prepayments with the debtors. If details are given in the notes to the accounts then deduct prepayments before making the calculation, otherwise you will have to assume they are not significant.

$$\text{Average credit period in days} = \frac{\text{Average creditors}}{\text{Total purchases}} \times 365$$

$$\text{Calculation of average creditors} = \frac{\text{Opening trade creditors} + \text{Closing trade creditors}}{2}$$

Calculation of total purchases Total purchases are different from cost of sales because of varying stock levels. The Trading Account is not usually included in published accounts therefore the purchases figure may not be available. An estimate can be made from the value added statement and stock levels but it may not be very accurate. If the resultant figure is outside the 30 to 60 day range then it is best to opt for a figure somewhere between 30 and 40 days. Although this seems a fairly crude measure it is necessary to make some allowance for trade credit when assessing the working capital cycle. Consider the following:

Methodical Manufacturing Limited – Estimated working capital cycle

	Days
Average stock turnover	120
Average debtor turnover	90
Average creditor turnover	(30)
Average time cash locked in working capital	180

Supercon Mailorder Limited – Estimated working capital cycle

	Days
Average stock turnover	40
Average holding of customers' cash	(40)
Average creditor turnover	(60)
Average time cash locked in working capital	(60)

Clearly Methodical and Supercon cannot be compared on liquidity ratios. They are two totally different types of commercial operations. Methodical needs a good quick ratio to see it through its 120 day stock and work in progress cycle, whereas Supercon has far more flexibility. The company's buying power probably allows it to occasionally squeeze its creditors and it can maintain a fast stock turnover ordering partly in relation to demand and keeping the customer waiting. Most of Supercon's cash flow would probably be going into its advertising and distribution.

3. **Cash Flow** There are two broad divisions for cash flows; short term and long term. The common accounting technique for short term cash flows is the cash budget. The technique for long term cash flows makes allowance for the time value of money and is commonly referred to as discounted cash flow or DFC. Cash budgets and discounted cash flows are operational accounting techniques and are not generally relevant for published accounts analysis because the required volume of detail is not available.

The term cash flow is widely abused because it is often used to represent the short and medium term funds generated by a business. Technically a cash flow cannot be a single figure, but as it is in general usage it needs to be defined.

Gross Cash Flow This is sometimes similar to the calculation in the funds flow statement of funds generated from operations. However some caution is needed because some fund statements use profit before tax in the sources of funds and taxation in application of funds, while others net off taxation and use profit after tax in the sources of funds. The gross cash flow is profit after tax, after adding back the increase in deferred tax, plus depreciation.

Net Cash Flow is the calculation we will concentrate on because it should represent the 'free cash' the company has available from the periods trading. The calculation is the gross cash flow less the dividends. As net cash flow has a specific meaning in DCF calculations the term 'free cash' is often used.

Company cash flows can be broken into two main categories: short term and long term.

Short term cash requirements increase due to two main factors: financing working capital and meeting rising costs. As sales increase a larger amount of cash is required to finance larger stocks and debtors. For example if a company had a turnover of £1 million, stocks of £300,000 and debtors of £200,000 then if turnover doubled then stocks and debtors would increase. The increased finance requirement would be up to a maximum of £500,000 depending on circumstances. A quick guide to the increase in working capital requirements from rising sales is calculated as follows:

$$\text{Working capital/sales ratio} = \frac{(\text{Stock} + \text{Debtors}) - \text{Creditors}}{\text{Sales}}\%$$

Cash is excluded from this calculation because it is affected by many factors outside the working capital equation. Taking the earlier example with creditors of say £100,000 the result would be:

$$\frac{(300{,}000 + 200{,}000) - 100{,}000}{1{,}000{,}000}\% = 40\%$$

Therefore if sales were expected to increase by £500,000 then there would be an approximate maximum additional working capital requirement of (500,000 × 4) £200,000.

Long term cash requirements are related to capital expenditure programmes. There are two aspects to consider concerning capital expenditure cash flows; paying for previous capital expenditure and commitments for future investment programmes. The debt/equity distinction of long term funding will be explained later. At this stage the concern is with the cash consequences of long term debt. How much it costs to service it and when it has to be repaid?

There is a banking principle that one should not borrow short to spend long. This basically means not to finance capital expenditure on overdraft or short term borrowing that may be needed for working capital. Assuming a company is borrowing long for capital projects then the main methods of repaying the principal are by installments with the interest, or in a lump sum, or several lump sums, at the end of a specified period. If a company does not have enough 'free cash' to meet debt repayments, investment commitments and/or working capital requirements then the courses of action open to it include the following:

(i) Short term financial action such as seeking increased bank overdraft facilities, invoice discounting, de-stocking and squeezing selected creditors.

(ii) Asset disposal through sale of investments and/or sale of assets. If the assets are needed then they may be sold and leased back.

(iii) Loss cutting programmes through tighter expenditure controls. Cutting back on expenditure programmes, trimming the labour force and possibly cutting back on the production of marginal income products.

(iv) Long term financial action such as issuing loan stock or a right. Possibly buying a company with 'chinese money' (i.e. paying for the company with shares not cash) that has a good cash flow or some property that can be sold or used as security for long term finance.

The majority of these types of company activities are not made public and if information does come to the surface there is a certain amount of cosmetic treatment making it difficult to identify the facts and figures.

4. **Gearing** There are the two main types of gearing; operational and financial. Operational gearing relates to cost volume profit relationships, whereas financial gearing is concerned with the financial structure of a company and tends to focus on the debt/equity relationship. Operational gearing refers to the level of fixed costs in relation to total costs at expected levels of output. Alternatively it can be viewed as a form of capital/labour relationship, because the function of increasing capital is usually to increase output per manhour. For example, a high geared company has a lot of machinery and is operationally geared for high levels of output. Conversely the low geared company depends on labour imput for increased output. This company is operationally geared for low output levels. The term *leverage* is often used instead of operational gearing to distinguish it from financial gearing.

Financial gearing There is a lot of theory and a few simple ratios relating to financial gearing. The theory revolves around a basic question: is there an optimal capital structure? For example if a company needed £1 million capital would the best mix be £1,000 equity and £999,000 debt or vice versa? As debt is supposed to be cheaper to service than equity, then one view suggest maximum debt offers the optimum mix. This view is challenged by the argument that as debt increases so the risk increases and therefore the cost of marginal debt increases. There are sometimes complicated calculations attached to these theories that make unrealistic assumptions such as rational investor behaviour and no tax or brokerage costs. What gearing ratios are trying to assess, is if the company had passed the optimal range. It is a fairly subjective assessment. For example if a company had a gearing ratio (debt/equity) of say 10% then it could probably manage a little more debt. But if it had a 60% ratio and the earnings forecast was low, then any additional finance should be with equity. High geared companies however, often resort to off balance sheet finance methods instead of opting for the lengthier and more costly alternative of issuing equity.

Off balance sheet finance is a recognised part of accounting practice that is sometimes described as 'window dressing' and or 'cosmetic reporting'. Basically, they all have the same objective – to present a favourable picture of the business. However the 'favourable view' can conflict with a 'true and fair view'. Leasing, renting and hiring are common ways of acquiring the use of assets without altering the balance sheet structure.

Figure 4.12 Quick Reference Table – Financial Ratios

Cash Flow

Gross cash flow — Profit after tax and adding back depreciation for the year and the increase in deferred tax.

Net cash flow — Gross cash flow less dividends.

Liquidity

$$\text{Current ratio} = \frac{\text{Current assets}}{\text{Current liabilities}}$$

$$\text{Quick ratio} = \frac{\text{Current assets} - \text{Stocks}}{\text{Current liabilities}}$$

Working Capital — Days

$$\text{Stock turnover} = \frac{\text{Average Stock}}{\text{Cost of Sales}} \times 365 = \quad X$$

$$\text{Debtor turnover} = \frac{\text{Average debtors}}{\text{Sales}} \times 365 = \quad X$$

$$\text{Credit turnover} = \frac{\text{Average creditors}}{\text{Total purchases}} \times 365 = \quad X$$

$$\text{Average Working Capital Cycle} = \quad \underline{\overline{X}}$$

$$\text{Working capital growth} = \frac{(\text{Stocks} + \text{Debtors}) - \text{Creditors}}{\text{Sales}} \%$$

Gearing

$$\text{Debt/Capital employed} = \frac{\text{Long term debt} + \text{Preference shares}}{\text{Capital employed} - \text{Minority interests}} \%$$

$$\text{Debt/Equity} = \frac{\text{Long term debt} + \text{Preference shares}}{\text{Ordinary shareholders' interests}} \%$$

$$\text{Interest cover} = \frac{\text{Profit before tax, minority interests, extraordinary items and interest.}}{\text{Total interest charges}}$$

$$\text{Hire charges/Depreciation} = \frac{\text{Hire charges}}{\text{Depreciation charges for the year}} \%$$

Investment Ratios

Generally speaking investors are concerned with three aspects of a company: investment security, future income potential and future capital growth potential. A company rarely offers all three, it is usually a trade off between risk and reward and payment/retention. A young fast growing dynamic company would normally adopt a retention policy to fund its growth, but there should be a high capital gain. Whereas the more mature company tends to have steady capital growth and steady dividends. One of the functions of portfolio analysis is to spread the investments in a portfolio across companies to achieve a balance between risk, reward, payment and retention.

Figure 4.13 Investor Ratio Structure

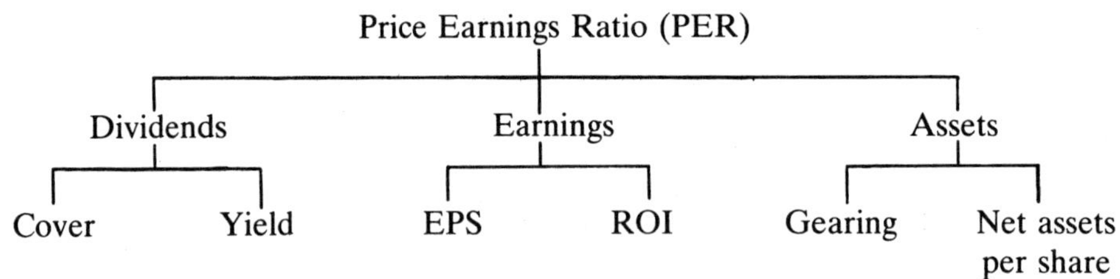

This brief introduction emphasises that investors are very concerned with the future income potential of a company and its retention policy. Thus the market capitalisation of a company (number of shares in issue multiplied by market price) is dependent more on expectations than on the historic cost accounts. Accordingly, a chairman of a listed company has to be constantly concerned with the corporate image, public statements by a chairman can have as much impact on the share price as the annual report. Also, external factors such as the expectation of a recession, industrial unrest or political uncertainty affect share prices. Thus historic cost accounts are not necessarily the most important factor for investment decisions.

Investor ratios draw upon two main figures in the accounts, profit after tax, and dividends. Sometimes the company's asset base and gearing is used but the most important accounting facts for the investor are how much the company has earned and how much it has paid out

1 **Earnings** An important quick reference ratio for investors is the price earnings ratio usually called the PE ratio.

Price Earnings (P/E) Basically the P/E ratio is the number of years earnings that is represented by the market price of the share. Consider the illustration in Figure 4.14

Figure 4.14 P/E ratio caculation

Detail: Profit attributable to ordinary shareholders £200,000
Number of ordinary shareholders 100,000
Market capitalization £1 million (i.e. £10 per share × 100,000 shares)
Earnings per share £2 (i.e. £200,000 ÷ 100,000)

P/E ratio calculation:

$$\frac{\text{Market capitalisation}}{\text{Earnings attributable to ordinary shareholders}} = \frac{1{,}000{,}000}{200{,}000} = 5$$

$$\text{or: } \frac{\text{share price}}{\text{Earnings per share}} = \frac{10}{2} = 5$$

What the P/E ratio of 5 is saying is that if £10 is paid for this share the investor is buying 5 years earnings at £2 a year. This is also called a capitalization factor. To protect past earnings as a constant into the future is a crude measure. However, it does highlight investor expectations, because few investors will buy, say, 25 years current earnings. Therefore when an escalating share price pulls the P/E ratio into large figures it is a measure of expected earnings. In short, therefore, although it is calculated on historic earnings, P/E is really a measure of expected earnings, and/or external factors influencing investment decisions.

The problem is that this calculation forms the basis of a company's marketing rating. The higher the P/E the higher the expectations of the market. When a company has a high market rating it is well positioned to grow by acquisition. For example the shareholders of a company with a P/E of say 5 would probably welcome a bid by a company with a P/E of 15 and may be prepared to accept shares instead of cash. Therefore this simple investment ratio can have a dramatic effect on companies. A company with a good cash flow and freehold property but a low P/E will be an obvious target for the company looking for an acquisition to provide cash to support its conglomerate and by the time the next accounts are published, the newly-acquired subsidiary may have been changed beyond recognition. Therefore a useful starting point for an analysis of a listed company, is to compare their P/E with other companies in the same industrial/commerical category.

Earnings Per Share (*EPS*) The explanation of the P/E ratio did not include the difficulty of defining earnings because this problem is usually associated with EPS which is used for calculating the P/E ratio. (Refer to Appendix 1 SSAP 3) The basic calculation is:

$$\text{EPS} \quad \frac{\text{Profit attributable to ordinary shareholders}}{\text{Number of ordinary shares in issue}}$$

Earnings per share basically represents earnings for shareholders expressed in simple terms. Thus what shareholders are looking for is a rising EPS. Because of the effect of EPS on shareholders' expectations and the company's market rating, the calculation has been subject to manipulation by companies, especially when it is adjusted in historical summaries. The adjustments to the EPS are not necessarily fraudulent. Calculation problems arise through rights issues, bonus issues, employee share option schemes and convertible debt. Thus a company that is strengthening its equity base may have a worsening EPS whilst a company that is gearing up may have an improving EPS.

Return on Investment (ROI) There are several opinions on what ROI represents. Some writers incorrectly substitute it for ROCE. Return on investment is precisely what it says: the return the investor gets on the investment. The earnings attributable to the ordinary shareholder is the return and the investment is the market price. Thus the formula is:-

$$\frac{\text{Earnings attributable to ordinary shareholders}}{\text{Market capitalisation}}$$

or:

$$\frac{\text{Earnings per share}}{\text{Market price per share}}$$

This is the reciprocal of the P/E ratio. It is often referred to as the *earnings yield*. Thus if shares with a market value of £10 per share have an EPS of £2, the return on current investment or earnings yield is 20%. Note that the ROI is based on current investment. There are some calculations where ROI is based on capital and income gains over the amount paid for the investment.

2. **Dividends** The theoretical objective of a dividend policy is to select a payout ratio that will maximise shareholders' wealth. In the real world, the payout ratio is often determined by government restrictions, cash availability, previous year's payment and maintenance of dividend stability and/or the risk of a take-over bid. The effect of dividend payments on share values is uncertain. Some theories claim an optimal payout ratio while others maintain dividends are irrelevant. Clearly investors are concerned about dividend payments and there are two main investor ratios that are used; dividend cover and dividend yield.

Dividend cover This is sometimes called the payout ratio and represents the relationship between earnings and dividends. For example if a company had profits attributable to ordinary shareholders of £200,000 and paid out £20,000 in dividends the dividend cover would be 10 times representing a payout ratio of 10% i.e.

Dividend cover $$\frac{\text{Profit attributable to ordinary shareholders}}{\text{Total gross dividend}}$$

or: $$\frac{\text{Earnings per share}}{\text{Gross dividend per share}}$$

Payout ratio $$\frac{\text{Total gross dividend}}{\text{Profit attributable to ordinary shareholders}} \%$$

or: $$\frac{\text{Gross dividend per share}}{\text{Earnings per share}} \%$$

Note that the ratio calculation used gross dividends, whereas under the Imputation System dividends are paid net of tax. The shareholder receives a net dividend payment and a tax credit calculated on the basic rate of income tax as illustrated in Figure 4.15.

Figure 4.15 Gross Dividend Calculation

	£
Net dividend	70,000
Advance Corporation Tax (3/7* of 70,000)	30,000
Gross dividend	100,000

Assume 100,000 shares then the shareholder receives £0.70 dividend and £0.30 tax credit per share.

* Basic rate of income tax @ 30%.

If the gross dividend is not given in the accounts it can be quickly calculated by the net dividend by dividing the net dividend by (1 – basic income tax rate). A negative dividend cover means that the company is paying dividends out of reserves and a high positive dividend cover indicates a safe dividend payment.

Dividend yield This represents the income gain to investors in relation to the share's market price. i.e.

$$\text{Dividend yield} \qquad \frac{\text{Total gross dividend payment}}{\text{Market capitalisation}}\ \%$$

$$\text{or;} \qquad \frac{\text{Gross dividend per ordinary share}}{\text{Market price per ordinary share}}\ \%$$

Dividend yield is distinguished from earnings yield in the example in Figure 4.16.

Figure 4.16 Earnings and Dividend Ratios

Detail: Number of ordinary shares in issue 100,000
Earnings attributable to ordinary shareholders £200,000
Gross dividends paid to ordinary shareholders £50,000
Market price per share £5

Calculations:

$$\text{P/E} \qquad \frac{(100{,}000 \times 5)}{200{,}000} = 2.5$$

$$\text{EPS} \qquad \frac{200{,}000}{100{,}000} = £2$$

$$\text{Earnings yield} \qquad \frac{2.5}{5}\ \% = 50\%$$

$$\text{Dividend cover} \qquad \frac{200{,}000}{50{,}000} = 4 \text{ times}$$

$$\text{Payout ratio} \qquad \frac{50{,}000}{200{,}000}\ \% = 25\%$$

$$\text{Dividend yield} \qquad \frac{50{,}000}{(100{,}000 \times 5)}\ \% = 10\%$$

3. **Assets** There are two aspects of a company's balance sheet that concern the investor. Firstly, the financial gearing, where the investor's concern is that a highly geared company places the equity at risk because of the company's potential inability to meet its debt commitments. The gearing ratios are the same as explained earlier, being Debt/equity % or debt/capital employed %. The other balance sheet aspect that

Figure 4.17 Quick Reference Tables – Investment Ratios

$$\text{Price/Earnings (P/E)} = \frac{\text{Market capitalisation}}{\text{Earnings attributable to ordinary shareholders}}$$

$$\text{or} \quad \frac{\text{Share price}}{\text{Earnings per share}}$$

$$\text{Earnings yield} = \frac{\text{Earnings attributable to ordinary shareholders}}{\text{Market capitalisation}} \%$$

$$\text{or} \quad \frac{\text{Earnings per share}}{\text{Share price}} \%$$

$$\text{Earnings per share (EPS)} = \frac{\text{Profit attributable to ordinary shareholders}}{\text{Number of ordinary shares in issue}}$$

$$\text{Dividend cover} = \frac{\text{Profit attributable to ordinary shareholders}}{\text{Total gross dividend}}$$

$$\text{or} \quad \frac{\text{Earnings per share}}{\text{Gross dividend per share}}$$

$$\text{Interest cover} = \frac{\text{Interest}}{\text{Pre-interest profit}}$$

$$\text{Payout ratio} = \frac{\text{Total gross dividend}}{\text{Profit attributable to ordinary shareholders}} \%$$

$$\text{or} \quad \frac{\text{Gross dividend per share}}{\text{Earnings per share}} \%$$

$$\text{Dividend yield} = \frac{\text{Total gross dividend payment}}{\text{Market capitalisation}} \%$$

$$\text{or} \quad \frac{\text{Gross dividend per ordinary share}}{\text{Market price per ordinary share}} \%$$

$$\text{Net assets per share} = \frac{\text{Net Assets}}{\text{Number of ordinary shares in issue}}$$

concerns the investor is the net assets. The ratio is sometimes referred to as *asset backing* or net assets per share, i.e.

$$\text{Net assets per share} \quad \frac{\text{Net Assets}}{\text{Number of ordinary shares in issue}}$$

The problem of time asset values weakens this ratio. As the ratio is meant to indicate the break up value per share the appropriate asset valuation model would be Net Realiseable Value (NRV). Therefore it would be wrong to use the Current Cost Balance sheet figures that are based on a value to the business valuation model which would tend to overstate the NRV.

Valuing a business

To the layman a balance sheet total may be considered to be the value of the business. This is completely wrong. Whilst the accounts may provide an indication of the value of a business there are many factors not shown in the accounts which could affect the valuation. The following list indicates some of the factors that need to be taken into consideration when valuing a business.

1. Type of business carried on, and its place in the range between necessities and luxuries
2. Locality and security of tenure of premises
3. Length of time established
4. Competition, actual and potential, and spread of customers
5. Present state of the order-load
6. Capital structure with special attention to priority classes of shares and to long-term liabilities, and the terms under which these have been issued or borrowed
7. Management, particularly with regard to the prospects of continuity of management, and whether one or several persons are actively managing the business
8. The nature and value of the tangible asset backing and whether the assets are likely to be difficult on realisation, are specially subject to obsolescence or are mainly of value only in the particular business involved
9. Extent of the cover given by earnings in relation to dividends on shares to be purchased
10. The steady maintenance, or otherwise, of available profits over the period and the trend of these profits at the date of valuation, the absence of material fluctuations in annual profits being a major factor
11. Repayment of obligations, if any, in respect of prior capital and loans.
12. Marketability of the shares, as affected by special restrictions on transfer, usually specified in the articles
13. The powers of directors under the articles, especially where there is control by one individual only
14. The value of the personal contacts of the management, if these are a material element in the business

Practical valuation methods

For a quoted company the value is often referred to as the 'market capitalisation' and is calculated as follows:

Market price per share × number of shares in issue.

For companies without a market price the following basic methods can provide an indication of value.

(i) $\dfrac{\text{Net Assets shown on the Balance Sheet}}{\text{Number of ordinary shares in issue}}$

There are many faults with this valuation method. The main one is the book value of the assets is unlikely to be the going concern value of the breakup value of the business.

(ii) $\dfrac{\text{Liquidation value of net assets}}{\text{Number of ordinary shares in issue}}$

This can be taken as the 'floor value', that is the lowest value. If the liquidation values included some good freehold property then this could be a good valuation especially if the purchaser was just interested in breaking up the business and selling the bits. Provisions would be made for labour disruption and redundancy payments.

(iii) $\dfrac{\text{Average of last two years profits} \times \text{appropriate number of years}}{\text{Number of ordinary shares in issue}}$

This method is simply asking how many years profit are being purchased. An average profit is calculated and multiplied by the number of years that the purchaser is prepared to buy. There are several variations on this method:

(a) The future profits may be estimated in cash flow terms and converted to present value

(b) If the business is in a rapidly expanding market and larger than normal profits (called 'super profits') are expected then the purchaser buys X years of super profits and Y years of normal profits.

It will be appreciated that the accounts are only a guide to the valuation of a business. The real value is what the market/individual is prepared to pay. This depends upon expectations of future profits and often the historic cost accounts are not the best indicator for the future.

Summary

The purpose of looking at company accounts is to assess performance. The assessment can be elementary such as seeing if sales have improved and if the company is trading profitably. But this kind of assessment still needs a yardstick against which a company's figures can be compared. The most commonly used yardstick are business ratios. Accordingly, an understanding of business ratios is needed to properly assess a company's performance.

There are hundreds of business ratios to choose from. This chapter has explained the important ones. The assessment process is made easier by the use of online data bases which can do all the calculations. For instance, a company's profit margin trend may seem good until it is compared with its industry profit margin average. Or, its liquidity may look bad until a comparison is made with other companies or the industry average which could show that low liquidity is a characteristic of the industry sector.

The next chapter explains how to use a financial database and will illustrate how quick and easy it is to assess a company with an online database.

5

HOW TO USE A FINANCIAL DATABASE

Introduction

The first four chapters in this book have provided reference material on UK companies and their legal disclosure requirements, sources of information, how to read accounts and how to assess company performance. All of this reference material is intended to help the non-financial specialist use a financial data base.

The online financial databases are truly remarkable and provide a very powerful tool for analysis of a single company, several companies and industries.

The examples used in this chapter are based on the ICC files that may be accessed either through Dialog, Datastar, Datastream, or ICC's own Viewdata Service.

Financial databases on UK companies draw much of their data from Companies House. This chapter will not be working through the keying instructions because these are clearly laid out in the user manuals provided for every database user. Instead this chapter explains some practical uses for a financial database. The first part of the chapter gives an outline of what a financial database can provide, followed by worked examples assuming a different user with different needs. For instance, an investor looking to invest in a specific industry may use the database to find out which are the largest and most profitable public companies and how their performance relates to the average performance of the industry. A worked example of this kind of problem is provided to illustrate how to use the database.

Another kind of user may be a businessman wanting to know something about his competitors. There is an example of getting details about competitors in an industry sector within a specific geographical area. Another use by a businessman would be a sales director looking for an up to date mailing list in a specific area. The example shows how a first class mailing list can be quickly compiled and printed out in ready to use label format, direct from a financial database.

Other examples are assessing customers for creditworthiness. This kind of check only takes a few minutes and is of vital importance if the customer wants credit for a very large contract. There is also an interesting example of an employee wanting to compare his salary with the average salary in his industry and getting a ranking of companies by who pays the most in his area.

This chapter will show that there are many uses for a financial database and it is hoped that the following examples will encourage the reader to use a database with confidence, becoming familiar with the specialist terms which appear on the screen. These terms are only a form of business finance shorthand and they are all explained in this book.

What databases provide

A financial database can provide several levels of information based upon the public records at Companies House. These levels are summarised below with brief details of different uses for the data.

Directory level

There are several directory level databases available, produced by ICC, Jordan & Son (Jordan Watch), Dun and Bradstreet (KBE). The ICC directory of companies contains 1,700,000 companies registered in England, Scotland, Wales, Ireland and the Irish Republic. Each directory record contains the following basic information:

Registered Company Number
Company Name
Registered Office Address
Accounts reference date
Date of latest annual return
Date of latest accounts

There are many uses for this kind of directory level database, for example,

(i) When setting up a company a search can be made to see if the chosen name is already in use. For instance, if a person named Haynes wanted to set up a publishing company a quick search could be made on the word Haynes as shown in Figure 5.1

Figure 5.1 Directory search on a company name

```
? SELEXPAND CO=HAYNES PUBLISHING
Ref Items   Index-term
E1      1  CO=HAYNES BROTHERS LTD
E2      1  CO=HAYNES FORD AND ELLIOT PLC
E3        *CO=HAYNES PUBLISHING
E4      1  CO=HAYNES PUBLISHING GROUP PLC
E5      1  CO=HAYS GROUP LTD
E6      1  CO=HAYSEECH FOUNDRY (BRIERLEY HILL)
E7      1  CO=HAYSSEN EUROPA LTD
E8      1  CO=HAYTERS PLC
```

(ii) Finding the address of a company's registered office.
(iii) Seeing when a company last filed its annual return and accounts.
(iv) Creating a mailing list for industry sectors within specified locations. For instance, the following list of electronic companies in Oxford was extracted from the ICC database via Dialog in less than 30 seconds.

Figure 5.2: Simple directory search for electronic companies in Oxford.

```
? TYPE 1/6/1-12
1/6/1
1507861                                  ** FULL DATASHEET AVAILABLE **
MEMEC (MEMORY & ELECT.COMPON) PLC


1/6/2
1499342                                  ** FULL DATASHEET AVAILABLE **
HYTEC MICROSYSTEMS LIMITED.


1/6/3
1319856                                  ** FULL DATASHEET AVAILABLE **
THAME COMPUTER SYSTEMS LTD


1/6/4
1038262                                  ** FULL DATASHEET AVAILABLE **
THAME COMPONENTS LTD


1/6/5
990211                               ** ABRIDGED DATASHEET AVAILABLE **
TELEVISIONS SYSTEMS & RESEARCH LTD


1/6/6
902205                                **ABRIDGED DATASHEET AVAILABLE **
SUHNER ELECTRONIC LTD


1/6/7
824412                                **ABRIDGED DATASHEET AVAILABLE **
ACADEMY SIGNS LTD


1/6/8
760747                                **ABRIDGED DATASHEET AVAILABLE **
TELSEC INSTRUMENTS LTD
```

Company Level

At the company data file level there is a wealth of information available and analysed by the computer in many ways to help the user. The Dialog ICC file gives the company name, number, registered office, trading address, names of the secretary and directors, principal and secondary activities with SIC codes and four year's summarised accounts with key business ratios.

In the example below it is worth noting just how much detail has been summarised in the statement. For instance, the key figures have been extracted from the balance sheet and profit and loss account, and a very wide choice of business ratios have been calculated. All of this valuable data is given for the latest four years of accounts filed at Companies House enabling trends to be established.

The same kind of company financial analysis is available through ICC Viewdata which also has a graphics program enabling companies to be compared by most of the ratios listed in the data file example below. An example of a bar chart inter company comparison by profit margin is given in Figure 5.4.

Figure 5.3 Example of financial data file for a company

```
1507861                                        ** FULL DATASHEET AVAILABLE **
MEMEC (MEMORY & ELECT. COMPON) PLC

TRADING OFFICE:
  Thame Park Road,
  Thame,
  Oxon OX9 3XD

REGD. OFFICE:
  Thame Park Road,
  Thame,
  Oxon OX9 3XD

SECRETARY: Stevens, C R
MANAGING DIRECTOR: R T Skipworth
DIRECTORS:
  E A L Sturmer
  C R Stevens
  W A Stolz
  M R Hargreaves

PRINCIPAL ACTIVITY: Co., through its subs., is principally engaged
in distribution of electronic components, microprocessor
systems and related equipment
PRIMARY UK SIC:
  6149. (Wholesale distribution of machinery, industrial
equipment)
SECONDARY UK SIC:
  8150. (Other financial institutions)
```

Memec (Memory & Elect Compon) plc

UNCONSOLIDATED ACCOUNTS (000's Sterling),

DATE OF ACCOUNTS	31Dec84	31Dec83	31Dec82	31Dec81
NUMBER OF WEEKS	52	52	52	52
Fixed Assets	1,925	1,219	638	662
Intangible Assets	0	0	0	0
Intermediate Assets	163	124	101	90
Stocks	7,867	2,426	1,953	1,338
Debtors	9,029	4,559	3,103	1,945
Other Current Assets	889	1,856	1,575	2,080
Total Current Assets	17,785	8,841	6,631	5,363
Creditors	7,561	2,853	1,710	1,738
Short Term Loans	1,079	0	0	0
Other Current Liab	3,816	2,251	2,079	1,426
Total Current Liab	12,456	5,104	3,789	3,164
Net Assets	7,417	5,080	3,581	2,951
Shareholders Funds	6,460	4,438	3,449	2,819
Long Term Loans	0	0	0	0
Other Long Term Liab	957	642	132	132
Capital Employed	7,417	5,080	3,581	2,951
Sales	34,425	18,002	12,228	8,021
U.K. Sales	NA	NA	NA	NA
Exports	NA	NA	NA	74
Profits	4,506	2,809	1,968	1,571
Interest Paid	36	0	0	1
Number of Employees	216	129	107	NA
Directors Remun	205	180	167	149
Employees Remun	2,757	1,528	1,105	NA
Depreciation	146	87	78	62
Non_trading Income	110	154	176	213

Memec (Memory & Elect Compon) plc

BUSINESS RATIOS

DATE OF ACCOUNTS	31Dec84	31Dec83	31Dec82	31Dec81
NUMBER OF WEEKS	52	52	52	52
Return on Capital (%)	60.8	55.3	55.0	53.2
Profitability (%)	22.7	27.6	26.7	25.7
Profit Margin (%)	13.1	15.6	16.1	19.6
Asset Utilization (%)	1.7	1.8	1.7	1.3
Sales/Fixed Assets (R)	17.9	14.8	19.2	12.1
Stock Turnover (R)	4.4	7.4	6.3	6.0
Credit Period (Days)	96.0	92.4	92.6	88.5
Working Cap/Sales (%)	15.5	20.8	23.2	27.4
Export Ratio (%)	NA	NA	NA	0.9
Liquidity (R)	1.4	1.7	1.8	1.7
Quick Ratio (R)	0.8	1.3	1.2	1.3
Creditors/Debtors (R)		0.6	0.6	0.9
Gearing Ratio I (R)	0.2	0.0	0.0	0.0
Gearing Ratio II (R)	0.3	0.4	0.5	0.5
Debt Gearing Ratio (R)	0.0	0.0	0.0	0.0
Gearing Ratio III (R)	0.8	0.0	0.0	0.1
Average Remun (£)	12,764	11,845	10,327	NA
Profit/Employee (£)	20,861	21,775	18,393	NA
Sales/Employee (£)	159,375	139,550	114,280	NA
Fix Ass/Employee (£)	8,912	9,450	5,963	NA
Wages/Sales (R)	0.1	0.1	0.1	NA
Return on Shrhldrs (R)	69.8	63.3	57.1	55.7

Figure 5.4 Illustration of a four company comparison by profit margin

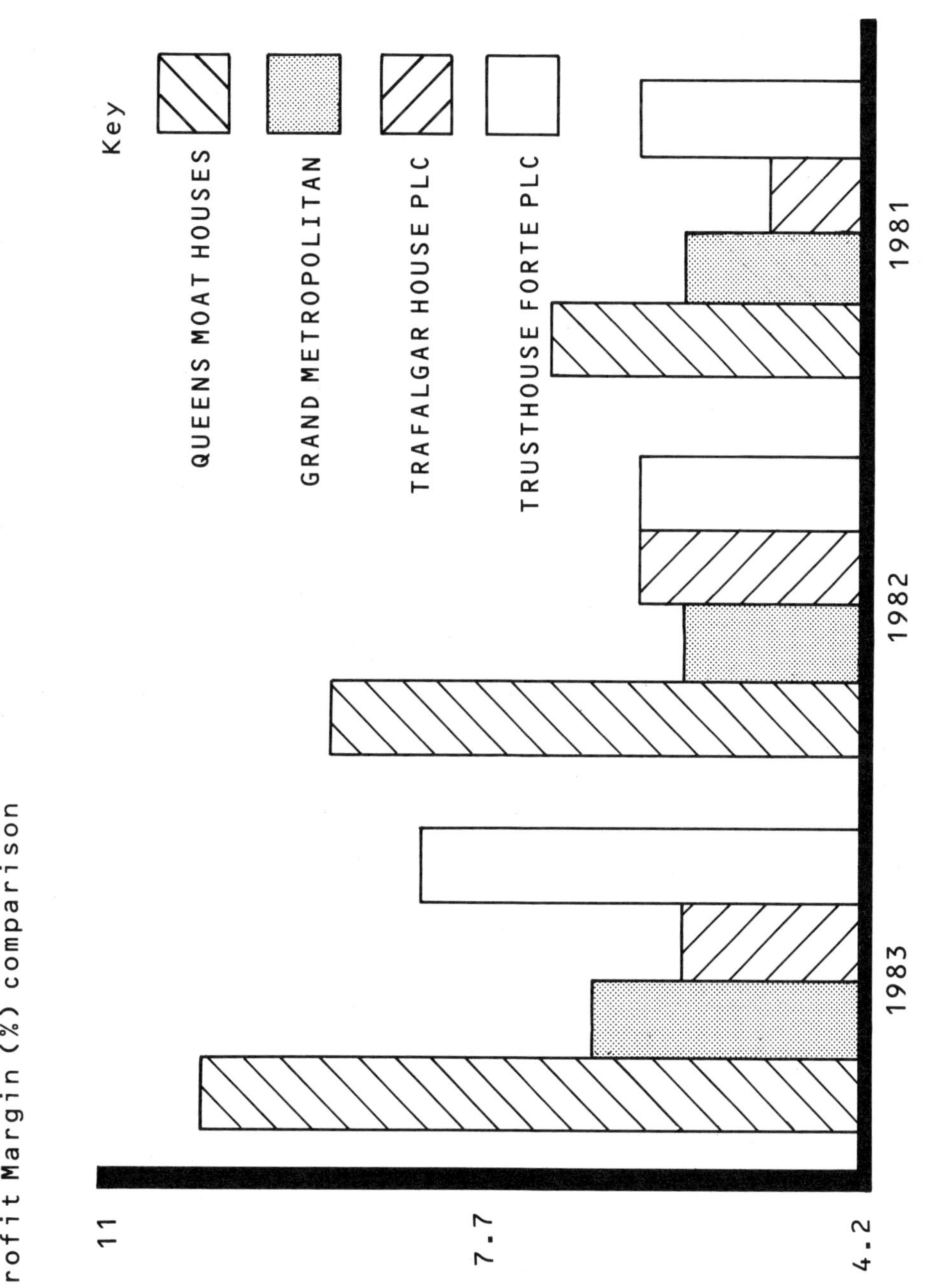

Industry sector level

This part of a financial database provides one of the best sets of financial yardsticks available. In the ICC company file database many years of trading are all aggregated into industry sub sectors. Thus a company in, for example, the electronics industry could compare their profit margins or returns on capital with the averages for the industry.

The appropriate industry sector for comparison can be identified through SIC's or through ICC's own industry sector definitions. Figure 5.5 shows a Viewdata printout of the industrial quartiles for Hotels, SIC 6650. The points to note about this example are:

(i) The large number of comparative measures that enable the user to choose the appropriate measures for the company comparison.
(ii) The quartiles that enable the user to see if the company is performing as well as the best, average or worst companies.
(iii) The number of years that enable trends to be established. The example only shows the latest two years, but many more are available on file.

The upper quartile represents the minimum performance achieved by the top 25% of companies. The lower quartile figure represents the maximum achieved by the bottom 25%. The median describes average performance.

Figure 5.5 Industrial Quartiles for SIC 6650 Hotels, 1983 and 1982

ICC INDUSTRIAL QUARTILES Enquiry Page 1
SIC Code 6650

Year to			31/12/83			31/12/82	
No. of Co.		43			70		
		Upper	Median	Lower	Upper	Median	Lower
Return on Capital	%	13.1	7.3	0.3	10.6	6.0	0.7
Profitability	%	9.4	6.3	0.3	7.4	3.9	0.5-
Profit Margin	%	8.4	5.6	0.6	7.7	4.8	0.8-
Asset Utilis	%	120.5	90.6	52.2	123.6	74.5	42.7
Sales/Fixed Assets	X	1.9	1.3	0.6	2.0	1.2	0.6
Stock Turnover	X	47.3	24.6	12.4	57.7	36.7	15.2
Credit Period Days		10	23	33	15	27	41
Working Capital/ Sales	%	17.4-	4.5-	3.3	36.7-	6.6-	4.8
Export	%	–	–	–	0.0	0.0	0.0
Liquidity	X	1.3	0.8	0.3	1.2	0.7	0.3

*/E/L/#

ICC INDUSTRIAL QUARTILES Enquiry Page 2
SIC Code 6650

Year to		31/12/83			31/12/82	
No. of Co.	43			70		
	Upper	Median	Lower	Upper	Median	Lower
Quick ratio	X 0.9	0.5	0.2	0.9	0.4	0.2
Creditors/ Debtors	X 1.7	1.2	0.8	2.1	1.3	0.8
Gearing Ratio I	X 0.2	0.4	0.6	0.2	0.4	0.8
Gearing Ratio II	X 0.7	0.6	0.3	0.7	0.5	0.2
Debt Gearing Ratio	X 0.0	0.1	0.3	0.0	0.2	0.5
Gearing Ratio III	X 5.0	15.3	34.5	2.4	15.2	45.0
Average Remun.	£ 4882	4435	3331	5119	4162	3245
Profit/ Employee	£ 1823	1251	195	1729	589	157-
Sales/ Employee	£ 26734	17762	12353	24545	15136	11169

ICC INDUSTRIAL QUARTILES Enquiry Page 3
SIC Code 6650

Year to		31/12/83			31/12/83	
No. of Co.	43			70		
	Upper	Median	Lower	Upper	Median	Lower
Capital Employed/ Employee	£ 25204	15060	10206	22419	13699	7046
Fixed Assets/ Employee	£ 22175	13396	9900	19467	13511	8441
Total Assets/ Employee	£ 27936	21392	13879	26821	19967	12205
Wages/ Sales	X 0.2	0.2	0.3	0.2	0.3	0.3
Return on Shrholders	% 17.6	8.6	2.2	16.7	7.7	1.0
Total Debt/ Wrkng Capl	X 2.4-	1.0-	0.3	2.2-	1.0-	0.3
Current Liab. Stock	X 14.0	6.5	2.6	21.2	10.4	4.0
Debtors/ Total Ass	% 0.1	0.0	0.0	0.1	0.1	0.0

The ICC Viewdata program also has a useful graphics capability that provides clear visual presentations of a company‘s performance in relation to the appropriate industry sector by any of the ratios listed in Figure 5.5.

Figure 5.6 Illustration of company and industry sector comparison by profit margin 1980–1983

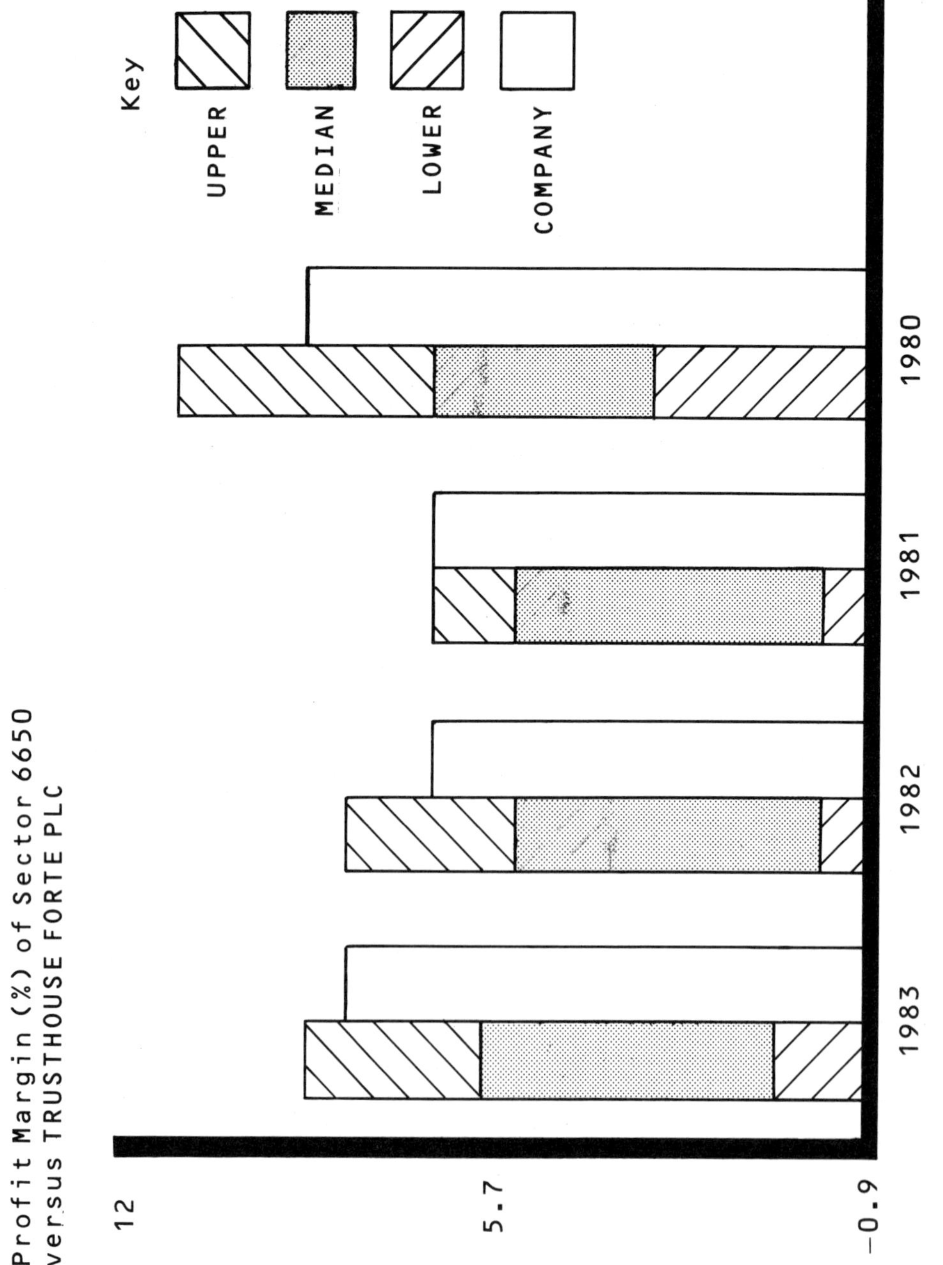

Figure 5.7 Illustration of company and industry sector comparison by sales per employee 1980–1983

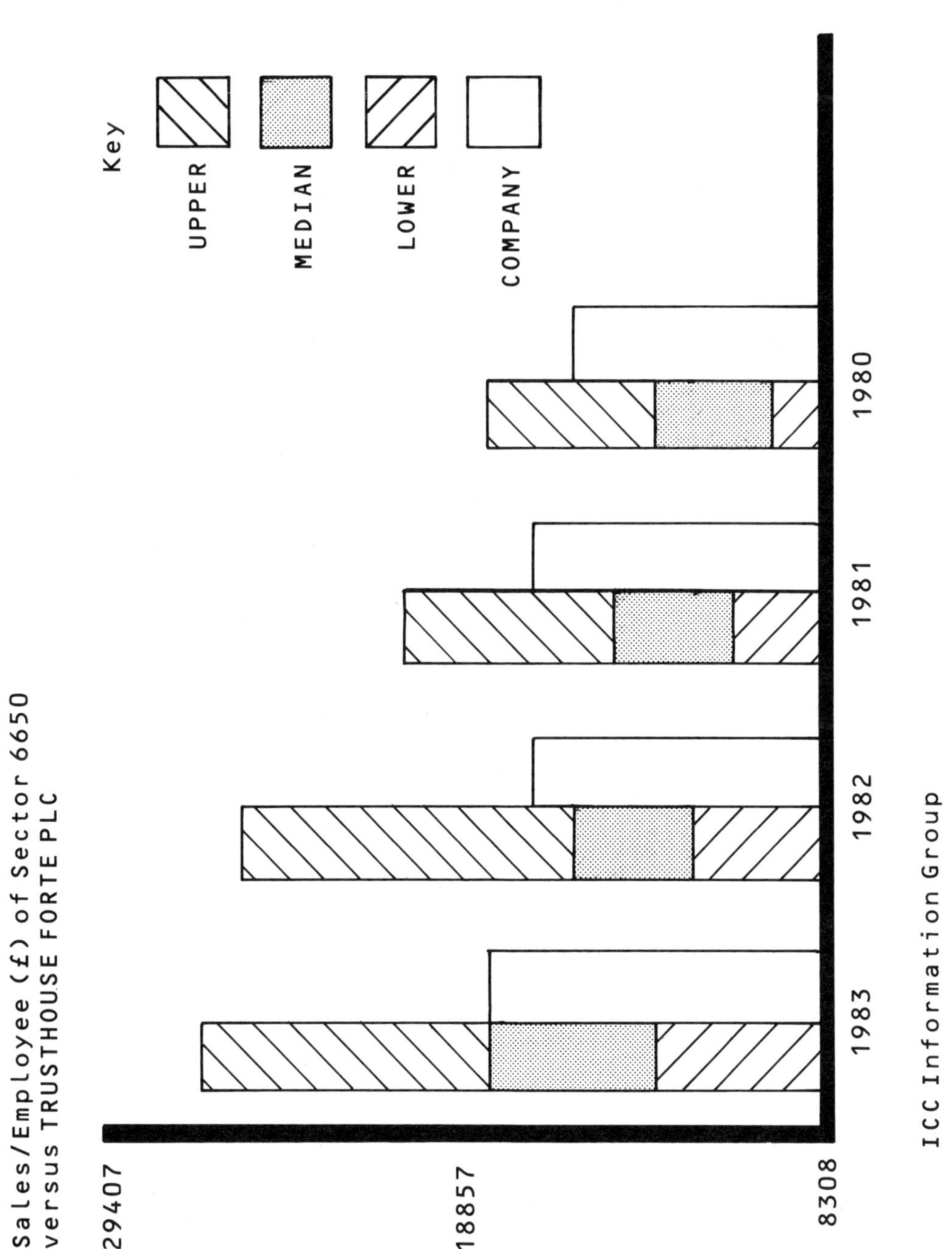

Examples of graphics comparisons are given in Figures 5.6 and 5.7. Figure 5.6 shows how Trusthouse Forte profit margins have been consistently above the median for the industry and in 1981 were comparable with the best. Figure 5.7 measures the company's performance in terms of sales per employee, where the company also shows it has been well above the median until 1983.

Company ranking

Another useful industry level analysis that can be undertaken is a company ranking by a wide range of criteria. For instance, in the Hotel industry using the broad industry definition of SIC 6650 the ten largest companies, or the ten most profitable companies could quickly be identified. Figure 5.8 lists the five largest companies in the SIC 6650 industry sector by turnover and Figure 5.9 the five most profitable companies in the industry as at the search date.

This ranking facility within an industry sector is used in the next part of the chapter on a financial data base search that may be carried out by an investor.

Figure 5.8 Listing of five largest companies in Hotel industry (SIC 6650) by turnover

```
?S HOTEL?/DE OR UC=66?
                 176 HOTEL?/DE
                 316 UC=66?
         1 369 HOTEL?/DE OR UC=66?
?.SORTI1/1-369/SA,D
?TYPE2/6/1-10
2/6/1
291848                                              ** FULL DATASHEET AVAILABLE **
GRAND METROPOLITAN PLC


2/6/2
074974                                              ** FULL DATASHEET AVAILABLE **
BRITISH_AMERICAN TOBACCO CO. LTD


2/6/3
689729                                              ** FULL DATASHEET AVAILABLE **
ALLIED_LYONS PLC


2/6/4
867281                                              ** FULL DATASHEET AVAILABLE **
TRAFALGAR HOUSE PLC


2/6/5
076230                                              ** FULL DATASHEET AVAILABLE **
TRUSTHOUSE FORTE PLC
```

Figure 5.9: Listing of five most profitable companies in Hotel industry (SIC 6650) by total profit (not profit margin).

```
?.SORTI1/1-369/PR,D
            3   369 1/1-369/PR,D
?TYPE3/6/1-10

3/6/2
291848                                        **FULL DATASHEET AVAILABLE**
GRAND METROPOLITAN PLC


3/6/3
689729                                        ** FULL DATASHEET AVAILABLE**
ALLIED_LYONS PLC


3/6/4
076230                                        **FULL DATASHEET AVAILABLE**
TRUSTHOUSE FORTE PLC


3/6/5
029423                                        **FULL DATASHEET AVAILABLE**
WHITBREAD & CO PLC


3/6/6
867282                                        ** FULL DATASHEET AVAILABLE**
TRAFALGAR HOUSE PLC
```

Investor Search

An investor will find a financial database an invaluable tool for making investment decisions. Through various commerical databases the investor has immediate access to the published financial records of over 60,000 companies including almost all of the public companies plus companies in the USM and OTC markets.

A typical investor search would be when an investor wants instant financial information about a company. This can be accessed through suppliers such as Datastream and ICC within less than a minute and the data printed out.

An important investor search than can be easily made using Datastream is large price gains and losses. This is particularly important for investors or fund managers with large portfolio responsibilities and quickly highlights equities that need to be investigated. Figure 5.10 lists the twenty industrial stocks with the largest price rises and Figure 5.11 the twenty largest price falls. A company chosen for deeper investigations can have four main forms of search undertaken:

(i) Share price, dividend and earnings records and analysis.

(ii) Published accounts records, analysis and comparisons with other companies and related industry sector.

(iii) Share ownership.

(iv) Related articles and news items.

Figure 5.10 The 20 UK Industrial Stocks showing the largest price gains yesterday or over the last week

COMPANY	CLOSING PRICE Y'DAY	GAIN ON WEEK (P)	%	DIV YIELD	PER	COVER
BARDSEY	11.00	5.00	+83.3	0.65		0.0
ELBAR INDUSTRIAL	50.00	20.00	+66.7	0.00		
CIFER	16.00	6.00	+60.0	0.00		
BROMSGROVE CAST.	36.00	11.00	+44.0	7.69	6.4	2.9
BAILEY,C.H.'B'	118.00	33.00	+38.8	0.00		
BULA RESOURCES	15.00	4.00	+36.4	0.00		
BURNETT&HALLAMS	50.00	13.00	+35.1	25.00	6.9	0.8
COPSON,F.	43.00	11.00	+34.4	4.98	20.6	1.7
GILL &DUFFUS	190.00	48.00	+33.8	7.52	14.3	1.5
DWEK GROUP	16.00	4.00	+33.3	0.00	15.3	
NEWMAN INDS.	44.00	11.00	+33.3	2.60	19.6	2.6
ENERGY CAPITAL	36.00	9.00	+33.3	0.00		
RICHARDS (LEICS.)	46.00	11.00	+31.4	0.00		
CLAYTON,SON HLD.	128.00	30.00	+30.6	6.70	6.7	3.2
ASSD.BRIT.ENGG.	6.50	1.50	+30.0	0.00		
PRIEST,BENJAMIN	12.25	2.75	+28.9	0.00		
BRAMMER	400.00	87.00	+27.8	2.77	21.8	2.4
RAYFORD SUPREME	225.00	45.00	+25.0	3.11	20.4	2.3
GOODMAN BROTHERS	20.00	4.00	+25.0	0.00		
HB ELTN.COMPNT.	56.00	11.00	+24.4	3.19	24.9	1.8

There are a wide variety of investigations which can be quickly and conveniently undertaken using online databases. The following example uses the Equity Research Service of Datastream. At the time of the search there was a lot of bid activity for department stores, which tended to pull up prices in related equities. Therefore a simple search would be to look at the share price history of quoted companies within the actuary group for department stores. Figure 5.12 shows the print out of this search that would enable the investor to pinpoint companies that warrant further investigation.

Figure 5.11 The 20 UK Industrial Stocks showing the largest price falls yesterday or over the last week

COMPANY	CLOSING PRICE Y'DAY	LOSS ON WEEK (P)	%	DIV YIELD	PER	COVER
MICRO FOCUS GRP.	375.00	365.00	-49.3	0.00		
MOLYNX HOLDINGS	57.00	18.00	-24.0	2.51	16.8	3.4
RADIO CITY A NV.	43.00	10.00	-18.9	12.62		0.0
PENGKALEN	450.00	100.00	-18.2	0.00		
SUNLEIGH ELECTR.	6.00	1.00	-14.3	5.83	14.5	1.7
INGRAM,HAROLD	120.00	20.00	-14.3	1.19	28.5	4.2
V.W.THERMAX	73.00	12.00	-14.1	10.27	7.9	1.8
TELECOMPUTING	420.00	65.00	-13.4	0.34	42.8	9.8
BARTON TRAN.DFD.	130.00	20.00	-13.3	17.58	5.1	1.4
VALOR	177.00	27.00	-13.2	3.71	13.6	2.8
BOGOD_PELEPAH'A'	20.00	3.00	-13.0	4.29	5.7	5.9
BENSONS CRISPS	55.00	8.00	-12.7	2.60		0.0
RELIANT MOTOR	52.00	7.00	-11.9	0.00	84.8	
ADAM LEISURE GP.	15.00	2.00	-11.8	9.52		0.0
FEB INTL.'A'	80.00	10.00	-11.1	5.19	13.8	1.9
TANJONG TIN	200.00	25.00	-11.1	0.00		
BALDWIN,H.J.	25.00	3.00	-10.7	0.00	11.2	
GREENFLD.BLACKS	46.50	5.50	-10.6	2.30		0.0
GREENALL WHITL.A	43.00	5.00	-10.4	3.06	16.9	2.6
SYS.DESIGN.INTL.	104.00	12.00	-10.3	0.47	56.2	5.4

Figure 5.12 Share price record of department stores related actuary group

NAME	PRICE	%CHANGE IN PRICE OVER			%GAIN/LOSS ON MARKET OVER		
		1MTH	3MTHS	12MTHS	1MTH	3MTHS	12MTHS
		STORES-DEPT.					
BEATTIE,JAMES'A'	150.00	+13.6	+26.1	+48.5	+9.4	+20.5	+16.8
BENTALLS	100.00	+14.9	+51.5	+143.9	+10.7	+44.9	+91.9
BREMNER	57.00	-6.6	+3.6	+32.6	-10.0	-0.9	+4.3
DEBENHAMS	366.00	+44.7	+75.1	+114.0	+39.3	+67.5	+68.4
ELYS (WIMBLEDON)	420.00	+2.4	+2.4	+44.8	-1.4	-2.0	+13.9
FORTNUM & MASON	232.00	0.0	+28.0	+60.0	-3.7	+22.4	+25.9
GOLDBERG,A.	55.00	-8.3	+19.6	-46.1	-11.7	+14.3	-57.6
LIBERTY	550.00	+14.6	+19.6	+103.7	+10.3	+14.3	+60.2
LIBERTY NV.	345.00	+30.2	+46.8	+91.7	+25.3	+40.4	+50.8
OWEN OWEN	235.00	+23.7	+30.6	+58.8	+19.1	+24.9	+24.9
STAVERT ZIGOMALA	305	0.0	0.0	+8.9	-3.7	-4.4	-14.3
UPTON,E.	40.00	+11.1	+33.3	0.0	+7.0	+27.5	-21.3
UPTON,E.'A',	34.00	+36.0	+41.7	+6.2	+30.9	+35.5	-16.4
WALKER & STAFF	35.00	-12.5	-10.3	+9.4	-15.8	-14.2	-14.0
WAREHOUSE GROUP	460.0	+17.9	+30.3	+35.3	+13.6	+24.6	+6.4
TOTAL INDUSTRY GROUP DATA							
STORES_DEPT.	+35.3	+61.6	+93.8	+30.3	+54.6	+52.5	

Staying with Datastream Equity Research Service and the department stores related actuary group, Figure 5.13 shows an equity search for Debenhams. A search on this system could also produce an analysis of the accounts, but this kind of search is covered in more detail in later examples. Most of Datastream's time series can be produced in the form of a graph as shown in Figure 5.14 for Debenhams share price record.

THE LIST FROM WHICH ITEMS MAY BE SELECTED IS:

1. PRICE AND RECENT CHANGE
2. PRICE HISTORY
3. RELATIVE PRICE AND RECENT CHANGE
4. PRICE INDEX RATIO HISTORY
5. BETA CALCULATIONS
6. YIELD AND PER
7. EARNINGS UNDER IMPUTATION TAX
8. GROWTH INDICES
9. GROWTH RATES
10. DIVIDEND YIELD RATIOS
11. YIELD AND DYR HISTORY
12. RELATIVE PER
13. PER AND RELATIVE PER HISTORY
14. CASH EARNINGS
15. ACCOUNTS ITEMS

Figure 5.13 Extract of share price, earnings, dividend and related data search for Debenhams

DEBENHAMS £ 0.25

PRICE		% CHANGE IN PRICE OVER		
CURRENT	RANGE(12MTH)	1MTH	3MTHS	12MTHS
366.00	366.00 – 152.00	+44.7	+75.1	+114.0

PRICE HISTORY

	1980	1981	1982	1983	1984	1985
RANGE-HIGH	90.00	109.00	108.00	156.00	219.00	366.00
LOW	65.00	66.00	67.00	90.00	141.00	189.00

PRICE ACTION RELATIVE TO THE FTA INDUSTRIAL INDEX

PRICE INDEX RATIO	% GAIN OR LOSS ON IND. INDEX OVER		
(BASE 1/65)	1 MTH	3 MTHS	12 MTHS
65	+38.7	+64.7	+61.2

PRICE ACTION RELATIVE TO THE FTA ALL-SHARE INDEX

PRICE INDEX RATIO	% GAIN OR LOSS ON MKT. INDEX OVER		
(BASE 1/65)	1 MTH	3 MTHS	12 MTHS
64	+39.3	+67.5	+68.4

PRICE INDEX RATIO HISTORY – ON THE FTA INDUSTRIAL INDEX

	1980	1981	1982	1983	1984	1985
RANGE-HIGH	47	43	32	40	46	64
LOW	32	27	25	27	34	36

PRICE INDEX RATIO HISTORY – ON THE FTA ALL-SHARE INDEX

	1980	1981	1982	1983	1984	1985
RANGE-HIGH	40	39	32	37	44	63
LOW	27	24	24	26	32	35

DIVIDEND AND EARNINGS DATA

DIVIDEND			EARNINGS (FULLY TAXED)		
LAST FIN.YR.ADJ.(P)	YIELD	COVER	LAST FIN YR (P)	LATEST 12MTH(P)	PER
10.20F (1/86)	3.98	1.5	15.0Y (1.85)		24.3

EARNINGS AND DIVIDEND COVER UNDER SSAP 15

LAST FIN.YR.EPS(P)	PER	COVER	LATEST 12MTH(P)	PER	COVER
20.6 (1/85)	17.8	2.3			

FULL, NIL AND NET EARNINGS ON A FULL TAX CHARGE

FULL			NIL		NET	
EARNS.(P)	PER	COVER	EARNS.(P)	PER	EARNS.(P)	PER
21.5	17.0	1.5	15.0	24.3	15.0	24.3

GROWTH INDICES

FIN YEAR ENDING IN:	1/79	1/80	1/81	1/82	1/83	1/84
PER SHARE DIVIDEND						
PENCE, (ADJ)	6.10	6.37	6.37	6.37	6.80	7.50
INDEX (BASE 1965=100)	180	188	188	188	200	221
PER SHARE EARNINGS						
PENCE. (ADJ)	7.4	3.4	7.2	4.1	7.1	10.7
INDEX (BASE 1965=100)	162	74	158	90	156	235
PER SHARE ASSETS						
PENCE. (ADJ)	183.1	175.2	225.0	226.3	222.5	227.5
INDEX (BASE 1965=100)	289	277	356	358	352	360

STATUS DATA ON THE FTA INDICES

DIVIDEND YIELD RATIO (ON IND.INDEX)				DIVIDEND YIELD RATIO (ON MKT.INDEX)			
CURRENT	12MTH RANGE	6M AVE	% DEV	CURRENT	12MTH RANGE	6M AVE	% DEV
104	157 – 98	129	–19.7	90	139 – 85	114	–20.9

STATUS HISTORY ON THE FTA INDICES

CALENDAR YRS:	1980	1981	1982	1983	1984	1985
DIV YIELD HISTORY						
RANGE-HIGH	13.99	13.78	13.57	10.10	7.05	5.90
LOW	10.10	8.34	8.42	6.37	5.09	3.83

Figure 5.14 Graph of share price data for Debenhams from 22/5/84 to 22/5/85 daily

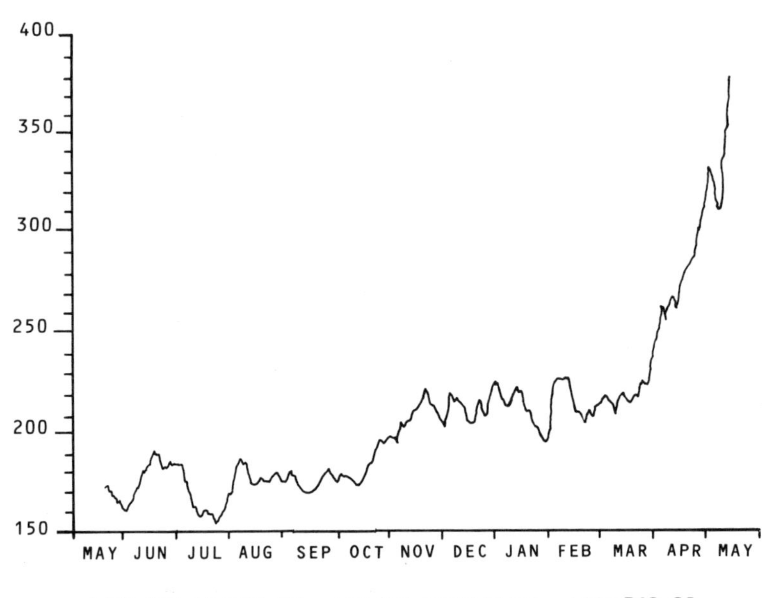

An area of investigation importance to investors is the ownership of shares in companies, industry sectors and share movements. A useful database that may be accessed for this information is the ICC Sharewatch service. The existing online service provides data on shareholdings down to 0.25% of the issued ordinary share capital of over 2,000 quoted companies on the London Stock Exchange and 80,000 shareholders. There is also a Newsline service revealing when large amounts of a company's equity are traded. Offline the Sharewatch service also provides five report options to subscribers:

(i) The largest investors in an actuary group listed alphabetically and by size of holding (Figure 5.15).
(ii) A list of major shareholdings in a specific company with shareholders' addresses (Figure 5.16). Also available on-line.
(iii) A listing of shareholdings above 0.25% in companies held by any individual shareholder or investing institution (Figure 5.17).
(iv) A concentration analysis of shareholdings in companies to see which company has control vested in a few shareholders. A variety of parameters can be set for this analysis (Figure 5.18)
(v) A detailed listing of shareholders in a specific company that can be used for mail list purposes (Figure 5.19).

Figure 5.15 Extract from listing of all companies in an actuary group sorted on share percentage holding

SHAREHOLDER NAME COMPANY NAME	ANNUAL RETURN DATE	HOLDING	%
PRITCHARD MAINTENANCE SERVICES LTD			
ICC OIL SERVICES PLC	28/09/84	22,124,442	42.93
MANX PETROLEUM LTD,			
CELTIC BASIN OIL EXPLORATION PLC	22/01/85	248,443	40.00
MORGAN NOMINEES LTD			
GOAL PETROLELEUM PLC	31/05/85	12,489,025	37.36
ENGLISH SHAREHOLDING NOMINEES LTD			
BRINT INVESTMENT PLC	26/02/85	1,087,725	28.09
SHAFCO NOMINEES LTD			
THE BESTWOOD PLC	29/10/84	384,000	24.62
BURNETT & HALLAMSHIRE HOLDINGS LTD			
BRINT INVESTMENT PLC	26/02/85	899,900	23.24
YULCAT LTD			
GOAL PETROLELEUM PLC	31/05/85	6,705,256	20.06
CLUFF OIL LTD,			
CELTIC BASIN OIL EXPLORATION PLC	20/06/85	115,171	18.54
TEMPLE INVESTMENT AND FINANCE CO LTD			
BRINT INVESTMENT PLC	26/02/85	516,000	13.32
THE CHARENTE STEAM SHIP CO LTD			
CLUFF OIL PLC	20/06/85	1,014,428	8.98
BARINGS NOMINEES LTD			
CLUFF OIL PLC	20/06/85	960,575	8.42
LONDON TRUST COMPANY LTD			
BRINT INVESTMENT PLC	26/02/85	300,000	7.75
HAMILTON INVESTMENT INCORPORATED			
HAMILTON OIL GREAT BRITAIN PLC	03/09/85	5,250,000	7.39
HAMILTON BROS PETROLEUM CO LTD			
HAMILTON OIL GREAT BRITAIN PLC	03/09/85	4,666,667	6.57
HAMILTON_HANNA PARTNERSHIP			
HAMILTON OIL GREAT BRITAIN PLC	03/09/85	4,376,259	6.16
HAMILTON CODY LTD			
HAMILTON OIL GREAT BRITAIN PLC	03/09/85	4,312,470	6.07

Note: The analysis/sort can be made in many different ways.

Figure 5.16 Extract from list of major shareholdings of a selected company

COMPANY NAME: TRICENTROL PLC   COMPANY NUMBER: 0145954

SHAREHOLDER NAME	ACCOUNT CODE	ADDRESS	HOLDING	%
GRACECHURCH TRUST COMPANY LTD	B	54 LOMBARD STREET LONDON	450,500	0.49
CUSHION TRUST LTD		21 MOORFIELDS LONDON	431,915	0.47
SINJUL NOMINEES LTD		21 NEW STREET BISHOPSGATE LONDON	424,289	0.46
EAGLE STAR INSURANCE COMPANY LTD	H	1 THREADNEEDLE ST LONDON	413,500	0.45
SUN LIFE ASSURANCE SOCIETY PLC		107 CHEAPSIDE LONDON	401,700	0.43
DRG PENSION INVESTMENTS LTD		1 REDCLIFFE STREET BRISTOL	400,000	0.43

Note: The analysis/sort can be made in many different ways.

Figure 5.17 An extract from a shareholder's portfolio of shareholdings above 0.25% in any company

SHAREHOLDER NAME: BISGENUS NOMINEES LTD   ADDRESS: 20TH FL, DRAPERS SON, 12 THROGMORTON ST, LONDON

COMPANY NAME: / COMPANY NUMBER:	SHARE TYPE: / ACCOUNT CODE:	ISSUED TOTAL / HOLDING:	SEARCH DATE / %
STOCKLEY PLC	ORDINARY	107,272,465	21/03/85
1767686	A	550,000	0.51
BOWATER INDUSTRIES PLC	ORDINARY	180,778,880	02/01/85
191285	A	1,000,000	0.55
FOSECO MINSEP PLC	ORDINARY	81,494,539	08/11/84
383505	A	650,000	0.80
FLIGHT REFUELLING (HOLDING) PLC	ORDINARY	47,582,388	08/11/84
30470	A	400,000	0.84

Note: The analysis/sort may be made in a number of different ways.

Figure 5.18 Concentration analysis of shareholdings in major companies within an actuary group

COMPANY NAME	COMPANY NUMBER	TOTAL NO. SHARE HOLDERS	ANALYSIS TOTAL NO OF HOLDERS	% CAPITAL
BRINT INVESTMENT PLC	0053044	305	24	91.2
CARLESS CAPEL & LEONARD PLC	0462696	7,980	92	61.2
CELTIC BASIN OIL EXPLORATION PLC	1021799	193	47	94.3
CLUFF OIL PLC	1087471	3,444	48	73.4
GOAL PETROLELEUM PLC	1061863	0	29	90.0
HAMILTON OIL GREAT BRITAIN PLC	0810819	2,738	54	61.2
ICC OIL SERVICES PLC	0303983	2,500	35	86.2
THE BESTWOOD PLC	0447987	372	54	85.9
TRICENTROL PLC	0145954	0	89	50.4

TOTAL NUMBER OF COMPANIES: 9 Sorted in alphabetical order

Note: The analysis sort can be made in many different ways.

Figure 5.19 Extract from a detailed shareholder listing for a specific company.

SHAREHOLDER NAME COMPANY NAME	DATE OF SEARCH	HOLDING	%
BOWATER INDUSTRIES PLC	02/01/85	1,000,000	0.55
CADBURY SCHWEPPES PLC	05/11/84	1,900,000	0.43
FLIGHT REFUELLING (HOLDING) PLC	08/11/84	400,000	0.84
FOSECO MINSEP PLC	08/11/84	650,000	0.80
FRESHBAKE FOODS GROUP PLC	21/12/84	75,000	0.27
MARLEY PLC	07/01/85	750,000	0.36
MARSTON THOMPSON & EVERSHED PLC	28/05/85	415,000	0.48
ROWNTREE MACKINTOSH PLC	29/01/85	400,000	0.25
SAATCHI & SAATCHI CO PLC	18/10/84	271,250	0.96
SCAPA GROUP PLC	09/11/84	637,500	1.96
SEARS HOLDINGS PLC	23/10/84	4,000,000	0.30
STOCKLEY PLC	21/03/85	550,000	0.51
VW THERMAX PLC	07/01/85	290,400	2.50
MCCARTHY & STONE PLC	14/06/85	200,000	2.48
AKROYD & SMITHERS PLC	13/06/85	100,000	0.44
UNIGROUP PLC	06/02/85	175,000	3.02

TOTAL NUMBER OF SHAREHOLDERS 20

In addition to details about a specific company or shareholder, the investor can make comparisons of a company's performance with other companies or the industry through Viewdata. The following example assumes that an investor wants to include in his portfolio a medium-sized printing and publishing company with growth potential. This is done in the following way:

(i) Set turnover parameters. The first search shows that there are 291 companies in this industry sector on file with a turnover above £5 million. As the search is for a medium sized company, an upper turnover limit is set for £30 million. This reduces the number of companies to 216.

(ii) Extract the public companies. This reduces the list to 24 companies.

(iii) Rank the 24 companies in order of profitability (Figure 5.20).

(iv) Select the Datasheet for the companies to be examined: Figure 5.21 shows the data sheets of four companies the investor could be interested in.

(v) Using Viewdata these four companies can be compared visually by a variety of ratio criteria. Figure 5.22 shows a comparison by profit margin.

(vi) Using Viewdata, a company's performance can be compared with the industry sector. Figure 5.23 uses Carlton Communications as an example.

Figure 5.20 Extract of ranking by profit margin of the 24 public companies in the printing and publishing industry sector in 1983

```
?TYPE 11/6/1-24
11/6/1
348312                                    **FULL DATASHEET AVAILABLE**
CARLTON COMMUNICATIONS PLC

11/6/2
171081                                    **FULL DATASHEET AVAILABLE**
CRADLEY PRINT PLC

11/6/3
872170                                    **FULL DATASHEET AVAILABLE**
LONDON & PROVINCL. POSTER GRP. LTD

11/6/4
659701                                    **FULL DATASHEET AVAILABLE**
HAYNES PUBLISHING GROUP PLC

11/6/5
695182                                    **FULL DATASHEET AVAILABLE**
FERRY PICKERING GROUP PLC

11/6/6
1010935                                   **FULL DATASHEET AVAILABLE**
INTEREUROPE TECHNOLOGY SERV. PLC
```

Figure 5.21 Selection of four companies for financial investigation as potential investments

11/8/1
348312
CARLTON COMMUNICATIONS PLC

BUSINESS RATIOS

DATE OF ACCOUNTS	30 Sep 84	30Sep83	30Sep82	31Mar82
NUMBER OF WEEKS	52	52	26	52
Return on Capital (%)	29.3	31.0	52.2	106.5
Profitability (%)	20.7	19.9	33.3	43.8
Profit Margin (%)	25.7	20.3	16.7	47.3
Asset Utilization (R)	0.8	1.0	2.0	0.9
Sales/Fixed Assets (R)	2.5	2.3	5.9	41.5
Stock Turnover (R)	22.4	26.0	94.4	–
Credit Period (Days)	89.0	85.0	43.9	13.4
Working Cap/Sales (%)	33.6	9.0	6.9	36.9
Export Ratio (%)	NA	NA	NA	4.0
Liquidity (R)	1.9	1.2	1.4	1.6
Quick Ratio (R)	1.8	1.1	1.3	1.6
Creditors (R)	39.0	41.0	46.0	60.0
Gearing Ratio I (R)	0.1	0.6	0.8	0.0
Gearing Ratio II (R)	0.5	0.3	0.3	0.2
Debt Gearing Ratio (R)	0.1	0.4	0.6	0.0
Gearing Ratio III (R)	1.4	2.5	0.9	1.0
Average Remun (£)	10,304	10,547	17,834	NA
Profit/Employee (£)	13,705	10,613	16,525	NA
Sales/Employee (£)	53,379	52,402	99,207	NA
Fix Assets/Employee (£)	21,468	22,594	16,958	NA
Wages/Sales (R)	0.2	0.2	0.2	NA
Return on Shrhldrs (R)	41.5	70.0	131.2	194.3

Note: (R) denotes that the figure expressed is a ratio.

11/8/2
171081
CRADLEY PRINT PLC

BUSINESS RATIOS

DATE OF ACCOUNTS	30Jun85	30Jun84	30Jun83	30Jun82
NUMBER OF WEEKS	52	52	52	52
Return on Capital (%)	20.0	11.9	26.3	19.1
Profitability (%)	12.8	7.5	20.3	12.4
Profit Margin (%)	12.7	7.5	17.4	12.5
Asset Utilization (R)	1.0	1.0	1.2	1.0
Sales/Fixed Assets (R)	2.2	2.0	2.6	1.8
Stock Turnover (R)	9.0	15.2	16.5	16.7
Credit Period (Days)	89.0	100.0	99.7	94.0
Working Cap/Sales (%)	15.9	11.5	27.0	9.4
Export Ratio (%)	0.0	0.0	0.0	0.0
Liquidity (R)	1.4	1.3	2.3	1.3
Quick Ratio (R)	1.1	1.1	2.0	1.1
Creditors (R)	45.0	34.0	38.0	54.0
Gearing Ratio I (R)	0.1	0.2	0.0	0.0
Gearing Ratio II (R)	0.4	0.2	0.5	0.6
Debt Gearing Ratio (R)	0.1	0.2	0.0	0.0
Gearing Ratio III (R)	3.7	5.6	0.0	0.0
Average Remun (£)	9,087	8,052	6,987	6,270
Profit/Employee (£)	4,159	2,063	4,170	2,510
Sales/Employee (£)	32,675	27,575	23,915	20,088
Fix Assets/Employee (£)	15.016	13,667	9,283	11,186
Wages/Sales (R)	0.3	0.3	0.3	0.3
Return on Shrhldrs (R)	28.8	17.8	37.3	24.5

Note: (R) denotes that the figure expressed is a ratio.

11/8/4
659701
HAYNES PUBLISHING GROUP PLC

BUSINESS RATIOS

DATE OF ACCOUNTS	31May85	31MAy84	31May83	31May82
NUMBER OF WEEKS	52	52	52	52
Return on Capital (%)	32.3	29.7	30.1	24.6
Profitability (%)	25.1	21.2	20.8	19.6
Profit Margin (%)	18.0	17.2	16.1	14.8
Asset Utilization (R)	1.4	1.2	1.3	1.3
Sales/Fixed Assets (R)	3.6	3.2	3.6	3.7
Stock Turnover (R)	5.0	4.8	4.5	4.5
Credit Period (Days)	68.0	79.0	77.2	84.5
Working Cap/Sales (%)	27.6	25.5	25.3	33.3
Export Ratio (%)	7.9	7.1	6.0	21.2
Liquidity (R)	2.7	2.1	2.1	3.2
Quick Ratio (R)	1.5	1.2	1.1	1.7
Creditors (R)	18.0	55.0	37.0	38.0
Gearing Ratio I (R)	0.0	0.0	0.0	0.0
Gearing Ratio II (R)	0.7	0.6	0.6	0.6
Debt Gearing Ratio (R)	0.0	0.0	0.0	0.0
Gearing Ratio III (R)	0.0	0.2	0.4	0.6
Average Remun (£)	9,117	8,237	7,4378	7,124
Profit/Employee (£)	6,619	5,701	4,815	3,951
Sales/Employee (£)	36,704	33,071	29,845	26,655
Fix Assets/Employee (£)	10,066	10,452	8,218	7,504
Wages/Sales (R)	0.2	0.2	0.2	0.2
Return on Shrhldrs (R)	35.9	33.6	35.4	32.7

Note: (R) denotes that the figure expressed is a ratio.

11/8/5
695182
FERRY PICKERING GROUP PLC

BUSINESS RATIOS

DATE OF ACCOUNTS	30Jun85	30Jun84	30Jun83	30Jun82
NUMBER OF WEEKS	52	52	52	52
Return on Capital (%)	18.5	16.7	19.2	23.2
Profitability (%)	14.7	13.4	15.6	17.4
Profit Margin (%)	13.8	13.4	15.1	17.6
Asset Utilization (%)	1.1	1.0	1.0	1.0
Sales/Fixed Assets (R)	2.5	2.3	2.4	2.5
Stock Turnover (R)	4.7	5.0	5.4	4.6
Credit Period (Days)	86.0	83.0	76.0	88.0
Working Cap/Sales (%)	33.4	36.3	37.1	34.4
Export Ratio (%)	NA	NA	NA	NA
Liquidity (R)	2.7	2.8	3.0	2.4
Quick Ratio (R)	1.6	1.8	2.0	1.5
Creditors/Debtors (R)			0.6	0.7
Gearing Ratio I (R)	0.0	0.0	0.0	0.0
Gearing Ratio II (R)	0.7	0.7	0.8	0.7
Debt Gearing Ratio (R)	0.0	0.0	0.0	0.0
Gearing Ratio III (R)	0.0	0.0	0.0	0.5
Average Remun (£)	7,763	7,232	6,682	6,454
Profit/Employee (£)	4,482	3,946	4,161	4,546
Sales/Employees (£)	32,396	29,425	27,482	25,898
Fix Assets/Employee (£)	13,006	12,741	11,218	10,441
Wages/Sales (R)	0.2	0.2	0.2	0.2
Return on Shrhldrs (R)	21.2	18.8	19.9	23.5

Note: (R) denotes that the figure expressed is a ratio.

Figure 5.22 Comparison of four possible companies suitable for investment by profit margins 1981 to 1983

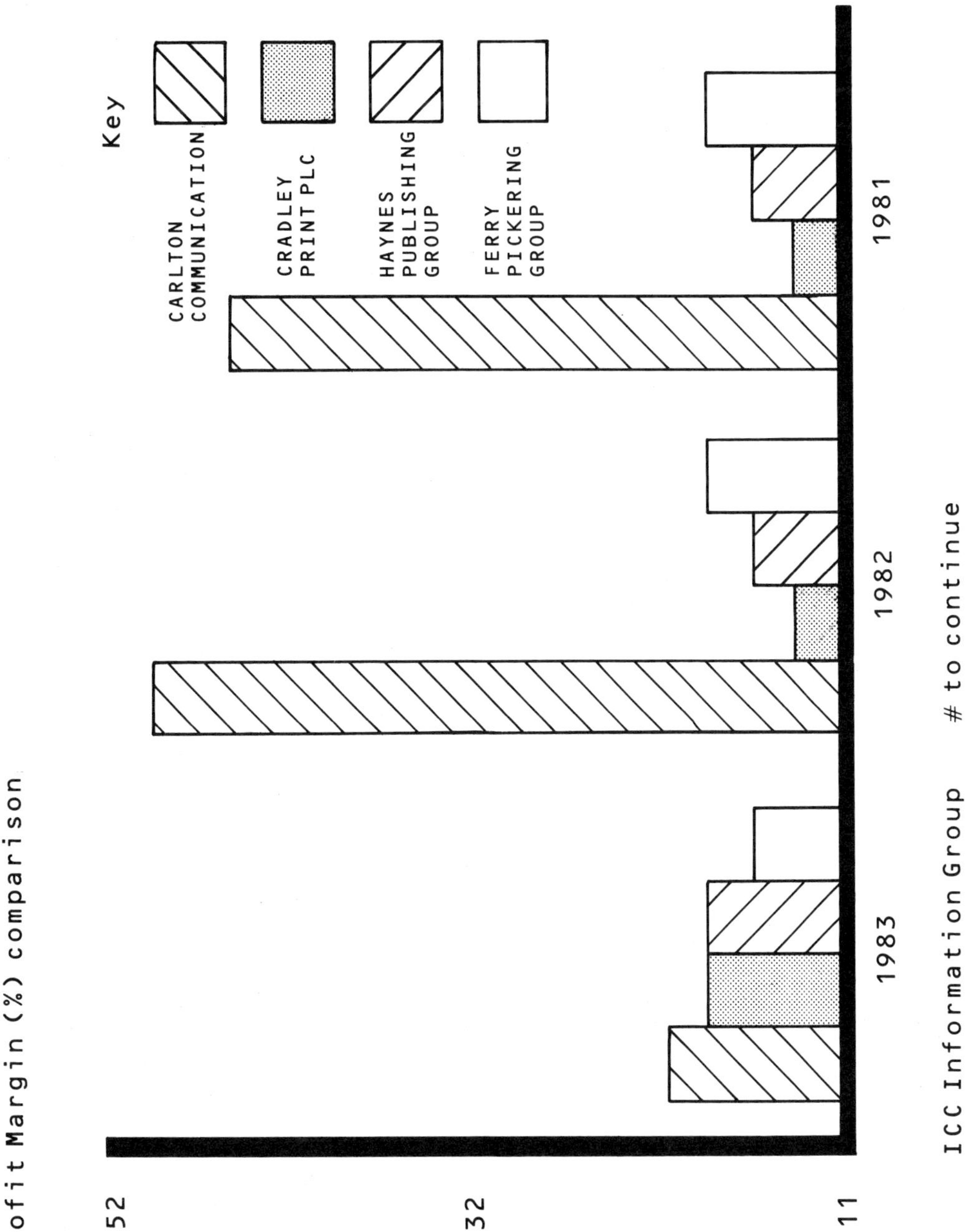

Figure 5.23 Profit margin comparison of selected company for investment with industry average 1980 to 1983

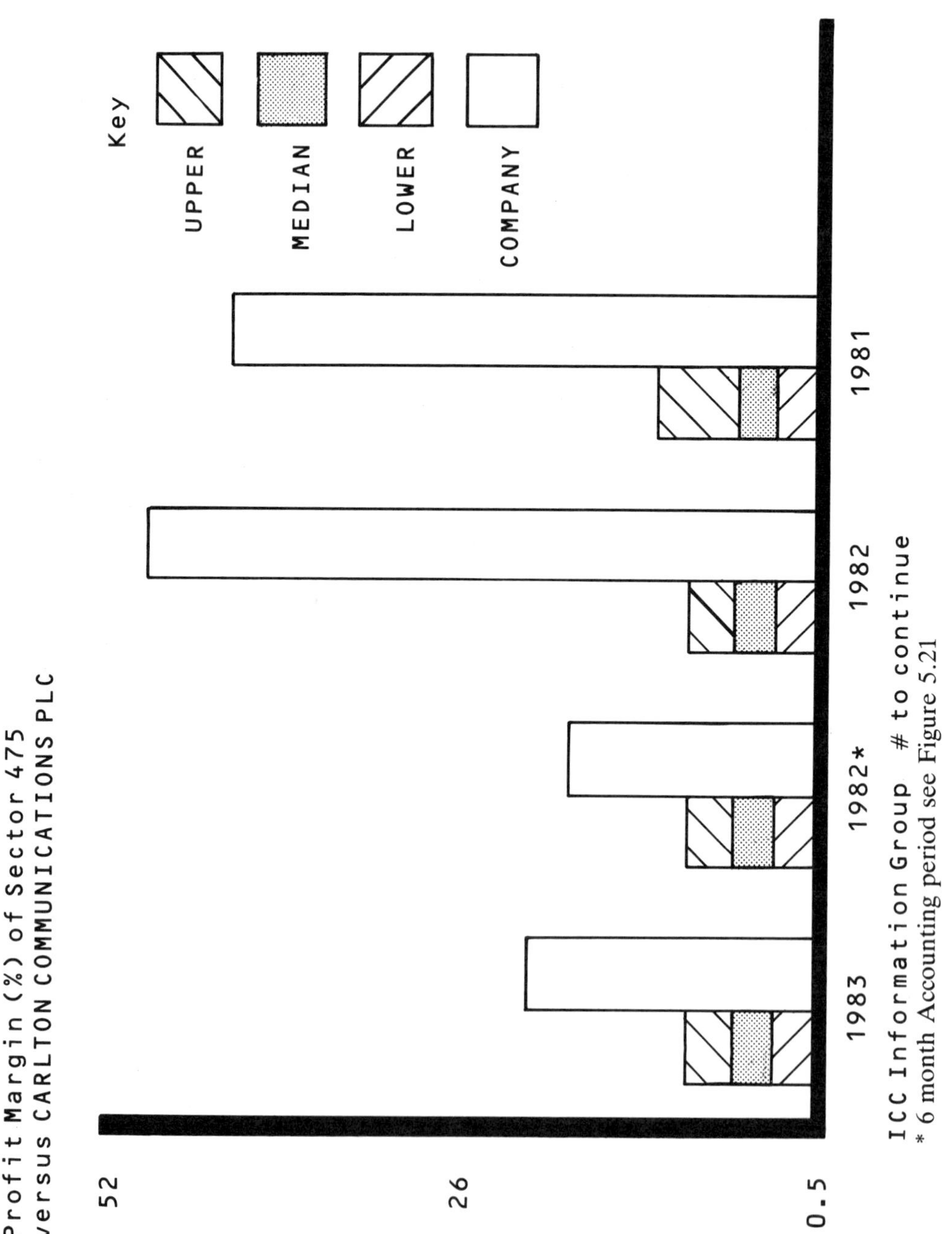

Competitor search

A company wanting to know something about its competitors can access a company financial database and extract the relevant financial details as shown in earlier examples. This kind of competitor search is easy and very useful.

The competitors could be compared graphically using Viewdata as shown earlier in Figure 5.22 or a specific competitor's performance could be compared with the industry averages as shown in Figure 5.23.

In this example however, it will be assumed that a businessman wants to set up a book retailing business in Cambridge and wants to know about his potential competitors. Using the ICC file he can quickly find out that he will have two main competitors as shown in Figure 5.24. If he wants to know more about these competitors their financial data sheets can be quickly printed out as shown in Figure 5.25.

A comparison of companies using different criteria could then be made using the ICC file Viewdata as shown earlier. In Figure 5.26 it is assumed that he decides only two of the companies are real competitors and produces a bar chart of their stock turnovers.

Figure 5.24 Extract listing of major book retailing businesses in Cambridge

```
? SELECT CAMBRIDGE/GE
15      242 CAMBRIDGE/GE
? COMBINE 14 AND 15
16      3 14 AND 15

16/6/2
223043                                    **FULL DATASHEET AVAILABLE**
GALLOWAY AND PORTER LTD
Most recent account date:  30Jun83

16/6/3
106348                                    **FULL DATASHEET AVAILABLE**
W.HEFFER & SONS LTD
Most recent account date:  31Mar83
```

This example of a competitor search for a businessman considering setting up in an area shows the flexibility of a company financial database. There is no other way this kind of information could be extracted so quickly, easily and cheaply.

Figure 5.25 Abridged financial data sheets on potential competitors in Cambridge area

16/5/2
223043 **FULL DATASHEET AVAILABLE**
GALLOWAY AND PORTER LTD

TRADING OFFICE:
30 Sidney Street,
Cambridge CB2 3HS

REGD. OFFICE:
30 Sidney Street,
Cambridge

SECRETARY: Porter, G E C
MANAGING DIRECTOR: G E C Porter
DIRECTORS:
D A Porter
C S Porter
P M Floate

PRINCIPAL ACTIVITY: Booksellers and office equipment suppliers
PRIMARY UK SIC:
6530. (Retail distribution of books, stationery & office supplies)

UNCONSOLIDATED ACCOUNTS (000's Sterling), GAZETTE DATE: 30Jun84

DATE OF ACCOUNTS	30Jun84	30Jun83	30Jun82	30Jun81
NUMBER OF WEEKS	52	52	52	52
Total Assets	280	220	199	183
Total Current Assets	217	175	162	149
Total Current Liab	132	116	109	99
Sales	1,650	1,395	1,202	1,098
Profits	44	24	9	7
Directors Remun	39	37	37	40

```
16/5/3
106348                                        **FULL DATASHEET AVAILABLE**
W.HEFFER & SONS LTD

TRADING OFFICE:
  19 Sidney Street,
  Cambridge CB2 3HL

REGD. OFFICE:
  20 Trinity Street
  Cambridge CB2 3NG

SECRETARY: Heffer,N
MANAGING DIRECTOR: N T Biggs
DIRECTORS:
  C W S Heffer
  J N M Heffer
  N Heffer
  R G Heffer
  S J Heffer
  R A Laming
  J F Welch

PRINCIPAL ACTIVITY: Booksellers, printers and stationers.
PRIMARY UK SIC:
  4753.(Printing and publishing of books)
SECONDARY UK SIC:
  6530.(Retail distribution of books, stationery & office
supplies)

CONSOLIDATED ACCOUNTS (000's Sterling), GAZETTE DATE: 31Mar85
```

DATE OF ACCOUNTS	31Mar85	31Mar84	31Mar83	31Mar82
NUMBER OF WEEKS	52	52	52	52
Total Assets	6,887	6,178	5,300	5,092
Total Current Assets	4,330	4,234	3,631	3,475
Total Current Liab	2,093	2,605	1,933	1,964
Sales	15,133	13,768	12,513	11,471
Profits	254	441	351	293
Directors Remun	151	166	146	135

Creditor search

The most common kind of search a creditor would make is to access the financial database for a specific company using the full data sheet on his potential debtor. As an example, assume a medium-sized printer has received a very large order from a publisher and wants to assure himself that the publisher is financially sound. For this example the publisher will be Haynes Publishing Group plc. Figure 5.27 shows the full ICC file data sheet on the company and enables the printer to make a financial assessment. A quick assessment could also be made using ICC file Viewdata. Figure 5.28 for example shows the company's quick ratio in relation to the industry average.

Figure 5.26 Comparison of two competitors by stock turnovers 1980 to 1984

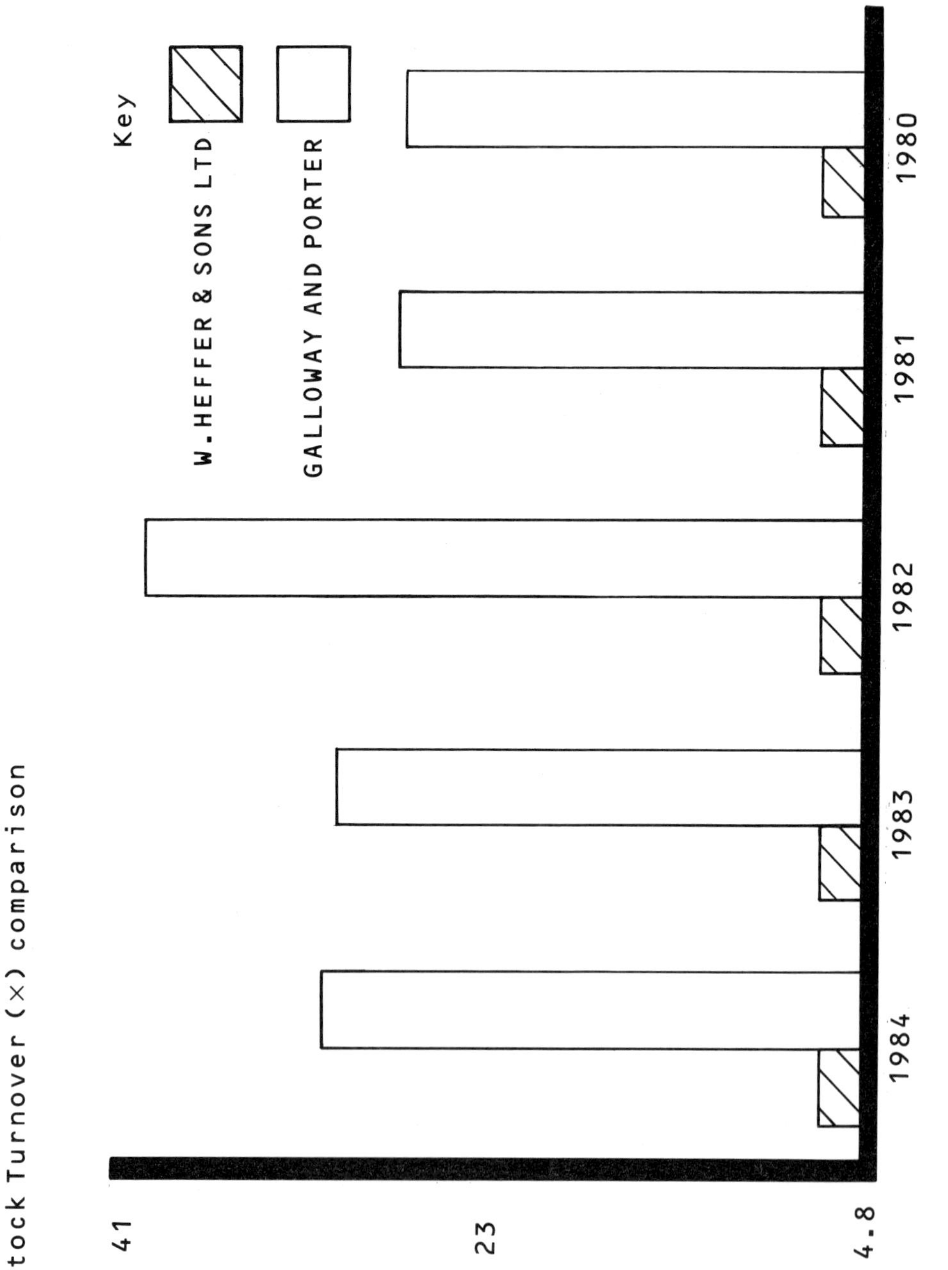

Figure 5.27 Full data sheet on possible debtor company

```
?TYPE18/5/1
18/5/1
659701                                          **FULL DATASHEET AVAILABLE**
HAYNES PUBLISHING GROUP PLC

TRADING OFFICE:
  Sparford,
  Yeovil,
  Somerset BA22 7JJ

REGD. OFFICE:
  Sparkford
  Yeovil
  Somerset BA22 7JJ

SECRETARY: Haynes, D M
MANAGING DIRECTOR: J H Haynes
DIRECTORS:
  D A Quayle
  A C Haynes (Mrs)
  D M Haynes

PRINCIPAL ACTIVITY: Printing,publishing and selling of books and
manuals subjects connected with motorcars and motorcylces.
PRIMARY UK SIC:
  4753. (Printing and publishing of books)

CONSOLIDATED ACCOUNTS (000's Sterling), GAZETTE DATE: 31May85
```

DATE OF ACCOUNTS	31May85	31May84	31May83	31May82
NUMBER OF WEEKS	52	52	52	52
Total Assets	6,784	6,495	5,403	4,662
Total Current Assets	4,123	3,910	3,434	2,922
Total Current Liab	1,576	1,876	1,673	918
Sales	9,433	7,970	6,954	6,024
Profits	1,701	1,374	1,122	893
Directors Remun	237	220	252	230

```
? TYPE18/7
18/7/1
659701
HAYNES PUBLISHING GROUP PLC

CONSOLIDATED ACCOUNTS (000's Sterling), GAZETTE DATE: 31May83
```

DATE OF ACCOUNTS	31May85	31May84	31May83	21May82
NUMBER OF WEEKS	52	52	52	52
Fixed Assets	2,587	2,519	1,915	1,626
Intangible Assets	0	0	0	0
Intermediate Assets	74	66	54	0
Stocks	1,883	1,646	1,551	1,347
Debtors	1,760	1,734	1,470	1,394
Other Current Assets	480	530	413	183
Total Current Assets	4,123	3,910	3,434	2,924
Creditors	470	1,194	707	816
Short Term Loans	10	0	0	0
Other Current Liab	1,036	682	966	102
Net Assets	5,268	4,619	3,730	3,632
Shareholders Funds	4,739	4,085	3,172	2,674
Long Term Loans	0	0	0	0
Other Long Term Liab	529	534	558	958
Capital Employed	5,268	4,619	3,730	3,632
Sales	9,433	7,970	6,954	6,024
U.K. Sales	–	NA	NA	NA
Exports	743	563	419	1,278
Profits	1,701	1,374	1,122	893
Interest Paid	0	3	5	5
Number of Employees	257	241	233	202
Directors Remun	237	220	252	230
Employees Remun	2,343	1,985	1,733	1,496
Depreciation	343	266	247	221
Non_trading Income	134	77	82	58

The consolidated accounts are followed by a ratio analysis. See page 137.

The creditor search example showed how a creditor could undertake a detailed investigation of a debtor or a simple comparison of key ratios of the company in relation to the industry sector averages. Figure 5.28 in the example, clearly shows that this debtor had a strong liquidity base in relation to the industry. (See Chapters 3 and 4).

Figure 5.28 Comparison of debtor company and industry sector quick ratios 1980 to 1983

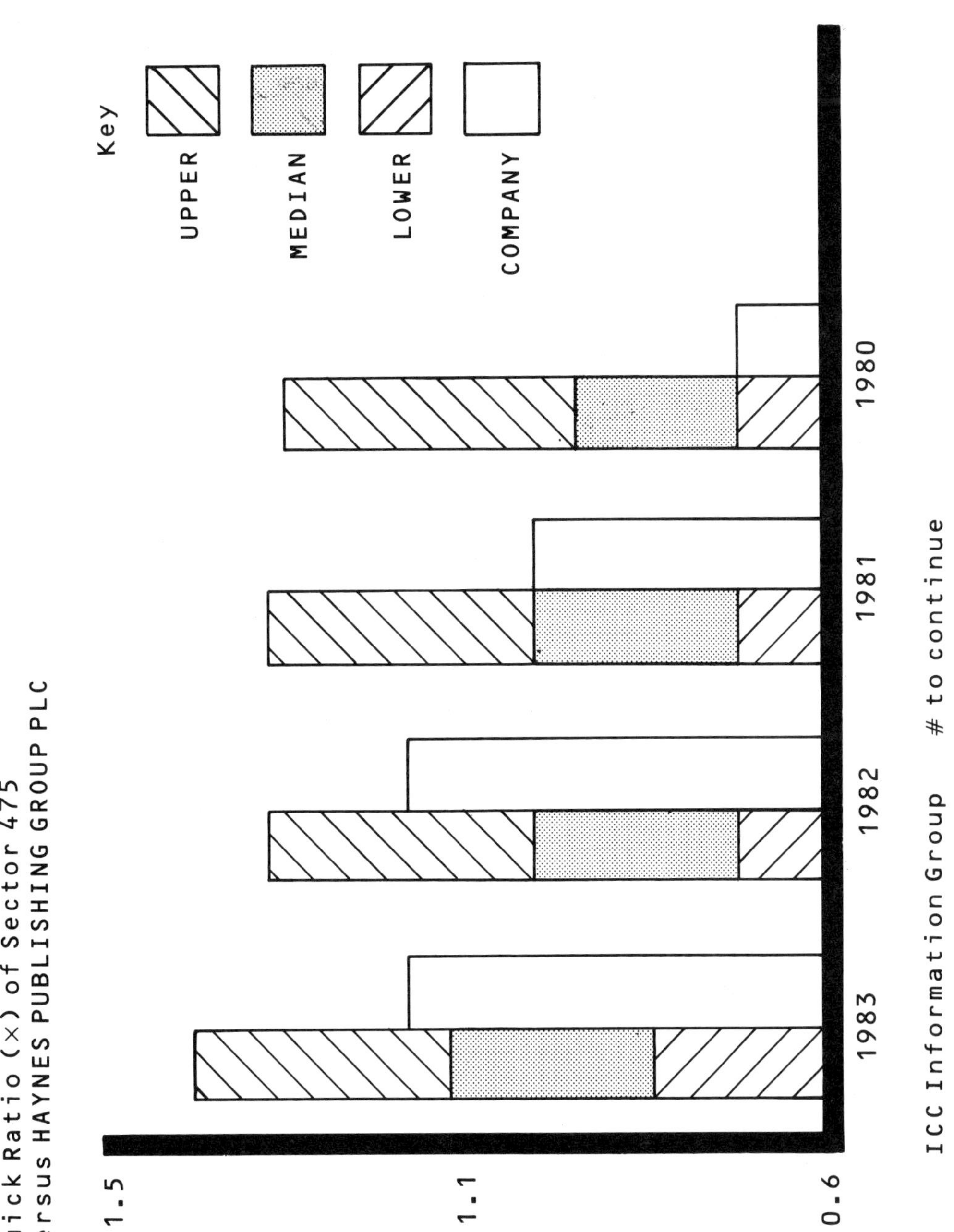

Sales Director Search

There are two main financial database facilities that would be useful for a sales director. Firstly, there is the abridged financial statement on a company which is quickly obtained. This is useful for a sales director or manager to have before seeing a client, because it gives him a clearer picture of the company's ability to meet its trade debts. For instance, if the accounts showed the company as having a turnover of a £100,000 and net assets of £20,000 and this company wanted to place a £1 million order, the deal would need very careful consideration.

The other useful database service for a sales department is the creation of up to date mailing lists. From the ICC file, the print out can be used directly as labels for a mailshot. For example, if a sales manager wanted to mount a sales campaign to say investment and financial institutions in the Manchester area this could be done by:

(i) Identifying post codes of target market.
(ii) Listing out all companies in those post codes with the word investment and/or finance in their names.

The beginning of such a print out is shown in Figure 5.29.

Figure 5.29 Extract from mailing list print out used as sales aid

FLEXIBLE INVESTMENT PLANNING LTD
43 FLIXTON ROAD
MANCHESTER
M31 3QT

1/3/2
1798300

ROBERTSDALE PROPERTY INVESTMENTS LTD
HOLLAND HOUSE
1 OAKFIELD
SALE
CHESHIRE M33 1NB

1/3/3
1775333

CRESCENT ISLAMIC INVESTMENT CO LTD
MAZDA HOUSE
40B RABY ST
MANCHESTER
M16 7EB

1/3/4
1772741

MILTON PARK INVESTMENTS LTD
THE ESTATE OFFICE
TRAFFORD PARK
MANCHESTER
M16 1AU

1/3/5
1771184

CHRISTALEX INVESTMENTS LTD
74 BLACKBURN ST
RADCLIFFE
MANCHESTER M26 9TS

1/3/6
1761509

BRINESTATE INVESTMENTS LTD
BANK HOUSE
CHARLOTTE STREET
MANCHESTER
M1 4ET

An address listing could also contain the name of the managing director if required. One of the advantages of this mailing list facility is that it is constantly updated as Companies House is notified in changes in the registered office.

Employee Search

To illustrate the wide variety of potential users of a financial database it is useful to look at an example of an employee who wants to know if his employer is paying the going rate. Assume a systems analyst working in London wants to see if it is worthwhile applying to other computer companies for a job.

Firstly he can search the ICC Dialog file for computer companies in London and get a print out ranked in order of the highest average remuneration. This list is shown in Figure 5.30 and lists the top 15 companies in terms of average remuneration.

The list shows that Intelligence (UK) pays the highest average wages. The analyst could then access the ICC Viewdata file to see how this company compares with the industry average. The comparison given in Figure 5.31 shows that the company pays far higher average wages than the industry. Further information about the company could then be obtained from a Dialog data sheet as shown in Figure 5.32.

Figure 5.30 List ranking the 15 highest average renumeration computer companies in London

```
30/6/1
1504047                                   **FULL DATASHEET AVAILABLE**
INTELLIGENCE (UK) PLC

30/6/2
1240677                                   **FULL DATASHEET AVAILABLE**
CAP_CPP GROUP LTD

30/6/3
1278274                                   **FULL DATASHEET AVAILABLE**
GENERAL COMPUTER SYSTEMS (UK)LTD

30/6/4
1310493                                   **FULL DATASHEET AVAILABLE**
COMPUTER SYSTEMS DEVELOPMENT (CS

30/6/5
1273380                                   **FULL DATASHEET AVAILABLE**
SUMLOCK BONDAIN LIMITED

30/6/6
537338                                    **FULL DATASHEET AVAILABLE**
THE WEBSTERS GROUP PLC

30/6/7
229231                                    **FULL DATASHEET AVAILABLE**
THORN EMI PLC

30/6/8
1709998                                   **FULL DATASHEET AVAILABLE**
MICRO FOCUS GROUP PLC
```

Figure 5.31 Comparison of a company and industry section average renumeration 1982–1983

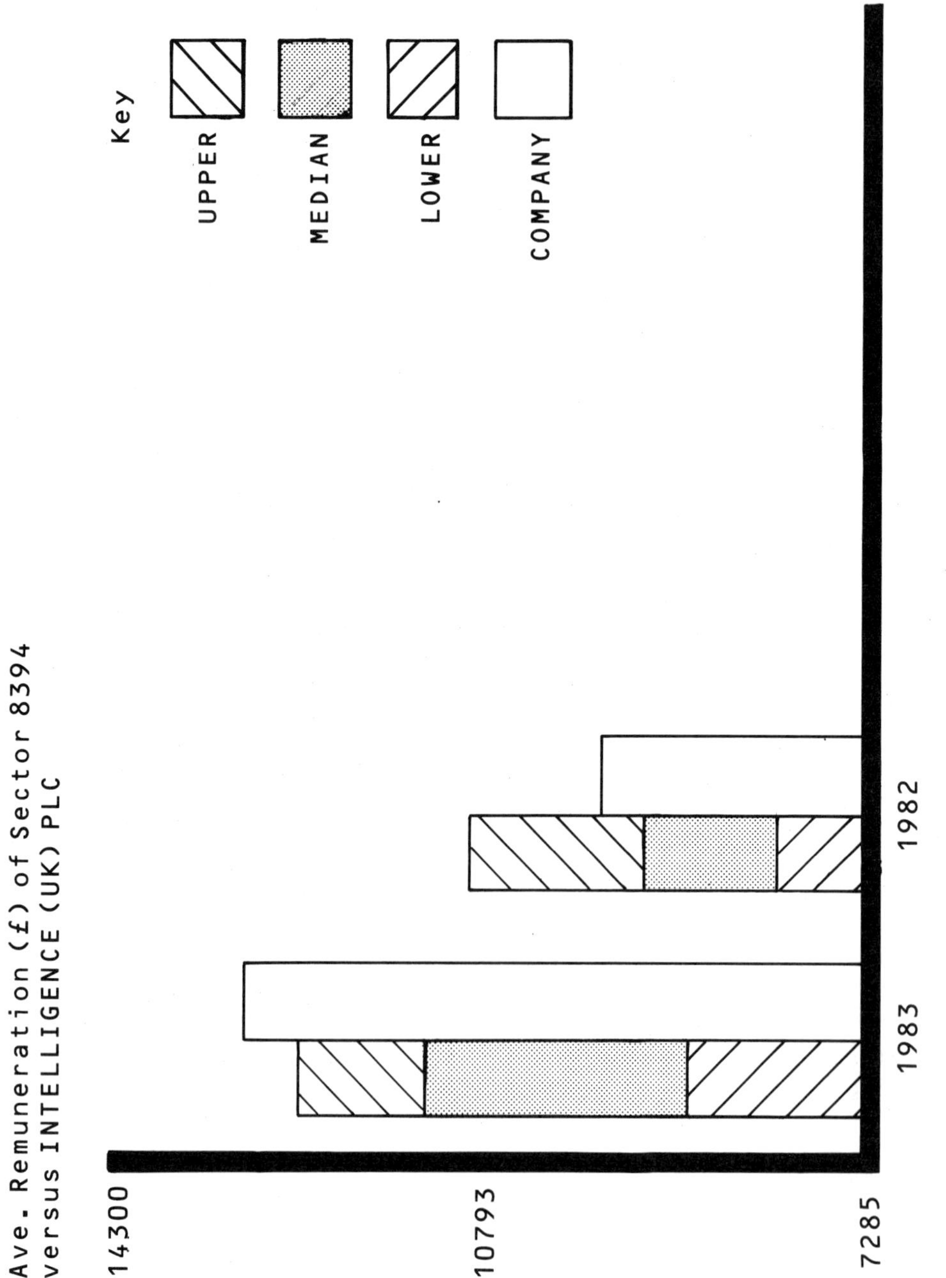

Figure 5.32 Data sheet on potential employer

? TYPE30/7/1-3
30/7/1
1504047
INTELLIGENCE (UK) PLC

UNCONSOLIDATED ACCOUNTS (000's Sterling), GAZETTE DATE: 30Jun83

DATE OF ACCOUNTS	30Jun83	30Jun82
NUMBER OF WEEKS	52	52
Fixed Assets	446	33
Intangible Assets	0	0
Intermediate Assets	0	0
Stocks	163	47
Debtors	464	289
Other Current Assets	33	224
Total Current Assets	660	560
Creditors	117	149
Short Term Loans	169	0
Other Current Liab	203	128
Total Current Liab	489	277
Net Assets	617	316
Shareholders Funds	275	266
Long Term Loans	338	50
Other Long Term Liab	4	0
Capital Employed	617	316
Sales	1,662	742
U.K. Sales	NA	NA
Exports	229	119
Profits	76	205
Interest Paid	35	3
Number of Employees	24	12
Directors Remun	50	27
Employees Remun	312	115
Depreciation	34	2
Non-trading Income	9	1

Summary

This final chapter has shown how valuable a company financial database can be to a wide variety of users. But to get the real value from the data base it is necessary for the user to know what he/she is looking for and then how to interpret the data.

APPENDICES

Acknowledgement: The summary of accounting standards has been kindly provided by Matthew Patient and Leslie Campbell of Deloitte Haskins and Sells.

1. ACCOUNTING STANDARDS

Introduction

Accounting standards in the UK are rules developed, written and enforced by the accountancy profession to ensure consistency and comparability between the financial statements of enterprises. The main objective of the rules is to narrow the area of discretion in accounting practices in specified areas such as: depreciation, stock valuation, exchange transactions, deferred tax, extraordinary items, associated companies, research and development, etc. Their function is not to establish rigid uniformity as say in the French system of accounting reports, but to provide an accounting framework that helps to meet the legal requirement of a 'true and fair view'. There are a number of accounting standards published by different bodies the most significant being:-

(a) The UK accounting standards called Statements of Standard Accounting Practice (SSAP's) issued by the Accounting Standards Committee (ASC) of the six chartered accountancy bodies (Refer to chapter 1 section 4).

(b) International accounting standards (IAS) issued by the International accounting standards committee (IASC) representing the major accountancy bodies from: Australia, Canada, France, Germany, Japan, Mexico, Netherlands, UK and the USA.

(c) American accounting standards issued by the Financial Accounting Standards Board (FASB) a government backed 'independent' institution.

In addition to these influential standards there are important pronouncements such as 'Statements on Auditing'. 'Recommendations on Accounting Principles' and discussion documents. All of these documents relating to accountancy come within the ambit of the broad objective of narrowing the choice in accounting practices.

SSAP 1 Accounting for associated companies

(Issued January 1971; amended August 1974; revised April 1982. Effective January 1982.)

An associated company is a company (other than a subsidiary of the investing group or company) over which the investing company can exercise a significant influence. Most 20 to 50 per cent investments are classified as associated companies. SSAP 1 requires investing groups to account for associated companies in their consolidated financial statements by the equity method. That is, the investing group should include, and should disclose, the underlying share of associated companies' earnings and net assets. The tax charge attributable to those earnings should be separately disclosed, and the goodwill element of the net assets should also be disclosed separately. The investing company's own financial statements should account for associated companies using the cost of investment/dividends receivable method rather than the equity method.

SSAP 2 Disclosure of accounting policies

(Issued November 1971. Effective January 1972.)

SSAP 2 defines four fundamental accounting

concepts, namely going concern, accruals, consistency and prudence. SSAP 2 states that these fundamental accounting concepts are regarded as having general acceptability. If financial statements are prepared on the basis of assumptions that differ materially from these concepts, then the facts should be explained. In the absence of a clear statement to the contrary, it is presumed that the four fundamental concepts have been observed. Financial statements should disclose the accounting policies followed for dealing with material items. The accounting policies should be described clearly, fairly and briefly.

SSAP 3 Earnings per share

(Issued Febuary 1972; revised August 1974. Effective January 1972.)

SSAP 3 applies to all listed companies other than banking, insurance and shipping companies. For the purposes of SSAP 3, earnings refers to consolidated profit after tax, minority interests and preference dividends, but before extraordinary items. 'Shares' means the number of equity shares in issue and ranking for dividend. The net basis of calculating earnings per share (EPS) includes any irrecoverable advance corporation tax and any unrelieved overseas tax, whereas the nil basis excludes such amounts.

The EPS figure, calculated on the net basis, should be disclosed on the face of the profit and loss account. The current year and the preceding year EPS figure should be disclosed. EPS on the nil basis should be also disclosed if this differs significantly from EPS on the net basis.

The basis of calculating EPS should be disclosed, and such disclosure should include the amount of earnings and the number of equity shares used in the calculation. Fully diluted EPS should also be disclosed.

SSAP 4 The accounting treatment of government grants

(Issued April 1974. Effective January 1974.)

Grants relating to fixed assets should be credited to revenue over the expected useful life of the asset. This may be achieved either by reducing the cost of the acquisition of the fixed asset by the amount of the grant or by treating the amount of the grant as a deferred credit, a portion of which is transferred annually to revenue. If the latter method is selected, then the amount of the deferred credit should, if material, be shown separately in the balance sheet. It should not be shown as part of shareholders' funds.

SSAP 5 Accounting for Value Added Tax

(Issued April 1974. Effective January 1974.)

Turnover shown in the profit and loss account should exclude VAT on taxable outputs. Irrecoverable VAT allocable to fixed assets and to other items disclosed separately in published accounts should be included in their cost where practicable and material.

SSAP 6 Extraordinary items and prior year adjustments

(Issued April 1974. Effective January 1974.)

Extraordinary items are defined as material, non-recurring items that derive from events or transactions outside the ordinary activities of the business. Prior year adjustments are defined as those material adjustments applicable to prior years arising from changes in accounting policies and from the correction of fundamental errors. SSAP 6 requires the profit and loss account to show a profit or loss after extraordinary items, reflecting all profits and losses recognised in the year other than prior year adjustments and unrealised surpluses on the revaluation of fixes assets. Extraordinary items should be disclosed separately in the profit and loss account after the results derived from ordinary activities. Their nature and size should be disclosed. Items of an abnormal size and incidence that are derived from the ordinary activities of the business should be separately disclosed and described, but should be included in the results derived from ordinary activities. Prior year adjustments should be accounted for by restating prior years, with the result that the opening balance of retained profits will be adjusted accordingly. A statement of retained profits/reserves showing any prior year adjustments should immediately follow the profit and loss account.

Provisional SSAP 7 Accounting for changes in the purchasing power of money

(Issued June 1974. Withdrawn January 1978.)

SSAP 8 The Treatment of taxation under the imputation system in the accounts of companies

(Issued August 1974. Effective in the UK January 1975. An appendix to SSAP 8 relating to the Republic of Ireland was issued in January 1978 and is effective from then.)

The following items should be included in the taxation charge in the profit and loss account and, where material, should be separately disclosed:-

(a) The amount of UK corporation tax, specifying:-

- (i) the charge for corporation tax on the year's income (including separate disclosure of transfers to and from the deferred taxation account where material);
- (ii) tax attributable to franked investment income;
- (iii) irrecoverable advance corporation tax (ACT);
- (iv) the relief for overseas taxation;

(b) Total overseas taxation.

Outgoing dividends should not include either the related ACT or the attributable tax credit. Incoming dividends from UK resident companies should be included at the amount of cash received or receivable plus the tax credit.

Proposed dividends should be included in current liabilities without the addition of the related ACT. The ACT on proposed dividends should be included as a current tax liability, and if it is regarded as recoverable it should be deducted from the deferred taxation account (if one exists) or shown as a deferred asset (if there is no deferred taxation account).

SSAP 9 Stocks and work in progress

(Issued May 1975. Effective January 1976.)

Stocks and work in progress (WIP), other than long-term contract WIP, should be included in financial statements at the lower of cost and net realisable value (NRV). The cost versus NRV comparison should be made for each item (of for groups of similar items) rather than in total. Long-term contract WIP should be valued at cost plus any attributable profit, less any foreseeable losses and progress payments received and receivable. There can be no attributable profit until the outcome of the contract can be assessed with reasonable certainty.

The financial statements should disclose the accounting policies used in calculating cost, NRV, attributable profit and forseeable losses. Stocks and WIP should be sub-classified in the balance sheet or notes to the financial statements in a manner appropriate to the business and so as to indicate the amounts held in each of the main categories. In relation to long-term contract WIP, the balance sheet or notes should disclose:-

(a) WIP at cost plus attributable profit, less attributable losses.
(b) Progress payments received and receivable.

SSAP 10 Statements of source and application of funds

(Issued July 1975. Effective January 1976.)

SSAP 10 does not apply to enterprises with turnover or gross income of less than £25,000 per annum.

Audited financial statements should include a statement of source and application of funds (with comparative figures for the preceding period). The statement should show the profit or loss for the period together with adjustments for items (such as depreciation) that did not use or provide funds. The statement should also show the following items (where material):-

(a) Dividends paid.
(b) Acquisitions and disposals of fixed and other non-current assets.

(c) Increases or decreases in medium or long-term loans and in issued capital.
(d) Increase or decrease in working capital sub-divided into its components, and movements in net liquid funds (defined as cash at bank and in hand and cash equivalents such as current investments, less bank overdrafts and other borrowings repayable within one year of the balance sheet date).

SSAP 11 Accounting for deferred taxation

(Issued September 1975. Withdrawn October 1978.)

SSAP 12 Accounting for depreciation

(Issued December 1977; revised November 1981. Effective January 1978.)

SSAP 12 does not apply to investment properties as defined by SSAP 19.

Fixed assets with a finite useful life should be depreciated by allocating the cost (or revalued amount) less estimated residual values as fairly as possible to the periods expected to benefit from their use. If the estimated useful life of an asset is revised, the unamortised cost should be charged over the remaining useful life. However, if at any time the unamortised cost is considered to be irrecoverable, then it should be written down immediately to the estimated recoverable amount which should be charged over the remaining useful life.

The financial statements should disclose the following for each major class of depreciable asset:-

(a) The depreciation methods used.
(b) The useful lives or depreciation rates used.
(c) The total depreciation allocated for the period.
(d) The gross amounts of depreciable assets and the related accumulated depreciation.

SSAP 13 Accounting for research and development

(Issued December 1977. Effective January 1978.)

SSAP 13 distinguishes between *research* expenditure (pure and applied) and *development* expenditure. Research expenditure involves original investigation in order to gain new scientific or technical knowledge. Development expenditure involves the use of scientific or technical knowledge to produce new or improved materials, products or processes prior to commercial production. Expenditure on pure and applied research should be written off in the year of expenditure. Development expenditure should be written off immediately except in certain circumstances, when it may be deferred to the extent that recovery is reasonably assured. The circumstances referred to are as follows:-

(a) There is a clearly defined project with separately identifiable expenditure.
(b) The technical and commerical viability of the project has been assessed with reasonable certainty.
(c) Future revenues will cover any further development costs.
(d) Adequate funds exist to complete the project.

The financial statements should separately disclose deferred development expenditure. It should not be included in current assets. Movements on deferred development expenditure, and opening and closing balances should be disclosed. The accounting policy followed should be clearly explained.

SSAP 14 Group accounts

(Issued September 1978. Effective January 1979.)

A holding company should generally prepare group accounts in the form of a single set of consolidated financial statements including all domestic and foreign subsidiaries. A subsidiary should be excluded from consolidation where its activities are materially different from the rest of the group, or where the holding company lacks effective control, or where the subsidiary operates under severe restrictions, or where control is intended to be temporary. SSAP 14 describes the alternative information to be given when a subsidiary is excluded from consolidation.

Uniform accounting policies and uniform accounting periods should, wherever practicable, be used throughout the group. Departures from uniformity should be disclosed and described, with reasons.

When subsidiaries are purchased, the purchase consideration should be allocated between the underlying net tangible and intangible assets (other than goodwill) on the basis of the fair value to the acquiring company. Any difference arising between purchase consideration and fair value will represent premium or discount on acquisition. Where there is a material disposal, the consolidated profit and loss account should include the subsidiary's results up to the date of disposal and should also include the gain or loss on the sale of the investment.

The group accounts should disclose the names of the principal subsidiaries, showing for each subsidiary the proportion of issued shares held by the group and an indication of the nature of its business. Minority interests should be disclosed separately in the consolidated balance sheet, and should not be shown as part of shareholders' funds. Minority interests should be shown separately in the consolidated profit and loss account after group profit or loss after tax but before extraordinary items.

SSAP 15 Accounting for deferred taxation

(Issued October 1978. Effective January 1979.)

SSAP 15 defines timing differences as differences between tax profits and accounting profits arising from the inclusion of income and expenditure items in tax computations in periods different from those in which they are included in the financial statements. Deferred taxation should be provided for on all short-term timing differences. Deferred taxation should be provided for on all other material timing differences other than those that can be demonstrated with reasonable probability to continue in the future. If only a proportion of the timing differences are likely to reverse then it may be appropriate to provide only part of the full potential deferred taxation. The notes to the financial statements should disclose the full potential deferred taxation, split into principal categories and showing for each category the amount actually provided.

Deferred taxation dealt with in the profit and loss account should be disclosed separately as part of the total tax charge or credit or in the notes. Deferred taxation account balances should be shown separately in the balance sheet. A note to the financial statements should indicate the nature and amount of the major elements of the net balance.

SSAP 16 Current cost accounting

(Issued March 1980. Effective January 1980. Being revised ED 35.)

SSAP 16 applies to large or listed companies other than authorised insurers, property investment and dealing entities, investment trusts, unit trusts and not-for-profit entities. Also, SSAP 16 does not apply to wholly-owned subsidiaries whose parent is registered in the UK or the Republic of Ireland.

The annual financial statements of entities coming within the scope of SSAP 16 should include a current cost balance sheet, profit and loss account and notes. The current cost accounts may be supplementary to the main historical cost accounts, or the current cost accounts may be the main accounts with supplementary historical cost accounts (or information).

The current cost profit and loss account should include a depreciation adjustment, a cost of sales adjustment (COSA), a monetary working capital adjustment and a gearing adjustment. The current cost balance sheet should include land and buildings, plant and machinery and stocks subject to a COSA at their value to the business (which is generally net current replacement cost). Reserves should include revaluation surpluses or deficits and adjustments made to allow for the impact of price changes in arriving at current cost profit attributable to shareholders. Listed companies should disclose current cost earnings per share.

SSAP 17 Accounting for post balance sheet events

(Issued August 1980. Effective September 1980.)

SSAP 17 defines post balance sheet events as

those events occurring between the balance sheet date and the date on which the financial statements are approved by the directors. Adjusting events are post balance sheet events that provide additional evidence of conditions existing at the balance sheet date. Non-adjusting events are post balance sheet events that concern conditions that did not exist at the balance sheet date.

A material post balance sheet event requires changes in the amounts to be included in financial statements where it is an adjusting event or where it raises doubts as to the applicability of the going concern concept. A material post balance sheet event should be disclosed where it is a non-adjusting event or where it involves window-dressing. Such disclosure should include details of the nature of the event and an estimate of the financial effect.

The financial statements should disclose the date on which the board of directors approved the financial statements.

SSAP 18 Accounting for contingencies

(Issued August 1980. Effective September 1980.)

SSAP 18 defines a contingency as a condition that exists at the balance sheet date, where the outcome will be confirmed only on the occurrence or non-occurrence of one or more uncertain future events.

A material contingent loss should be accrued where it is probable that a future event will confirm a loss that can be estimated with reasonable accuracy at the date on which the directors approve the financial statements. A material contingent loss that is not accrued should be disclosed except where the possibility of loss is remote. Contingent gains should not be accrued, and should be disclosed only if material and if it is probable that the gain will be realised.

The disclosure of each contingency should include details of the nature of the contingency, the uncertainties that are expected to affect the ultimate outcome, and a prudent estimate of the potential financial effect.

SSAP 19 Accounting for investment properties

(Issued November 1981. Effective July 1981.)

SSAP 19 does not apply to investment properties owned by charities.

SSAP 19 defines an investment property as an interest in land and/or buildings in respect of which construction work and development have been completed and which is held for its investment potential, any rental income being negotiated at arm's length. However, a property that is owned and occupied by a company for its own purposes is not an investment property, nor is a property let to and occupied by another group company.

Investment properties should not be subject to periodic depreciation charges, except for properties held on short-term leases. Investment properties should be included in the balance sheet at their open market value. The names or qualifications of the persons making the valuation should be disclosed. If the valuer is an employee or officer of the company, this should be disclosed. Changes in the value of investment properties should not be taken to the profit and loss account but should be disclosed as a movement on an investment revaluation reserve. The carrying value of investment properties and the investment valuation reserve should be displayed prominently in the financial statements.

SSAP 20 Foreign currency translation

(Issued April 1983. Effective April 1983.)

When preparing the financial statements of an individual company, each asset, liability, revenue or cost arising from a transaction denominated in a foreign currency should be translated into the local currency at the exchange rate in operation on the date on which the transaction occurred. No subsequent translations should normally be made once non-monetary assets have been translated and recorded. The only exception to this is in the case of foreign equity investments financed by foreign currency borrowings, where the investments may be retranslated each year. Any exchange differences arising should be taken to reserves, and exchange differences on the foreign currency borrowings should be offset against these exchange differences as a reserve movement (the 'offset procedure'). Monetary assets and liabilities should be retranslated at the year-end. Exchange differences arising from this retranslation process and exchange differences on settled transactions should be included as part of the profit or loss from ordinary activities (unless they result from transactions that are classified as extraordinary items).

When preparing consolidated financial statements, the net investment in the foreign enterprise should be translated using the closing exchange rate. Exchange differences arising from the retranslation of the opening net investment at the closing rate should be taken to reserves. The profit and loss account of a foreign enterprise should be translated at the closing rate or at an average rate. Where foreign equity investments are financed by foreign currency borrowings, exchange differences can be offset through reserves in a similar manner to that described above in the individual company stage.

The financial statements should disclose the methods used in the translation of the financial statements of foreign enterprises and the treatment accorded to exchange differences. The net amount of exchange gains and losses on foreign currency borrowings less deposits should be disclosed, identifying separately:-

(a) The amount offset in reserves under the 'offset procedure' described above.
(b) The net amount charged or credited to the profit and loss account.

The net movement on reserves arising from exchange differences should also be disclosed.

SSAP 21 (Proposed) Accounting for leases and hire purchase contracts

(Based on ED 29, which was issued in October 1981. The comments below relate to the latest draft of SSAP 21.)

The standard distinguishes two types of leases: finance leases and operating leases. Finance leases are leases that transfer substantially all the risks and rewards of ownership of a leased asset (other than legal title itself) to the lessee. All other leases are classified as operating leases. Under proposed SSAP 21 the lessee will capitalise his rights to use assets held under a finance lease and recognise the obligation to make future payments. The lessee will recognise the implicit finance charges over the period of the lease on a constant rate of charge basis. In this way, the lessee's treatment of a finance lease is similar to his treatment of owned assets that are financed by borrowing. In comparison, the lessee's treatment of operating leases will be simply to treat operating rentals as a revenue expense. The lessor's treatment of finance leases follows the same concepts as those applied to the lessee. That is, the lessor will account for finance leases as amounts receivable in the same way as instalment debt. The finance income from finance leases will be recognised on a constant rate of return based on the amount of funds the lessor has invested in the lease. In comparison, the lessor will treat assets leased under operating leases as fixed assets and depreciate them over their useful lives. Under proposed SSAP 21 lessees and lessors will need to make certain specific disclosures amplifying the balance sheet and loss information.

2. BUSINESS INFORMATION FROM COMMERCIAL SOURCES

The traditional commercial sources of business information have been from specialist publishers, trade associations and professional bodies producing directories, reports and surveys. These publications still provide useful information, but many of the hard copy publications are being replaced or supplemented by electronic publishing in the form of an online data bases.

This appendix provides addresses of some relevant trade associations, professional bodies and specialist publishers. There is also a summary of database suppliers, with brief details of their databases. Much of this listing is based on an excellent publication Accountants Digest 166 produced by the Institute of Chartered Accountants in England & Wales. For further details such as communication links, costs and an excellent analysis of online systems, readers are recommended to refer to this publication.

UK Accountancy Bodies

Chartered Accountancy Bodies

The Institute of Chartered Accountants in England and Wales (ICAEW)
Chartered Accountants' Hall
Moorgate Place
London EC2P 2BJ
01–628 7060

The Association of Certified Accountants (ACA)
29 Lincoln's Inn Fields
London WC2A 3EE
01–242 6855

The Institute of Cost and Management Accountants (ICMA)
63 Portland Place
London W1N 4AB
01–637 2311

The Institute of Chartered Accountants of Scotland (ICAS)
27 Queen Street
Edinburgh EH2 1LA
031–225 5673

The Chartered Institute of Public Finance and Accountancy (CIPFA)
3 Robert Street
London WC2N 6BH
01–930 3456

The Institute of Chartered Accountants in Ireland (ICAI)
7 Fitzwilliam Place
Dublin 2
0001 760288 and at
11 Donegal Square South,
Belfast BT1 NJE
0232 221600

The Chartered Accountancy Bodies

The Institute of Administrative Accountants (IAA)
Burford House
44 London Road
Sevenoaks
Kent TN13 1AS
0732 458080

The Society of Company and Commercial Accountants (SCCA)
40 Tyndalls Park Road
Bristol BS8 1PL
0272 738261

The Association of International Accountants (AIA)
2–10 St John's Street
Bedford MK42 ODW
0234 213557/8

The Association of Cost and Executive Accountants (ACEA)
Tower House
141–149 Fonthill Road
London N4 3HF
01–272 3925

The Association of Authorised Public Accountants (AAPA)
c/o 29 Lincoln's Inn Fields
London WC2A 3EE
01–242 6855

The Association of Corporate Treasurers (ACT)
16 Park Crescent
London W1W 4AH
01–631 1991

The Institute of Certified Public Accountants in Ireland
22 Upper Fitzwilliam Street
Dublin 2
0001 767353

Institute of Incorporated Public Accountants
60 Lower Bagot Street
Dublin 2
0001 785302

Quasi Accountancy Bodies

Institute of Internal Auditors United Kingdom Ltd
82Z Portland Place
London W1N 3DH
01–580 0101

The Institute of Taxation
3 Grosvenor Crescent
London SW1X 7EL
01–235 8847

Insolvency Practitioners Association
St Paul's House
Park Square
Leeds LS1 2PJ
0532 438222

Professional and Trade Associations

Accepting Houses Committee
Granite House
101 Cannon Street
London EC3N 2NJ
01–481 1896

Advertising Association (The)
Abford House
15 Wilton Road
London SW1V 1NJ
01–828 2771

Anglo-Japanese Economic Institute
342 Grand Buildings
Trafalgar Square
London WC2
01–930 5567

Associated Australian Banks in London (The)
71 Cornhill
London EC3V 3PR

Association of British Chambers of Commerce
212 Shaftesbury Avenue
London WC2
01–240 5831

Association of British Factors Ltd
Moor House
London Wall
London EC2Y 5HE
01–638 4090

Association of Consortium Banks
International Mexican Bank Ltd
29 Gresham Street
London EC2V 7ES
01–600 0880

Association of Consulting Actuaries (The)
Rolls House
7 Rolls Buildings
Fetter Lane
London EC4A 1NH
01–831 7130

Association of Corporate Trustees (The)
2 Withdean Rise
Brighton
East Sussex BN1 6YN
0273 504276

Association of Independent Businesses
Trowbray House
108 Weston Street
London SE1 3QB
01–403 4066

Association of Independent Contract Research Organisations Ltd
Bridge Works
Shoreham-by-Sea
West Sussex BN4 5FG
(079 17) 5611

Association of Independent Investment Managers (The)
19 Widegate Street
off Bishopsgate
London E1 7HP
01–247 2229

Association of Insurance & Risk Managers in Industry & Commerce
Plantation House
31–35 Fenchurch Street
London EC3M 7DX
01–621 0337

Association of International Bond Dealers (The)
c/o Orion Royal Bank Ltd
1 London Wall
London EC2Y 5JX
01–600 6222

Association of Investment Trust Companies (The)
6th Floor
Park House
16 Finsbury Circus
London EC2M 7JJ
01–588 5347

Aviation Insurance Offices Association
110–112 Fenchurch Street
London EC3M 5JJ
01–283 7101

Baltic Exchange [The]
St Mary Axe
London EC3A 8BU
01–623 5501

Banking Information Service
10 Lombard Street
London EC3V 9AR
01–626 8486

Booksellers Assoc. of Great Britain & Ireland
154 Buckingham Palace Rd.
London SW1W 9TZ
01–730 8214

British Bankers Association
10 Lombard Street
London EC3V 9EL
01–623 4001

British Computer Society
13 Mansfield Street
London W1M 0BP
01–637 0471

British Export Houses Association
69 Cannon Street
London EC4N 5AB
01–248 4444

British Importers Confederation
69 Cannon Street
London EC4N 5AB
01–248 4444

British Institute of Management
Management House
Parker Street
London WC2B 5PT
01–405 3456

British Insurance Association
Aldermary House
Queen Street
London EC4N 1TU
01–248 4477

British Insurance Brokers' Association [The]
Fountain House
130 Fenchurch Street
London EC3M 5DJ
01–623 9043

British Overseas & Commonwealth Banks Association
10 Clements Lane
London EC4N 7AB
01–623 7500

British Footwear Manufacturers Federation
Royalty House
72 Dean Street
London
W1V 5HB
01–437 5573

British Printing Industries Federation
11 Bedford Row
London
WC1R 4DX
01–242 6904

British Security Industry Association Ltd [The]
21 Whitefriars Street
London EC4Y 8AL
01–353 6760

British Shippers' Council
Hermes House
St John's Road
Tunbridge Wells
Kent TN4 7UZ
0892 26171

British Trade Corporation
65 South Audley Street
London W1
01–486 2700

British Venture Capital Association [The]
Electra House
Temple Place
Victoria Embankment
London WC2R 3HP
01–836 7766

Building Societies Association
[The]
3 Savile Row
London W1X 1AF
01–437 0655

Business Archives Council
Denmark House
15 Tooley Street
London SE1 2PN
01–407 6110

Charities Aid Foundation
48 Pembury Rd
Tonbridge
Kent
0732 356323

Chartered Institute of Arbitrators
69–75 Cannon Street
London EC4N 5BH
01–236 8761

Chartered Institute of Loss Adjusters
[The]
Manfield House
376 Strand
London WC2R 0LR
01–240 1496

Chartered Insurance Institute [The]
20 Aldermanbury
London EC2V 7HY
01–606 3835

Committee of London Clearing Bankers
10 Lombard Street
London EC3V 9AP
01–283 8866

Committee of Scottish Clearing Bankers
[The]
19 Rutland Square
Edinburgh EH1 2DD
031–229 1326

Company Pensions Information Centre
7 Old Park Lane
London W1Y 3LJ
01–493 4757

Computing Services Association
5th Floor
Hanover House
73–74 High Holborn
London WC1V 6LE
01–405 2171

Confederation of British Industry
(CBI)
Centre Point
New Oxford St
London WC1
01–379 7400

Consumer Credit Trade Association
3 Berners Street
London W1E 4JZ
01–636 7564

Co-operative Union Ltd
Holyoake House
Hanover Street
Manchester M60 0AS
061–834 0975

Electronic Components Industry
Federation
7/8 Saville Row
London W1X 1AF
01–437 4127

Engineering Employer's Federation
Broadway House
Tothill Street
London SW1H 9NQ
01–222 7777

Equipment Leasing Association
18 Upper Grosvenor Street
London W1X 9PB
01–491 2783

Faculty of Actuaries
23 St Andrew Square
Edinburgh EH2 1AQ
031–556 6791

Faculty of Architects & Surveyors
St Mary's House
St Mary's Street
Chippenham
Wiltshire
0249 55397

Fed. of British Hand Tool Manufacturers
Light Trades House
Melbourne Avenue
Sheffield S10 2QJ
0742 663084

Federation of Commodity Associations [The]
Plantation House
Mincing Lane
London EC3M 3HT
01–626 1745

Finance Houses Association
18 Upper Grosvenor Street
London W1X 9PB
01–491 2783

Foreign Banks Association
3 Bishopsgate
London EC2N 4AD
01–283 1080

Foreign Exchange and Currency Deposit Brokers Association
c/o Kirkland-Whittaker Group Ltd
67 Chiswell Street
London EC1Y 4XX
01–638 9354

Freight Transport Association Ltd [The]
Hermes House
St John's Road
Tunbridge Wells
Kent TN4 9UZ
Tunbridge Wells (0892) 26171

Industrial Life Offices Association
Aldermary House
Queen Street
London EC4N 1TL
01–248 4477

Institute for Fiscal Studies
1–2 Castle Lane
London SW1E 6DR
01–828 7545

Institute of Actuaries
Staple Inn Hall
High Holborn
London WC1V 7QJ
01–242 0106

Institute of Bankers [The]
10 Lombard Street
London EC3V 9AS
01–623 3531

Institute of Bankers in Ireland [The]
Nassau House
Nassau Street
Dublin 2
0001 777199

Institute of Bankers in Scotland [The]
20 Rutland Square
Edinburgh EH1 2BB
031–229 9869

Institute of Chartered Secretaries and Administrators
16 Park Crescent
London W1N 4AH
01–580 4741

Institute of Chartered Shipbrokers
24 St Mary Axe
London EC3A 8DE
01–283 1361

Institute of Directors
116 Pall Mall
London SW1Y 5ED
01–839 1233

Institute of Economic Affairs
2 Lord North Street
London SW1P 3LB
01–799 3745

Institute of Export
Europe House
World Trade Centre
East Smithfield
London E1 9AA
01–488 4766

Institute of Management Consultants Ltd
23–24 Cromwell Place
London SW7 2LG
01–584 7285

Institute of Personnel Management [The]
IPM House
35 Camp Road
London SW19 4UW
01–946 9100

Institute of Practitioners in Advertising
44 Belgrave Square
London SW1X 8QS
01–235 7020

Institute of Public Relations
Gate House
St John's Square
London EC1M 4DH
01–253 5151

International Commodities Clearing House Ltd
Roman Wall House
1–2 Crutched Friars
London EC3N 2AN
01–488 3200

Issuing Houses Association
Granite House
101 Cannon Street
London EC4N 5BA
01–283 7334

Law Society [The]
113 Chancery Lane
London WC2A 1PL
01–242 1222

Leather Producers Association
9 St Thomas Street
London SE1 9SA
01–407 1522

Life Offices' Association [The]
Aldermary House
Queen Street
London EC4N 1TP
01–236 1101

Lloyd's Insurance Brokers' Committee
Fountain House
130 Fenchurch Street
London EC3M 5DJ
01–623 9043

Lloyd's of London
Lime Street
London EC3M 7HA
01–623 7100

Lloyd's Register of Shipping
71 Fenchurch Street
London EC3M 4BS
01–709 9166

Lloyd's Shipping Information Services
4 Lloyd's Avenue
London EC3N 3ED
01–709 9166

London Chamber of Commerce & Industry
69 Cannon Street
London EC4N 5AB
01–248 4444

London Commodity Exchange Co Ltd [The]
Cereal House
58 Mark Lane
London EC3R 7NE
01–481 2080

London Discount Market Association
39 Cornhill
London EC3V 3NU
01–623 1020

London International Financial Futures Exchange [The]
Royal Exchange
London EC3V 3PJ
01–623 0444

Management Consultants Association Ltd
23–24 Cromwell Place
London SW7 2LG
01–584 7283

Market Research Society [The]
15 Belgrave Square
London SW1X 8PF
01–236 4709

Motor Agents Association
201 Gt Portland Street
London W1N 6AB
01–580 9122

Motor Insurance Bureau
Aldermary House
Queen Street
London EC4N 1TR
01–248 4477

National Association of Estate Agents
Central London Branch
c/o Eastern Estate Office
63 Broadway
London E15
01–555 0521

National Association of Pension Funds [The]
Sunley House
Bedford Park
Croydon CR0 0XF
01–681 2017

National Chamber of Trade
Enterprise House
Henley-on-Thames
Oxfordshire RG9 1TU
Henley-on-Thames
0491 576161

National Federation of Self-Employed & Small Businesses Ltd
32 St Anne's Road West
Lytham St Anne's
Lancashire FY8 1NY
0253 720911
also at
140 Lower Marsh
Westminster Bridge
London SE1 7AE
01–928 9272

National Institute of Economic & Social Research
2 Dean Trench Street
London SW1P 3HE
01–222 7665

National Pharmaceutical Association Ltd
40–42 St Peter's Street
St Albans
Herts AL1 3ND
0727 32161

Newspaper Society
Whitefriars House
Carmelite Street
London EC4
01–353 4722

Northern Ireland Bankers Association
Fountain House
19 Donegal Place
Belfast BT1 5AB
0232 227551

Occupational Pensions Board
Lynwood Road
Thames Ditton
Surrey KT7 0DP
01–398 4242

Panel on Take-overs and Mergers
PO Box 226
The Stock Exchange Building
London EC2P 2JX
01–628 2318

Public Relations Consultants Association
37 Cadogan Street
Sloane Square
London SW3 2PR
01–581 3951

Radio Equipment Manufacturers Association
Twentieth Century House
31 Soho Square
London W1V 5DG
01–734 7471

Rating & Valuation Association
115 Ebury Street
London SW1
01-730 7258

Ready Mixed Concrete Association
Shepperton House
Green Lane
Shepperton
Middlesex
09322 43232

Registrar of Companies [The]
Companies Registration Office
Crown Way
Maindy
0222 388588

The Registry of Friendly Societies
15–17 Gt Marlborough Street
London W1N 2AY
01–437 9992

Reinsurance Offices Association
Aldermary House
Queen Street
London EC4N 1ST
01–248 4477

Royal Institute of International Affairs
Chatham House
10 St James' Square
London SW1Y 4LE
01–930 2233

Royal Institute of Public Administration
3 Birdcage Walk
London SW1H 9JJ
01–222 2248

Royal Institution of Chartered Surveyors
12 Great George Street
Parliament Square
London SW1P 3AD
01–222 7000

Savings Bank Central Board (Trustee)
P.O. Box 33
3 Copthall Avenue
London EC2P 2AB
01–588 9292

Society of Investment Analysts
211–213 High Street
Bromley
Kent BR1 1NY
01–464 0811

Society of Pensions Consultants [The]
Ludgate House
Ludgate Circus
London EC4A 2AB
01–353 1688

Unit Trust Association
Park House
16 Finsbury Circus
London EC2M 7JP
01–628 0871

Published Sources

A and C Black
35 Bedford Row
London WC1R 4JH
01–242 0946

British Institute of Management
Management House
Parker St
London WC2
01–363 5802

Confederation of British Industry (CBI)
Centre Point
New Oxford St
London WC1
01–379 7400

Dun & Bradstreet Ltd
26-32 Clifton St
London EC2P 2LY
01–377 4377

The Economist
25 St James's St
London SW1
01–839 7000

ELC International
Sinclair House
The Avenue
West Ealing
London W13 8BR
01–998 8812

Extel Statistical Services Ltd
37 Paul St
London EC2
01–353 3400

Financial Times Business Information Ltd
102 Clerkenwell Rd
LondonEC1
01-603 4688

Financial Times Newspapers
Bracken House
Cannon St
London EC4
01-248 8000

ICC Informational Group
28–42 Banner St
London EC1Y 8QE
01-253 3906

Information Services Ltd
Windsor Court
East Grinstead House
East Grinstead
W. Sussex RH19 1XA

Jordan and Sons Ltd
Jordan House
Brunswick Place
London N1 6EE
01–253 3030

Key Note Publications Ltd
28–42 Banner St
London EC1Y 8QE
01–253 3006

Longman Group Ltd
Professional, Reference and Information Division
Westgate House
The High
Harlow
Essex CM20 1NE
0279 442601

Macmillan Publishers Ltd
Houndmills Estate
Basingstoke
Hants RG21 2XS
0256 29242

McCarthy Information Ltd
Manor House
Ash Walk
Warminster
Wilts BA12 0JP
0985 215151

The Stock Exchange
London EC2
01-588 2355

Times Books Ltd
16 Golden Sq
London W1
01–434 3767

Online Information Services

A.D.P. Network Services Ltd
179–193 Great Portland St
London W1N 5TB
01–637 1355

A.D.P. operates a range of financial and business databases covering banking, business and economic conditions, major international companies, mergers and acquisitions. Sources include the Bank of England, Standard and Poors', Extel, OECD and the international press.

Butterworths (Telepublishing) Ltd
4-5 Bell Yard
London WC2A 2JR
01–404 4097
Operates *Lexis* (UK tax law, US and UK law, French and EEC cases) *Naars* (last five years annual accounts of US corporations) and *Nexis* (News database dating from 1975, mainly US).

Chase Econometrics/Interactive Data Corp
80 Colman St
London EC2R 5BJ
01-588 4807
Operate Standard and Poors' Compustat Service and *Exstat*, Extel's database deriving from the established card services.

CISI (Wharton Econometric Forecasting Associates)
Ebury Gate
23 Lower Belgrave St
London SW1W 0NW
01–730 8171
Economic and banking databases deriving from the Bank of England, CSO, OECD and the *Financial Times*.

Control Data Ltd
Control Data house
179/199 Shaftesbury Ave
London WC2H 8AR
01-240 3400
and
Genesis Centre
Garrett Field
Birchwood Science Park
Birchwood
Warrington
Cheshire WA3 7BH
(0925) 824757
Operates a number of databases giving data on US companies and stocks.

Datasolve Ltd
Datasolve House
99 Staines Rd West
Sunbury-on-Thames
Middlesex TW16 7AH
(09327) 85566
Operates *World Reporter*, a news, political and commercial information database comprising BBC Summary of World Broadcasts and External Services News, *The Economist*, *The Guardian*, the *Financial Times*, the *Washington Post*, the Asahi News Service, *Keesing's Contemporary Archives*, and the Associated Press Wire Services. Datasolve also operates *World Exporter* providing data on major projects, mostly from developing countries.

Data-Star
The Plaza Suite
114 Jermyn St
London SW1Y 6HJ
01-930 5503
Operates a range of business, economic and financial databases, deriving from the *Financial Times*, *Harvard Business Review* and a number of directories covering companies in Austria, Netherlands and W. Germany. Data-Star also provides online access to the ICC company file and the *Predicasts* series of publications.

Datastream
Monmouth House
58–64 City Rd
London EC1Y 2AL
01–250 3000
Computer based information and computation services including investment research, investment accounting and portfolio valuations. Datastream is described in more detail in Chapter 2.

Dialog Information Services Inc
PO Box 8
Abingdon
Oxford OX13 6EG
(0865) 730969
Dialog is a major database host operating business, financial, market forecasts, investment research, patents and trademarks databases. Sources include Dun & Bradstreet (International), Business International Corp (US), ICC Information Group (UK), *Harvard Business Review*, *Management Contents*, Moody's Investors' Services, *Predicasts* and Standard and Poors'.

DRI Europe Ltd
30 Old Queen St
St James's Park
London SW1H 9HP
01–222 9571
Databases offered include *Exstat* and Standard and Poors' *Compustat* service.

Dun & Bradstreet Ltd
26–32 Clifton St
London EC2P 2LY
01–377 4377
Major International business information company offering search and rating services on and off line. For further details see Chapter 2.

EDS (Electronic Data Systems)
Queens house West
Greenhill Way
Harrow
Middx HA1 IGR
01–861 2233
Database host offering trade statistics collated from official sources from Belgium, France, Germany, Italy, Japan, Netherlands, UK and USA. Data on 1600 products in chemical and related fields.

Extel Computing Ltd
Lowndes House
1/9 City Rd
London EC1Y 1AA
01–638 5544
Operates UK financial and business information databases. Services offered include Extel's own *Exstat* service, deriving from the company card service (see page 0) as well as *Exshare*, compiled from information from Reuters and the Stock Exchange, *Exbond*, detailing terms and conditions for over 5000 international bonds, and *Esprit* and *Examiner*, two services compiled from various sources covering UK share, gilt prices and data, exchange rates, commodity prices and an international news service.

Finsbury Data Service
68–74 Carter Lane
London EC4V 5EA
01–248 9828
Operates two databases *Newsline* and *Textline*, largely deriving from UK and international press, company reports, reports from the BBC World Monitoring Services and press releases. A new service, *Dataline*, was launched late in 1984 to provide financial data on 3000 international companies, using data deriving from the *Exstat* company service.

ICC Information Group
ICC House
81 City Rd
London EC1Y 1BD
01–250 3922
Provide a range of financial and business information services. The main publicly available databases operated are the. *Directory of Companies*, *Financial Data* and *Sharewatch*. For further details see Chapter 2.

IRS-Dialtech
Room 392
Ashdown House
123 Victoria St
London SW1E 6RB
01–212 5638/8225
Database host operating a number of business news and economic databases. Services include *ABI/Inform* (coverage of 550 business periodicals) *Newsline* and *Textline* (compiled by Finsbury Data Services), and *Pricedata*, a database of world market prices of commodities, major currencies and international price trends of new materials.

Pergamon Infoline Ltd
12 Vandy St
London EC2A 2DE
01–377 4650
Operates a variety of scientific and technical databases. Pergamon-Infoline is also expanding its business/company information range of databases and now operates *KBE* (Key British Enterprises) and *Who Owns Whom* online for Dun & Bradstreet, and *Jordanwatch* (Jordan & Sons Ltd).

Prestel Citiservice
Woodsted House
72 Chertsey Rd
Woking
Surrey GU21 5BJ
(04862) 27431
Online information service offering access to share prices, foreign exchange rates and commodity prices, market commentaries and investment recommendations from brokers. A 'Telebroking' service is also available allowing orders to buy and sell shares to be placed electronically. All data is from the Stock Exchange.

SCICON
49 Berners St
London W1P 4AQ
01–580 5599

Operates a series of databases providing information on parliamentary proceedings comprising *Polis* – an index system of parliamentary information – and *Hansard*. Other databases, *Acompline* and *Urbaline* are derived from data held by the GLC Research Library and cover local government news and sources.

SDC Information Services
Stuart House
Crown St
Reading
Berkshire RG1 2SG
0734 866811

Bibliographic database host offering accountancy and management references mainly from the USA.

IP Sharp Associates Ltd
132 Buckingham Palace Rd
London SW1W 9SA
01-730 4567
International host running databases covering economic forecasts, commodities UK share prices and company accounts, money market rates, unit trusts and statistics from OECD, United Nations, Central Statistical Office and statistics from Eastern Bloc countries derived from the Vienna Institute for Comparative Economic Studies.

3. BUSINESS INFORMATION FROM GOVERNMENT SOURCES

The British government statistical service provides a wide range of data that can be of use to industry and commerce. There are also many government departments and agencies that produce reports and guidance leaflets on specific topics that may also be of use.

This appendix provides a substantial listing of addresses and telephone numbers of government departments, agencies and corporations where initial enquiries can be made. There is also an outline of government statistics and a detailed listing of Business Monitors.

Government statistics

A major source of UK business statistics are published by the Business Statistics Office in the form of Business Monitors. The coding of the Business Monitors is alpha numeric. The main codes are:

P = Production series
SD = Service and Distribution series
M = Miscellaneous series
A = Annual series
Q = Quarterly series
M = Monthly series
O = Occasional

Most of the Business Monitors are in the Production Series and produced annually, quarterly, monthly or occassionally. Thus the alpha codes will be PA, PQ, PM or PO followed by the number which denotes the industry sector. The same coding principles are applied in the SD and M series.

The P series contains industry sales, imports and exports which are generally broken down into detailed product groups. The PA series are very detailed and contain data such as employment, wages, and capital expenditure.

The SD series give data such as aggregate retail sales by sector, hire purchase sales, computer service work done and distribution.

The M series provides data on some parts of the financial sector such as insurance, pension funds, company finance and mergers plus other areas such as travel and tourism.

The industry sectors covered by Business Monitors are listed below.

Production Series

Mining and quarrying

Chalk, clay, sand and gravel extraction	PQ 103
Coal mining	PQ 101
Miscellaneous mining and quarrying	PQ 109.2
Petroleum and natural gas	PQ 104
Salt	PQ 109.3
Stone and slate quarrying and mining	PQ 102

Food, drink and tobacco

Animal and poultry foods	PQ 219
Bacon curing, meat and fish products	PQ 214

Biscuits	PQ 213
Bread and flour confectionery	PQ 212
Brewing and malting	PQ 231
British wines, cider and perry	PQ 239.2
Cocoa, chocolate and sugar confectionery	PQ 217
Fruit and vegetable products	PQ 218
Grain milling	PQ 211
Margarine	PQ 229.1
Milk and milk products	PQ 215
Soft drinks	PQ 232
Spirit distilling and compounding	PQ 239.1
Starch and miscellaneous foods	PQ 229.2
Sugar	PQ 216
Tobacco	PQ 240
Vegetable and animal oils and fats	PQ 221

Coal and petroleum products

Lubricating oils and greases	PQ 263
Mineral oil refining	PQ 262

Chemical and allied industries

Dyestuffs and pigments	PQ 277
Fertilizers	PQ 278
Formulated adhesives, gelatine, etc	PQ 279.2
Formulated pesticides, etc	PQ 279.4
Inorganic chemicals	PQ 271.1
Miscellaneous chemicals	PQ 271.3
Organic chemicals	PQ 271.2
Paint	PQ 274
Pharmaceutical chemicals and preparations	PQ 272
Photographic chemical materials	PQ 279.7
Polishes (including waxes) etc	PQ 279.1
Printing ink	PQ 279.5
Soap and detergents	PQ 275
Surgical bandages, etc	PQ 279.6
Synthetic resins and plastics materials	PQ 276.1
Synthetic rubber: see 'Rubber' under 'Other manufacturing industries'	
Toilet preparations	PQ 273

Metal manufacture

Aluminium and aluminium alloys	PQ 321
Copper, brass and other copper alloys	PQ 322
Miscellaneous base metals	PQ 323

Mechanical, instrument and electrical engineering

Engineering (volume indices of sales and orders)	PM 33–36 (1 vol.)
Engineering (volume indices of sales and orders)	PQ 33–36 (1 vol.)

Mechanical engineering

Agriculture machinery (except tractors)	PQ 331
Ball, roller, plain and other bearings	PQ 349.1
Compressors and fluid-power equipment	PQ 333.3
Construction and earth-moving equipment	PQ 336
Constructional steelwork	PQ 341.4
Food and drink processing machinery and packaging and bottling machinery	PQ 339.7
Industrial engines	PQ 334
Industrial (including process) plant and fabricated steelwork	PQ 341.5
Mechanical handling equipment	PQ 337
Metal-working machine tools	PQ 332
Metal-working machine tools: orders and deliveries	PM 332
Mining machinery	PQ 339.1
Miscellaneous (non-electrical) machinery	PQ 339.9
Office machinery See also 'Office equipment' under 'Monitors covering more than one industry')	PQ 338
Ordnance and small arms	PQ 342
Precision chains and other mechanical engineering	PQ 349.2
Printing, bookbinding and paper goods machinery	PQ 339.2
Pumps	PQ 333.1
Refrigerating machinery, space-heating, ventilating and air-conditioned equipment	PQ 339.3
Scales and weighing machinery and portable power tools	PQ 339.5

Textile machinery and accessories	PQ 335
Valves	PQ 333.2

Instrument engineering

Office equipment	
See under 'Monitors covering more than one industry'	
See also 'Office machinery' under 'Mechanical engineering'	
Photographic and document copying equipment	PQ 351
Scientific and industrial instruments and systems	PQ 354
Surgical instruments and appliances	PQ 353
Watches and clocks	PQ 352

Electrical engineering

Broadcast receiving and sound reproducing equipment	PQ 365.2
Electrical appliances primarily for domestic use	PQ 368
Electric lamps, electric light fittings, wiring accessories, etc	PQ 369.4
Electrical equipment for motor vehicles, cycles and aircraft	PQ 369.1
Electrical machinery	PQ 361
Electronic computers	PQ 366
Gramophone records and tape recordings	PQ 365.1
Insulated wires and cables	PQ 362
Primary and secondary batteries	PQ 369.2
Radio and electronic components	PQ 364
Radio, radar and electronic capital goods	PQ 367
Telegraph and telephone apparatus and equipment	PQ 363

Shipbuilding and marine engineering

Ship and boat building, repairing and marine engineering	PQ 370

Vehicles

Aerospace equipment manufacturing and repairing	PQ 383
Cars and commercial vehicle production	PM 381
Locomotives, railway track equipment, railway carriages, wagons and trams	PQ 384
Motor cycle, tricycle and pedal cycle manufacturing	PQ 382
Motor vehicle manufacturing	PQ 381.1
Trailers, caravans and freight containers	PQ 381.2
Wheeled tractor manufacturing	PQ 380

Metal goods

Bolts, nuts, screws, rivets, etc	PQ 393
Cans and metal boxes	PQ 395
Cutlery, spoons, forks and plated tableware (including safety razors and blades)	PQ 392
Domestic gas appliances	PQ 399.9
Drop forgings, etc	PQ 399.5
Engineers' small tools and gauges	PQ 390
Hand tools and implements	PQ 391
Jewellery	PQ 396.2
Metal finishing	PQ 399.11
Metal furniture	PQ 399.1
Metal hollow-ware	PQ 399.6
Metal windows and door frames	PQ 399.2
Metallic closures	PQ 399.10
Miscellaneous metal goods	PQ 399.12
Needles, pins, fish-hooks and other metal small-wares	PQ 399.8
Safes, locks, latches, keys and springs	PQ 399.3
Wire and wire manufactures	PQ 394

Textiles

Asbestos	PQ 429.1
Canvas goods and sacks and other made-up textiles	PQ 422.2
Carpets	PQ 419
Hosiery and other knitted goods	PQ 417.1
Household textiles and handkerchiefs	PQ 422.1
Jute	PQ 415
Lace	PQ 418
Miscellaneous textile industries	PQ 429.2
Narrow fabrics	PQ 421
Production of man-made fibres	PQ 411
Rope, twine and net	PQ 416
Spinning and doubling on the cotton and flax systems	PQ 412
Textile finishing	PQ 423
Warp knitting	PQ 417.2
Weaving of cotton, linen and man-made fibres	PQ 413
Wollen and worsted	PQ 414

Leather, leather goods and fur

Fur	PQ 433
Leather (tanning and dressing) and fellmongery	PQ 431
Leather goods	PQ 432

Clothing and footwear

Corsets and miscellaneous dress industries	PQ 449.1
Footwear	PQ 450
Gloves	PQ 449.2
Hats, caps and millinery	PQ 446
Men's and boys' tailored outerwear	PQ 442
Overalls and men's shirts, underwear, etc	PQ 444
Weatherproof outerwear	PQ 441
Women's and girls' light outerwear, lingerie, infants' wear, etc	PQ 445
Women's and girls' tailored outwear	PQ 443

Bricks, pottery, glass, cement, etc

Abrasives	PQ 469.1
Cement	PQ 464
Clay building bricks and other non-refractory goods	PQ 461.2
Glass	PQ 463
Miscellaneous building materials and mineral products	PQ 469.2
Pottery	PQ 462
Refractory goods	PQ 461.1

Timber, furniture, etc

Bedding and soft furnishings	PQ 473
Imported timber	PM 476
Miscellaneous wood and cork manufacturers	PQ 479
Shop and office fitting	PQ 474
Timber (sawmilling, etc, and builders' woodwork)	PQ 471
Wood chipboard	PM 471.1
Wooden containers and baskets	PQ 475
Wooden furniture and upholstery	PQ 472

Paper, printing and publishing

Cardboard boxes, cartons and fibreboard packing cases	PQ 482.1
General printing and publishing	PQ 489
Manufactured stationery	PQ 483
Miscellaneous manufactures of paper and board	PQ 484.2
Miscellaneous packaging products of paper and film	PQ 482.2
Newspapers and periodicals	PQ 485
Paper and board	PQ 481
Paper and paper making materials	PM 481
Wallcoverings	PQ 484.1

Other manufacturing industries

Brushes and brooms	PQ 493
Linoleum, plastics floorcovering, leathercloth. etc	PQ 492
Miscellaneous manufacturing industries	PQ 499.2
Miscellaneous stationers' goods	PQ 495
Musical instruments	PQ 499.1
Plastics products	PQ 496
Rubber manufactures	PQ 491
Rubber (including synthetic rubber)	PM 491
Sports equipment	PQ 494.3
Toys, games and children's carriages	PQ 494.1

Gas, electricity and water

Electricity	PQ 602
Gas	PQ 601
Water supply	PQ 603

Monitors covering more than one industry

Guide to short term statistics of manufacturers' sales	PO 1001
Index to commodities	PO 1000
Manufacturing industries total sales	PQ 1002
Office equipment	PQ 1005
Packaging products	PQ 480
Statistics of product concentration of UK manufacturers	PQ 1006

Annual Census of Production Reports

Mining and quarrying

Chalk, clay, sand and gravel extraction	PA 103
Coal mining	PA 101
Miscellaneous mining and quarrying	PA 109
Petroleum and natural gas	PA 104
Stone and slate quarrying and mining	PA 102

Food, drink and tobacco

Animal and poultry foods	PA 219
Bacon curing, meat and fish products	PA 214
Biscuits	PA 213
Bread and flour confectionery	PA 212
Brewing and malting	PA 231
British wines, cider and perry	PA 239.2
Cocoa, chocolate and sugar confectionery	PA 217
Fruit and vegetable products	PA 218
Grain milling	PA 211
Margarine	PA 229.1
Milk and milk products	PA 215
Soft drinks	PA 232

Spirit distilling and compounding	PA 239.1
Starch and miscellaneous foods	PA 229.2
Sugar	PA 216
Tobacco	PA 240
Vegetable and animal oils and fats	PA 221

Coal and petroleum products

Coke ovens and manufactured fuel	PA 261
Lubricating oils and greases	PA 263
Mineral oil refining	PA 262

Chemicals and allied industries

Dyestuffs and pigments	PA 277
Explosives and fireworks	PA 279.3
Fertilizers	PA 278
Formulated adhesives, gelatine, etc	PA 279.2
Formulated pesticides, etc	PA 279.4
Inorganic chemicals	PA 271.1
Miscellaneous chemicals	PA 271.3
Organic chemicals	PA 271.2
Paint	PA 274
Pharmaceutical chemicals and preparations	PA 272
Photographic chemical materials	PA 279.7
Polishes	PA 279.1
Printing ink	PA 279.5
Soap and detergents	PA 275
Surgical bandages, etc	PA 279.6
Synthetic resins and plastics materials and synthetic rubber	PA 276
Toilet preparations	PA 273

Metal manufacture

Aluminium and aluminium alloys	PA 321
Copper, brass and other copper alloys	PA 322
Iron and steel (general)	PA 311
Iron castings, etc	PA 313
Miscellaneous base metals	PA 323
Steel tubes	PA 312

Mechanical engineering

Agricultural machinery (except tractors)	PA 331
Ball, roller, plain and other bearings	PA 349.1
Compressors and fluid power equipment	PA 333.3
Construction and earth-moving equipment	PA 336
Food and drink processing machinery and packaging and bottling machinery	PA 339.7
Industrial engines	PA 334
Industrial (including process) plant and steelwork	PA 341
Mechanical handling equipment	PA 337
Metal-working machine tools	PA 332
Mining machinery	PA 339.1
Miscellaneous (non-electrical) machinery	PA 339.9
Office machinery	PA 338
Ordnance and small arms	PA 342
Precision chains and other mechanical engineering	PA 349.2
Printing, bookbinding and paper goods machinery	PA 339.2
Pumps	PA 333.1
Refrigerating machinery, space-heating, ventilating and air-conditioning equipment	PA 339.3
Scales and weighing machinery and portable power tools	PA 339.5
Textile machinery and accessories	PA 335
Valves	PA 333.2

Instrument engineering

Photographic and document copying equipment	PA 351
Scientific and industrial instruments and systems	PA 354
Surgical instruments and appliances	PA 353
Watches and clocks	PA 352

Electrical engineering

Broadcast receiving and sound reproducing equipment	PA 365.2
Electric lamps, electric light fittings, wiring accessories, etc	PA 369.4
Electrical appliances primarily for domestic use	PA 368
Electrical equipment for motor vehicles, cycles and aircraft	PA 369.1
Electrical machinery	PA 361
Electronic computers	PA 366
Gramophone records and tape recordings	PA 365.1
Insulated wires and cables	PA 362
Primary and secondary batteries	PA 369.2
Radio and electronic components	PA 364
Radio, radar and electronic capital goods	PA 367
Telegraph and telephone apparatus and equipment	PA 363

Shipbuilding and marine engineering

Shipbuilding and marine engineering	PA 370

Vehicles

Aerospace equipment, manufacturing and repairing	PA 383

Locomotives, railway track equipment, railway carriages, wagons and trams	PA 384
Motor cycle, tricycle and pedal cycle manufacturing	PA 382
Motor vehicle manufacturing	PA 381.1
Trailers, caravans and freight containers	PA 381.2
Wheeled tractor manufacturing	PA 380
Metal goods, not elsewhere specified	
Bolts, nuts, screws, rivets etc	PA 393
Cans and metal boxes	PA 395
Cutlery, spoons, forks and plated tableware, etc	PA 392
Drop forgings, etc	PA 399.5
Engineers' small tools and gauges	PA 390
Hand tools and implements	PA 391
Jewellery and precious metals	PA 396
Metal furniture	PA 399.1
Metal hollow-ware	PA 399.6
Miscellaneous metal manufacture	PA 399.8
Wire and wire manufactures	PA 394
Textiles	
Asbestos	PA 429.1
Canvas goods and sacks and other made-up textiles	PA 422.2
Carpets	PA 419
Hosiery and other knitted goods	PA 417.1
Household textiles and handkerchiefs	PA 422.1
Jute	PA 415
Lace	PA 418
Miscellaneous textile industry	PA 429.2
Narrow fabrics	PA 421
Production of man-made fibres	PA 411
Rope, twine and net	PA 416
Spinning and doubling on the cotton and flax systems	PA 412
Textile finishing	PA 423
Warp knitting	PA 417.2
Weaving of cotton, linen and man-made fibres	PA 413
Woollen and worsted	PA 414
Leather, leather goods and fur	
Fur	PA 433
Leather goods	PA 432
Leather (tanning and dressing) and fellmongery	PA 431
Clothing And footwear	
Corsets and miscellaneous industries	PA 449.1
Dresses, lingerie, infants' wear, etc	PA 445
Footwear	PA 450
Gloves	PA 449.2
Hats, caps and millinery	PA 446
Men's and boys' tailored outerwear	PA 442
Overalls and men's shirts, underwear,. etc	PA 444
Weatherproof outerwear	PA 441
Women's and girls' outerwear	PA 443
Bricks, pottery, glass, cement, etc	
Abrasives	PA 469.1
Building bricks and non-refractory goods	PA 461.2
Cement	PA 464
Glass	PA 463
Miscellaneous building materials and mineral products	PA 469.2
Pottery	PA 462
Refractory goods	PA 461.1
Timber, furniture, etc	
Bedding, etc	PA 473
Furniture and upholstery	PA 472
Miscellaneous wood and cork manufactures	PA 479
Shop and office fitting	PA 474
Timber	PA 471
Wooden containers and baskets	PA 475
Paper, printing and publishing	
Cardboard boxes, cartons and fibreboard packing cases	PA 482.1
General printing and publishing	PA 489
Manufactured stationery	PA 483
Miscellaneous manufactures of paper and board	PA 484.2
Packaging products of paper and associated materials	PA 482.2
Paper and board	PA 481
Printing, publishing of newspapers and periodicals	PA 485
Wallcoverings	PA 484.1
Other manufacturing industries	
Brushes and brooms	PA 493
Linoleum, plastics floor-covering, leathercloth, etc	PA 492
Miscellaneous manufacturing industries	PA 499.2
Miscellaneous stationers' goods	PA 495
Musical instruments	PA 499.1
Plastics products	PA 496

Rubber	PA 491
Sports equipment	PA 494.3
Toys, games and children's carriages	PA 494.1
Construction	
Construction	PA 500
Gas, electricity and water	
Electricity	PA 602
Gas	PA 601
Water supply	PA 603
Monitors covering more than one industry	
Analyses of UK manufacturing (local) units by employment size	PA 1003
Classified list of manufacturing businesses 1979 issued in 10 parts	PA 1007
Input/output tables for the UK	PA 1004
Introductory notes	PA 1001
Minerals	PA 1007
Provisional results	PA 1000
Summary tables (the combined 1974/1975 summary tables are published in two volumes: establishment analyses and enterprise analyses	PA 1002

Service and Distributive Series

(SDO10–24 renumbered from SD10–24
SDQ5 Catering trades
SDM6 Finance houses and other consumer credit grantors
SDQ7 Assets and liabilities of finance houses and other consumer credit companies
SDM8 Instalment credit business of retailers
SDQ9 Computer services

Useful addresses: government sources

Advisory, Conciliation and Arbitration Service (ACAS)
11–12 St James's Sq
London SW1Y 4LA
01-214 6000

Agricultural and Food Research Council
160 Great Portland St
London W1N 6DT
01-580 6655

Agriculture, Fisheries & Food, Ministry of
3 Whitehall Place
London SW1A 2HH
01-233 3000

Bank of England
Threadneedle St
London EC2R 8AH
01-601 4444

British Airports Authority (BAA)
Head Office: Gatwick Airport
West Sussex RH6 OHZ
(0293) 517755

British Broadcasting Corporation (BBC)
Broadcasting House
London W1A 1AA
01-580 4468

British Council
10 Spring Gardens
London SW1A 2BN
01-930 8466

British Gas Corporation
Rivermill House
152 Grosvenor Rd
London SW1V 3JL
01-821 1444

British Library
2 Sheraton St
London W1V 4BH
01-636 1544

British Overseas Trade Board
Headquarters
1 Victoria St
London SW1H 0ET
01–215 7877

BOTB Regional Offices

South Eastern
Ebury Bridge House
Ebury Bridge Rd
London SW1W 8QD
01–730 9678

North Eastern
Stanegate House
2 Groat Market
Newcastle upon Tyne NE1 1YN
0632–324722

Yorkshire and Humberside
Priestley House
Park Row
Leeds LS1 5LF
0532–443171

West Midlands
Ladywood House
Stephenson Street
Birmingham B2 4DT
021 632 4111

North Western
Sunley Building
Piccadilly Plaza
Manchester M1 4BA
061–236 2171

East Midlands
Severns House
20 Middle Pavement
Nottingham
NG1 7DW
0602–506181

South Western
The Pithay
Bristol BS1 2PB
0272–291071

The following also act as BOTB Regional Offices:

Welsh Office
New Crown Building
Cathays Park
Cardiff CF1 3NQ
0222–825111

Scottish Export Office
Industry Department for Scotland
Alhambra House
45 Waterloo St
Glasgow G2 6AT
041–248 2855

Industrial Development Board for Northern Ireland
IDB House
64 Chichester St
Belfast BT1 4JX
(0232) 233233

British Standards Institution (BST)
2 Park St
London W1A 2BS
01-629 9000

British Steel Corporation
9 Albert Embankment
London SE1 7SN
01-735 7654

British Technology Group (BTG)
101 Newington Causeway
London SE1 6BU
01-403 6666

British Tourist Authority
Queen's House
64 St James's St
London SW1A 1NF
01-629 9191

British Waterways Board
Melbury House
Melbury Terrace
London NW1 6JX
01-262 6711

Business Statistics Office
Government Buildings
Cardiff Rd
Newport
Gwent NPT 1XG
0633 56111 ext 2973

Central Electricity Generating Board (CEGB)
Sudbury House
15 Newgate St
London EC1A 7AU
01-634 5111

Central Statistical Office (CSO)
Great George St,
London SW1P 3AQ
01–223 + extension number

Income/expenditure, balance of payments etc	6135/6193
Surrey Control Unit	7341
Macro-Economic Databank	5401
Price index numbers for Current Cost Accounting	7718/7661

Charity Commission
14 Ryder St
St James's,
London SW1Y 6AH
01–214 6000

Civil Aviation Authority
CAA House
45–59 Kingsway
London WC2B 6TE
01–379 7311

Civil Service Commission
Alencon Link
Basingstoke
Hants RG21 1JB
(0256; 29222

Companies Registration Office

England
Companies House
55 City Rd
London EC1
01–253 9393

Wales
Companies House
Crown Way
Maindy
Cardiff CF4 3U2
0222–388588

Scotland
Companies House
Exchequer Chambers
102 George St
Edinburgh EH2 3DJ
031–225 5774

Ireland
Companies Office
Dublin Castle
Dublin
0001 713511

Co-operative Development Agency
Broadmead House
21 Planton St
London SW1Y 4DR
01-839 2988

Council for Small Industries in Rural Areas (CoSIRA)
Head office
141 Castle St
Salisbury
Wilt
SP1 3TP
(0722) 336255

Crown Agents for Overseas Governments and Administrations
Information Office:
4 Millbank,
London SW1P 3JD
01–222 7730

HM Customs and Excise
King's Beam House
Mark Lane
London EC3R 7HE
01–626 1515

Ministry of Defence
Main Building
Whithall
London SW1A sHB
01–218 9000

Development Commission
11 Cowley Street
London SW1Y 4SU
01–222 9134

Economic and Social Research Council
1 Temple Avenue
London SW1P 0BD
01–353 5252

Department of Education and Science
Elizabeth House
York Road
London SE1 7PH
01–928 9222

Electricity Council
30 Millbank, London SW1P 4RD
01-834 2333

Department of Employment
Caxton House, Tothill St
London SW1H 9NF
01-213 3000

Regional Offices

North
Wellbar House
Gallowgate
Newcastle upon Tyne NE1 41P
0632 327575

North West
Sunley Bldg
Piccadilly Plaza
Manchester M60 7JS
061–832 9111

Yorkshire and Humberside
City House
Leeds LS14JH
0532 438232

Midlands
2 Duchess Place
Hagley Rd
Birmingham M16 8NS
021–445 7111

London and South East
Hanway House
Red Lion Sq.
London WC1R 4HN
01-405 8454

South West
The Pithay
Bristol BS1 2NQ
0272 291071

Scotland
Pentland House
47 Robb's Loan
Edinburgh EH14 1UE
031-443 8731

Wales
Companies House
Crown Way
Maindy
Cardiff CF4 3UW
0222 388588

Department of Energy
Thames House South
Millbank
London SW1P 4QJ
01-211 3000

English Tourist Board
4 Grosvenor Gardens
London SW1W 0DW
01-730 3400

Department of the Environment
2 Marsham St
London SW1P 3EB
01-212 3434

Regional Offices

Northern
Wellbar House
Gallowgate
Newcastle-upon-Tyne NE1U 4TD
0632 327575

North West
Sunley Bldg
Manchester M1 4BE
061-832 9111

Yorkshire and Humberside
City House
Leeds LS1 4JD
0532 438232

East Midlands
Cranbrook House
Cranbrook St
Nottingham BG1 1EY
0602 476121

East and South East
Charles House
375 Kensington High St
London W14 8QH
01-603 3444

South West
Tollgate House
Moulton St
Bristol B52 9DJ
0272 218811

Enterprise Zones
England

Corby
0536662571

Dudley
0384 55433

Glanford (Flixborough)
0652 52441

Hartlepool
0429 66522

Isle of Dogs
01-515 3000

Middlesbrough
0642 222279

North East Lancashire
0282 37411

North West Kent
0634 826233

Rotherham
0709 72099

Salford/Trafford
Salford, 061-793 3237 or
061-7944711; Trafford, 061-872 2101

Scunthorpe
0724 862141

Speke (Liverpool)
051-227 3911, ext. 394

Telford
0952 502277

Tyneside/Gateshead
Tyneside, 0632 328520;
Gateshead, 0632 771011

Wakefield
0924 370211

Wellingborough
0933 229777

Workington (Allerdale)
0900 65656

Scotland
Clydebank
041-952 0084

Invergordan
0349 853666

Tayside (Arbroath)
0307 65101

Wales
Delyn
03526 4004

Lower Swansea Valley
0792 50821

Milford Haven Waterway
0437 4551

Northern Ireland
Belfast
0232 248449

Londonderry
0504 263992

European Communities, Commission of the (UK Office)
8 Storey's Gate
London SW1P 3AT
01-222 8122

European Parliament Information Office
2 Queen Anne's Gate
London SW1H 9AA
01-222 0411

Export Credits Guarantee Department (ECGD)
Aldermanbury House
Aldermanbury
London EC2P 2EL
01-382 7000

and at
Crown Building
Cathays Park
Cardiff
CF1 3NH
0222 824100

ECGD Regional Offices

Belfast
12th Floor
Windsor House
9–15 Bedford Street,
Belfast
BT2 7EG
(0232)231734

Birmingham
Colmore Centre
115 Colmore Row
Birmingham
B3 3SB
021-233 1771

Bristol
1 Redcliffe Street
Bristol
BS1 6NP
(0272)299971

Cambridge
Three Crowns House
72–80 Hills Road
Cambridge
CB2 1NJ
(0223)68801

City of London
PO Box 46
Clements House
14–18 Gresham Street
London
EC2V 7JE
(01-726-4050

Croydon
Sunley House
Bedford Park
Croydon
CR9 4HL
01-680 5030

Glasgow
Fleming House
134 Renfrew Street
Glasgow
G3 6TL
041-332 8707

Leeds
West Riding House
67 Albion Street
Leeds
LS1 5AA
0532-450631

Manchester
6th Floor, Townbury House
Blackfriars Street
Salford
M3 5AL
061-834 8181

Fair Trading, Office of
Field House
Breams Bldgs
London EC4A 1PR
01-242 2858

Foreign and Commonwealth Office
Old Admiralty Bldg
London SW1A 2AF
01-273 3000

Forestry Commission
231 Corstorphine Rd
Edinburgh EH12 7AT
031-334 0303

Freeports (sources of information)

Northern Ireland Airports Ltd
Belfast International Airport
Belfast BT29 4AB
(0232) 229271 ext. 203

West Midlands Freeport Ltd
County Hall
1 Lancaster Circus
Queensway
Birmingham B4 7DJ
021-300 6771

Mersey Docks and Harbour Company
Pier Head
Liverpool L3 1BZ
051-200 2173

Kyle and Carrick District Council
Burns House
Burns Statue Square
Ayr KA7 1UT
0292 281511

Associated British Ports
Melbury House
Melbury Terrace
London NW1 6JY
01-486 6621

Health and Safety Executive
St Hughes House
Stanley Precinct
Bootle L20 3QY
051-951 4000

Department of Health and Social Security
Alexander Fleming House
London SE1 6BY
01-407 5522

Health Service Commissioner (Ombudsman)
Church House,
Great Smith Street,
London SW1P 3BW
01-928 2345

Her Majesty's Stationery Office (HMSO)
49 High Holborn
London WC1V 6HB
01-928 6977
(personal callers only)
and
PO Box 569
London SE1 9NH
01-928 1321
(telephone and mail orders only)
Branches

13A Castle St
Edinburgh EH2 3AR
031-225 6333

80 Chichester St
Belfast BT1 4JY
0232 34488

41 The Hayes
Cardiff
CF1 1JW
0222 23654

258 Broad St
Birmingham B1 2HE
021-643 3740

Southey House
Wine St
Bristol BS1 2BQ
0272 24306

Brazenose St
Manchester M60 8AS
061-834 7201

St Crispins
Duke St
Norwich NR3 1PD
0603 22211

Home Office
Queen Anne's Gate,
London SW1 9AT
01-213-3000

House of Commons
London SW1A 0AA
01-219 4272

House of Lords
London SW1A OPW
01-219 3107

Central Office of (COI) Information
Hercules Rd
London SE1 7DU
01-928 2345

COI Regional Offices

North Eastern
13th Floor
Welbar House
Gallowgate
Newcastle upon Tyne NE1 4TB
0632 327575

Yorkshire and Humberside
City House
New Station St
Leeds LS1 4JG
0532 438232

Eastern
Three Crowns House
72–80 Hills Rd
Cambridge CB2 1LL
0223 358911

London and South Eastern
Atlantic House
Holborn Viaduct
London EC1N 2PD
01-583 5744

South Western
The Pithay
Bristol BS1 2NF
0272 291071

Board of Inland Revenue
Somerset House
London WC2R 1LB
01-438 6622

Intervention Board of Agricultural Produce
Fountain House
2 Queen's Walk
Reading RG1 7QW
0734 583626

Land Registry
Lincoln's Inn Fields
London WC2A 3PH
01-405 3488

Lord Chancellor's Department
Neville House
Page St
London SW1P 4LS
01-211-3000

Manpower Economics, Office of
22 Kingsway, London WC2B 6JY
01-405 5944

Manpower Services Commission
Moorfoot, Sheffield S1 4PQ
0742 753275

MSC Training Division Regional Offices:

North
Broadacre House
Market Street
Newcastle upon Tyne
NE1 6HH
0632 326181

North West
Washington House
The Capital Centre
New Bailey Street
Manchester
M3 5ER
061-833 0251

Yorkshire and Humberside
Jubilee House
33–41 Park Place
Leeds
LS1 2RL
0532 446299

Midlands
Alpha Tower
Suffolk Street
Queensway
Birmingham
B1 1UR
021-632 4144

London
Selkirk House
166 High Holborn
London
WC1V 6PF
01-836-1213

South East
Telford House
Hamilton Close
Basingstoke
Hants
RG21 2UZ
0256 29266

South West
4th Floor
The Pithay
Bristol
BS1 2NQ
0272 291071

Wales
Companies House
Crown Way
Maindy
Cardiff CF4 3UT
0222 388588

Scotland
Training Division
9 St Andrew Square
Edinburgh EH2 2QX
031-225 8500

National Economic Development Office
Millbank Tower
Millbank
London SW1P 4QX
01-211 3000

Department for National Savings
Charles House
375 Kensington High St
London W14 8SD
01-603 2000

Northern Ireland Office
Whitehall
London SW1A 2AZ
01-273 3000

Overseas Development Administration
Eland House
Stag Place
London SW1E 5DH
01-213 3000

Office of Population Censuses and Surveys
St Catherines House
10 Kingsway
London WC2B 6JP
01-242 0262

Public Record Office
Ruskin Ave
Kew
Richmond
Surrey TW9 4DU
01-876 3444

Science and Engineering Research Council
Polaris House,
North Star Avenue,
Swindon SN2 1ET
0793 26222

Scottish Information Office
New St Andrew's House,
Edinburgh EH1 3td
031-556 8400

Small Firms Centres

Birmingham
Sixth Floor
Ladywood House
Stephenson Street
Birmingham B2 4DT
021-643 3344

Bristol
Fifth Floor
The Pithay
Bristol
BS1 2NB
0272 294546

Cambridge
24 Brooklands Avenue
Cambridge
CB2 2BU
0223 63312

Cardiff
16 St David's House
Wood Street
Cardiff
CF1 1ER
0222 396116

Glasgow
120 Bothwell Street
Glasgow G2 6TU
041-248 6014

Leeds
1 Park Row
City Square
Leeds LS1 5NR
0532 445151

Liverpool
Graeme House
Derby Square
Liverpool L3 9HJ
051-236 5756

London
Ebury Bridge House
2–18 Ebury Bridge Road
London SW1W 8QD
01-730 8451

Manchester
Third Floor
320–325 Royal Exchange Buildings
St Ann's Square
Manchester M2 7AH
061-832 5282

Newcastle
Centro House
3 Cloth Street
Newcastle upon Tyne NE1 3EE
0632 325353

Nottingham
Severns House
20 Middle Pavement
Nottingham NG1 7DW
0602 581205

Reading
Abbey Hall
Abbey Square
Reading RG1 3BE
0734 591733

Department of Trade and Industry
1 Victoria St
London SW1H 0ET
01-215 7877

Regional Offices

North East
Stanegate House
2 Groat Market
Newcastle upon Tyne NE1 1YN
(0632) 324722

North West
Sunley Building
Piccadilly Plaza
Manchester M1 4BA
061-236 2171

Merseyside
Graeme House
Derby Square
Liverpool L2 7UJ
051-227 4111

Yorkshire and Humberside
Priestley House
1 Park Row
City Square
Leeds LS1 5LF
0532 443171

West Midlands
Ladywood House
Stephenson Street
Birmingham B2 4DT
021-632 4111

East Midlands
Severns House
20 Middle Pavement
Nottingham NG1 7DW
0602 56181

South Eastern
Charles House
375 Kensington High Street
London W14 8QH
01-603 2060

South West
The Pithay
Bristol BS1 2PB
0272 291071

Export Data Branch
1 Victoria St
London SW1H OET
01-215 3496

Department of Transport
2 Marsham St
London SW1P 3EB
01-212 3434

HM Treasury
Information Division, Treasury Chambers, Parliament St
London SW1P 3AG
01-233 3415

United Kingdom Atomic Energy Authority
11 Charles II St
London SW1Y 4QP
01-930 5454

United Nations
14–15 Stratford Place, London W1N 9AF
01-629 6411

Water Authorities Association
1 Queen Anne's Gate
London SW1H 9BT
01-222 8111

Welsh Office
Information Division
Cathays Park
Cardiff CF1 3NQ
0222 825111

4. FORMS REQUIRED BY THE REGISTRAR OF COMPANIES

Most UK registered companies are legally required to provide the Registrar of Companies with accounts as described in Chapter 3 and completed forms relating to any changes that may have occurred. The accounts and completed forms then become part of the public record and are available in microfiche.

This appendix provides examples of the more common forms such as:

6a Annual return of of a company having a share capital
9b Notice of change of directors or secretaries or in their particulars
4a Notice of change in situation of registered office
3a Notice of new accounting reference date given after the end of an accounting reference period

There are many forms relating to a wide range of circumstances which companies may have to complete. A list of the form numbers and their descriptions are given in this appendix.

Any of the forms are available from The Registrar of Companies, Companies House, Crown Way, Maindy, Cardiff CF4 3U2, telephone (0222) 388588.

Forms required by Companies Registration Office

UK registered companies are required to notify the companies Registration Office of any changes by using the appropriate form.

Form No	Title
2	Notice of accounting reference date
3	Notice of new accounting reference date given during the course of an accounting reference period
3a	Notice of new accounting date given after the end of an accounting reference period
4a	Notice of change in situation of registered office
5	Notice of overseas interests
6a	Annual return of a company having a share capital
7	Annual return of a company not having a share capital
8	Application by a public company to commence business and declaration of particulars
9b	Notice of change of directors or secretaries or in their particulars (plus continuation sheet)
10	Notice of increase in nominal capital
11	Notice of increase in number of members
14	Notice of passing of resolution removing an auditor
17	Application by an existing joint stock for registration as a company limited by shares or limited by guarantee
17a	Application by an existing company other than a joint stock company for registration as a company limited by guarantee

17b	Application by an existing joint stock company for registration as a private company limited by share or limited by guarantee
17c	Application by an existing company other than a joint stock company for registration as a private company limited by guarantee
17d	Application by an existing joint stock company for registration as a public company limited by shares
17e	Registration of an existing joint stock company. Declaration of compliance in connection with registration as a public company
18	Application by an existing joint stock company for registration as an unlimited company
18a	Application by an existing company other than a joint stock company for registration as an unlimited company
18b	Application by an existing joint stock company for registration as an unlimited company
18c	Application by an existing company other than a joint stock company for registration as an unlimited company
19	Registration of an existing joint stock company list of members
21	Registration of an existing joint stock company as a limited company Statement of Particulars
23	Registration of an existing joint stock company declaration verifying documents delivered to the Registrar of Companies with application for registration
24	Statement of places of business of banks
25	Notice of intention to carry on business as an investment company
25a	Revocation of notice to carry on business as an investment company
26	Notice of place where copies of directors' service contracts or memorandums thereof are kept or of any change in that place
27	Notice of place where register of directors' interest in shares etc is kept or of any change in that place
27a	Notice of place for inspection of a register of a register of directors' interest in shares which is kept by recording the matters in question other than in a legible form or of any change in that place
28	Notice of consolidation division, conversion, sub-division, redemption or cancellation of shares or re-conversion of stock into shares
29	Notice of the situation of the office where a dominion register is kept or of any change in, or discontinuance of, any such office
29a	Notice of place for inspection of a dominion register which is kept by recording the matters in question otherwise than in a legible form or of any change in that place
33	Statement of particulars of rights attached to shares allotted not otherwise registerable
33a	Statement of particulars of variation of rights attached to shares not otherwise registerable
33b	Notice of assignments of name or new name to any class of shares not otherwise registerable
39c	Members' voluntary winding up notice of appointment of liquidator
39d	Creditors' voluntary winding up notice of appointment of liquidator
39e	Notice of appointment of liquidator (members') (creditors') voluntary winding up
41a	Declaration of compliance with the requirements on application for registration of a company
44	Declaration that the conditions of section 109 (1) (a) (b) and (c) of the Companies Act 1948
44a	Declaration that the provisions of section 109 (2) (b) of the Companies Act 1948 have been complied with
47	Particulars of a mortgage or charge
47 (Scot)	Particulars of a mortgage or charge in Scotland
47a	Particulars of a series of debentures
47a (Scot)	Particulars of a series of debentures (Scotland)
47b	Particulars of a mortgage or charge subject to which property has been acquired
47b (Scot)	Particulars of a mortgage or charge subject to which property has been acquired in Scotland

47c	Certificate of registration in Scotland or Northern Ireland of a charge comprising property situate there
48	Particulars of an issue of debentures in a series
48 (Scot)	Particulars of an issue of debentures in Scotland
48a (Scot)	Particulars of an instrument of alteration to a floating charge created by a company registered in Scotland
49	Memorandum of complete satisfaction of mortgage or charge
49 (Scot)	Memorandum of complete satisfaction of mortgage or charge (Scotland)
49a	Memorandum of (1) partial payment or satisfaction of mortgage or charge (2) release of part of property or undertaking from mortgage or charge
49a (Scot)	Memorandum of (1) partial payment or satisfaction of charge (2) release of part of property or undertaking from charge (Scotland)
49b	Memorandum of fact that part of property or undertaking mortgaged or charged has ceased to form part of property or undertaking or company
49b (Scot)	Memorandum of fact that part of the property or undertaking mortgaged or charged has ceased to form part of the property or undertaking of company (Scotland)
52	Particulars of a contract relating to shares allotted as fully paid up otherwise than in cash
53	Notice of appointment of receiver or manager
53a (Scot)	Notice of Registrar of appointment of a receiver (Scotland)
53b (Scot)	Notice of Registrar of appointment of a receiver (Scotland)
53c	Notice to company of appointment of receiver or manager
57	Receiver or manager's abstract of receipts and payments
57 (Scot)	Receiver's abstracts of receipts and payments (Scotland)
57a	Notice of ceasing to act as receiver or manager
58a	Statement of the amount or rate per cent of the commission payable in respect of shares and of the number of shares for which persons have agreed for a commission to subscribe absolutely
91 (Scot)	Register of Charges alteration to charges and memorandum of satisfaction (Scotland)
100	Notice of dissenting shareholders
100a	Notice to dissenting shareholders
100b	Notice to transferee company by dissenting shareholder
101	Notice of application made to the Court for the cancellation of an alteration made by special resolution to the provisions of the memorandum of the company
101a	Notice of application made to the Court of the cancellation of a special resolution regarding re-registration
102	Notice of place where a register of holders of debentures or a duplicate thereof is kept or of any charge in that place
102a	Notice of place for inspection of a register of holders of debentures which is kept by recording the matters in question otherwise than in a legible form or of any change in that place
103	Notice of place where register of members is kept or of any change in that place
103a	Notice of place for inspection of a register of members which is kept by recording the matters in question otherwise than in a legible form or of any change in that place
109	Statement as to affairs in the matter of a debenture or series of debentures registered on............19
109 (Scot)	Statement as to affairs of a company (Scotland)
109a	Statement as to affairs in the High Court of Justice chancery division
110/111	Liquidator's statement of accounts and return of final meeting (members' winding up)
110/112	Liquidator's statement of accounts and return of final meeting (creditors' winding up)

PUC2	Return of allotments of shares issued for cash
PUC3	Return of allotments of shares issued wholly or in part for a consideration other than cash
PUC4	Claim for credit or relief from capital duty under section 49(5) of the Finance Act 1973
PUC5	Statement of amounts or further amounts paid on nil paid or partly paid shares (under pt V of Finance Act 1973)
PUC6	Statement relating to a chargeable transaction of a capital company
PUC7	Return of allotments of shares issued by way of capitalisation of reserves

R1	Application by a limited company to be re-registered as unlimited
R2	Members' assent to company being re-registered as unlimited
R3	Application by an unlimited company to be re-registered as limited
R4	Declaration by directors as to members' assent to re-registration
R5	Application by a private company for re-registration as a public company
R6	Declaration of compliance with the requirements by a private company for re-registration as a public company
R7	Application by an old public company for re-registration as a public company
R8	Declaration by Director or Secretary on application by an old public company for re-registration as a public company
R9	Declaration by old public company that it does not meet the requirements for a public company
R10	Application by a public company for re-registration as a private company
R11	Application by a public company for re-registration as a private company following a Court Order
R12	Application by a public company for re-registration as a private company following cancellation of shares and diminution of share capital

The companies Act 1981 (also 1980 Companies Act) introduced some new registration forms to meet the new definitions of companies. These new forms are summarised below.

New form 8 'Application by a public company to commence business and declaration of particulars'
Form 17b replacing form 17 'Application by an existing joint stock company for registration as a private company limited by shares or limited by guarantee'
Form 17c replacing form 17a 'Application by an existinh company other than a joint stock company for registration as a private company limited by guarantee.'
New form 17d 'Application by an existing joint stock company for registration as a public company limited by shares.'
New form 17e 'Registration of an existing joint stock company. Declaration of compliance in connection with registration as a public company.'
Form 18b replacing form 18 'Application by an existing joint stock company for registration as an unlimited company.'
Form 18c replacing form 18a 'Application by an existing company other than a joint stock company for registration as an unlimited company.'
New form 25 'Notice on intention to carry on business as an investment company.'
New form 25a 'Revocation of notice to carry on business as an investing company.'
New form 33 'Statement of particulars of rights attached to shares allotted not otherwise registerable.'
New form 33a 'Statement of particulars of variation of rights attached to shares not otherwise registerable.'
New form 33b 'Notice of assignment of name or new name to any class of shares not otherwise registerable.'
Form 41a replacing form 41 'Declaration of compliance with the requirements on application for registration of a company.'
Form 58a replacing form 58 'Statement of the amount or rate per cent of the commission payable in respect of shares and of the number of shares for which persons have agreed for a commission to subscribe absolutely.'
New form 101a 'Notice of application made to the Court for the cancellation of a special resolution regarding re-registration.'

New form R5 'Application by a private company for re-registration as a public company.'
New form R6 'Declaration of compliance with the requirements by a private company for re-registration as a public company.'
New form R7 'Application by an old public company for re-registration as a public company.'
New form R8 'Declaration by director or secretary on application by an old public company for re-registration as a public company.'
New form R9 'Declaration by old public company that it does not meet the requirements for a public company.'
New form R10 'Application by a public company for re-registration as a private company.'
New form R11 'Application by a public company for re-registration as a private company following a court order.'
New form R12 'Application by a public company for re-registration as a private company following cancellation of shares and diminution of share capital.'

A

THE COMPANIES ACTS 1948 TO 1981

Form No. 6a

6a

Annual return of a company having a share capital

Pursuant to sections 124 and 126 of the Companies Act 1948

Please do not write in this binding margin

To the Registrar of Companies

For official use

Company number

Annual return of

Please complete legibly, preferably in black type, or bold block lettering.

Limited*

made up to the ....19........... (hereinafter called 'the date of this return') being the fourteenth day after the date of the annual general meeting for the year 19..........

* delete if inappropriate

Address of registered office of the company

Total amount of indebtedness of the company in respect of all mortgages and charges which are required to be registered with the Registrar of Companies (note 1). †

† Scottish companies see also note 2

If the register of members or any register of debenture holders is kept at a place other than the registered office, insert the address of the place where it is kept, or, if such a register is kept otherwise than in a legible form and the place for inspection of the register is elsewhere than at the registered office, insert the address where inspection may be made. (see note 3)

Register of members

Register of debenture holders

Particulars of the person who is the secretary at the date of this return

Name (notes 4, 5 and 6)

Previous name(s) (note 4)

Address (notes 5, 6 and 7)

We certify this return which comprises pages 1, 2 and 3 [plus ‡ ____________ continuation sheets] *

‡ enter number of continuation sheets attached

Signed ____________________ Director, and ____________________________ Secretary

Presentor's name, address and reference (if any):

For official use

General section

Post room

Please do not write in this binding margin

Please complete legibly, preferably in black type, or bold block lettering

Summary of share capital and debentures

Nominal share capital	£		
divided into:-	Number of shares	Class	Nominal value of each share
			£
			£
			£
			£

Issued share capital and debentures

	Amount	Number	Class
1 Number of shares of each class taken up to the date of this return (which must agree with the total shown in the list as held by existing members)			
2 Number of shares of each class issued subject to payment wholly in cash			
3 Number of shares of each class issued as fully paid up for a consideration other than cash			
4 Number of shares of each class issued as partly paid up for a consideration other than cash and extent to which each such share is so paid up	£ *		
5 Number of shares (if any) of each class issued at a discount			
6 Amount of discount on the issue of shares which has not been written off at the date of this return			
7 Amount called up on number of shares of each class	£ *		
8 Total amount of calls received (note 8)	£		
9 Total amount (if any) agreed to be considered as paid on number of shares of each class issued as fully paid up for a consideration other than cash	£		
10 Total amount (if any) agreed to be considered as paid on number of shares of each class issued as partly paid up for a consideration other than cash	£		
11 Total amount of calls unpaid	£		
12 Total amount of sums (if any) paid by way of commission in respect of any shares or debentures	£		
13 Total amount of the sums (if any) allowed by way of discount for any debentures since the date of the last return	£		
14 Total number of shares of each class forfeited			
15 Total amount paid (if any) on shares forfeited	£		
16 Total amount of shares for which share warrants to bearer are outstanding	£		
17 Total amount of share warrants to bearer issued and surrendered respectively since the date of the last return — ISSUED	£		
SURRENDERED	£		
18 Number of shares comprised in each share warrant to bearer, specifying in the case of warrants of different kinds, particulars of each kind			

*per share

LIST OF PAST

Folio in register ledger containing particulars	Names and addresses

Please do not write in this binding margin

Please complete legibly, preferably in black type, or bold block lettering

Important
The particulars to be given are those referred to in section 200 of the Companies Act 1948 as amended by section 95 of the Companies Act 1981.

*enter particulars of other directorships held or previously held (see note 10). If this space is insufficient use a continuation sheet.

Particulars of the director(s) of the company at the date of the return (note 9)

Name (note 4)	Business occupation
Previous name(s) (note 4)	Nationality
Address (note 7)	Date of birth (note 11)
Other directorships *	

Name (note 4)	Business occupation
Previous name(s) (note 4)	Nationality
Address (note 7)	Date of birth (note 11)
Other directorships *	

Name (note 4)	Business occupation
Previous name(s) (note 4)	Nationality
Address (note 7)	Date of birth (note 11)
Other directorships *	

AND PRESENT MEMBERS (notes 12, 13 and 14)

Account of shares				
Number of shares or amount of stock held by existing members at date of return. (notes 15 and 16)	Particulars of shares transferred since the date of the last return, or, in the case of the first return, of the incorporation of the company, by (a) persons who are still members, and (b) persons who have ceased to be members (note 17)			Remarks
	Number (note 16)	Date of registration of transfer (a)	(b)	

Form No. 9b

G

THE COMPANIES ACTS 1948 TO 1981

Notice of change of directors or secretaries or in their particulars

Pursuant to section 200 of the Companies Act 1948
as amended by section 22 of the Companies Act 1976
and section 95 of the Companies Act 1981

Please do not write in this binding margin.

To the Registrar of Companies

For official use

Company number

Please complete legibly, preferably in black type, or bold block lettering

Name of Company

Limited*

* delete if inappropriate

hereby notifies you of the following change(s):

†

† specify the change and date thereof and if this consists of the appointment of a new director or secretary complete the box below. If this space is insufficient use a continuation sheet.

Particulars of new director or secretary (see note 1)

Name (notes 2 & 3)

Business occupation ‡

Previous name(s) (note 2)

Nationality ‡

Address (notes 3 & 4)

Date of birth (where applicable) (note 5) ‡

‡ Applicable to directors only.

Other directorships ‡ +

+ Enter particulars of other directorships held or previously held (see note 6). If this space is insufficient use a continuation sheet.

I hereby consent to act as [director] [secretary] § of the above-named company

Signature Date

§ delete as appropriate

Name (notes 2 & 3)

Business occupation ‡

Previous name(s) (note 2)

Nationality ‡

Address (notes 3 & 4)

Date of birth (where applicable) (note 5) ‡

Other directorships ‡ +

I hereby consent to act as [director] [secretary] § of the above-named company

Signature Date

number of continuation sheets attached (see note 7)

Signature [Director] [Secretary] § Date

Presentor's name, address and reference (if any):

For official use
General section | Post room

G

Form No. 4a

THE COMPANIES ACTS 1948 TO 1976

Notice of change in situation of registered office

Pursuant to section 23 (3) of the Companies Act 1976

Please do not write in this binding margin

Please complete legibly, preferably in black type, or bold block lettering

To the Registrar of Companies

For official use

Company number

Name of company

*delete if inappropriate

Limited*

hereby gives you notice in accordance with section 23 (3) of the Companies Act 1976 that the situation of the registered office of the company has been changed to:

†delete as appropriate

Signed [Director] [Secretary]† Date

Presentor's name, address and reference (if any):

For official use

General section	Post room

Form No. 3a

THE COMPANIES ACTS 1948 TO 1976

Notice of new accounting reference date given after the end of an accounting reference period

Pursuant to section 3(2) of the Companies Act 1976

Please do not write in this binding margin

Please complete legibly, preferably in black type, or bold block lettering

To the Registrar of Companies

For official use

Company number

Name of company

*delete if inappropriate

Limited*

Note

Please read notes 1 to 5 overleaf before completing this form

hereby gives you notice in accordance with section 3(2) of the Companies Act 1976 that the company's new accounting reference date on which the previous accounting reference period and each subsequent accounting reference period of the company is to be treated as coming, or as having come, to an end is as shown below:

Day Month

†delete as appropriate

The previous accounting reference period of the company is to be treated as [shortened] [extended]† and [is to be treated as having come to an end] [will come to an end]† on

Day Month Year

1 9

‡delete as appropriate

The company is a [subsidiary] [holding company]‡ of ______

______

______, company number ______

the accounting reference date of which is ______

§delete as appropriate

Signed [Director] [Secretary]§ Date

Presentor's name, address and reference (if any):

For official use
General section
Post room

5. GLOSSARY OF FINANCE AND ACCOUNTING

This glossary has been extracted from Accountancy for non-accountants, Financial Accounting by Paul Norkett, published by Longman Group Ltd.

Above the line A journalistic term used to describe charges against profit.
Account A chronological record of pecuniary transactions for a specific category of income or expenditure.
Account balance The difference between the total debits and total credits in an account.
Accounting bases The methods used for applying accounting concepts.
Accounting concepts The basic assumption which underlie accounting statements.
Accounting period The time period when accounts are regularly balanced and analysed. Usually annually.
Accounting policies Statements in published accounts that explain the assumptions upon which the accounts are based.
Accounting standards A set of rules produced by the accountancy profession to reduce the variety of accounting practice and attempt to achieve consistency and comparability between the financial statements of enterprises.
Accruals Amounts due for payment at the end of an accounting period. Not trade creditors.
Added value A concept based on the basic calculation of sales less bought in materials and services.
Added value ratios A set of operating ratios based on added value.
Added value statement Usually a re-statement of the trading and profit and loss account detail that separates bought in materials and services.
Advance Corporation Tax (ACT) An amount payable in advance of the main corporation tax payment calculated of 3/7ths of dividend payments.
Amalgamation Joining together of companies.
Amortisation Often substituted for depreciation, especially by Americans. Frequently used to describe the writing down of specific assets such as a lease.
Annual General Meeting (AGM) A statutory general meeting of the company's shareholders to be held every calendar year with not more than 15 months interval between meetings.
Appropriation Usually refers to the appropriation of profits, being what is done with the profit after tax. Be certain of the distinction between appropriations and charges.
Arms length The transfer between group companies of costs and revenues at open market values.
Assets Things a business owns, leases or rents to increase its income earning potential.
Asset turnover A ratio where turnover is divided by average net assets to give some indication of capital usage.
Associate company Joined to another company by more than 20% of its issued share capital, but not controlled by it. Distinguish from subsidiary company.
Audit An independent verification of the books of account.
Audit Committee A committee usually comprising of directors not associated with finance in the company whose main function is to independently review internal control in relation to the audit report.
Audit report Most common audit report is

attached to the published accounts of limited companies in accordance with company law and accounting practice.
Audit trail A complete record of bookkeeping transaction on computer print out.
Auditor An independent person appointed by the ordinary shareholders to audit the accounts.

Bad debt provision A specific sum or percentage set aside to allow for non-payment of debts.
Balance sheet A statement of assets and liabilities.
Below the line A journalistic term used to describe appropriations of profit.
Book value Usually refers to the value of assets entered in the books of account at their depreciated historic cost. Often a meaningless value.
Bought ledger A grouping of accounts relating to goods that have been purchased.
Budget Detailed estimates of future income and/or expenditure used as a management control technique.

Capital The amount belonging to the owners of a business.
Capital allowance A tax allowance for most items of business capital expenditure. Compare with notes on depreciation and timing differences.
Capital employed Total assets minus current liabilities. The same value as Net Assets.
Capital expenditure Expenditure from which the benefit is derived for longer than one accounting period.
Capital reserves Amounts set aside for specific purposes. Some classes of capital reserve are not available for distribution.
Capitalisation factor A figure which converts income (or revenue expenditure) into a figure that is treated as capital. i.e. The P/E ratio multiplied by the historic cost earnings attributable to the ordinary shareholders produces the market value of the share.
Cash budget A calculation of expected future cash flows.
Cash flow Management of cash through a business.
Cash flow accounting A cash based accounting system that ignores many accounting concepts.
Chairman's statement The published statement by the chairman included in the annual accounts. Distinguish from directors' report.
Class rights The legal rights attached to certain classes of shares and loan stock. Mainly prevents motions being passed at the AGM that will directly affect class rights.
Computer audit program A powerful audit tool that can carry out a wide range of audit tests and enquiries on a computer data base and its associated systems.
Conglomerate An industrial or general holding company that has a diversified range of group company activities.
Conservatism A concept that requires an accountant to be a pessimist.
Consistency A concept that requires accounts to be comparable by consistent treatment of book-keeping items.
Consolidated accounts Adding together the accounts of subsidiary companies into the group company accounts.
Contingent liabilities A liability that may arise if certain events take place.
Convertible preference shares of debentures These are issued usually as convertible to ordinary shares at an agreed date on an agreed basis of valuation. They often have the alternative of cash redemption.
Corporation A legal entity that is separate from its members and can only be destroyed by a legal process.
Corporation sole An office that has perpetual existence such as the Sovereign or Bishop.
Corporation tax An amount charged on company taxable profits at 52% with relief for 'small' profits charged at 40%.
Corporate Report Name sometimes used to describe the statutory published accounts of limited companies. Also used as the title for an important document published by the accountancy profession.
Cost of Sales Purchase price of goods sold or their cost of manufacture.
Cost of sales adjustment (COSA) An inflation accounting adjustment that makes allowance for the rising cost of replacing stock.
Conversion costs Usually refers to the costs of stock that are added to the purchase costs. The costs of conversion include direct costs of production and attributable overheads to bring the product or service to its present location and condition.
Credit One side (usually on the right) of a

double entry book-keeping system. Abbreviation Cr.
Crisis policies The strategies adopted by management to quickly solve urgent problems.
Cum pref A common abbreviation for cumulative preference shares where dividend rights are carried forward if the business does not generate sufficient profits to pay during one or more years.
Current assets Mainly stock, debtors and cash.
Current cost In most instances this is the replacement cost.
Current cost accounting (CCA) An accounting system based on the valuation concept of value to the business. For practical purposes this is in most instances the current replacement cost.
Current purchasing power (CPP) A system of inflation accounting that converted historic cost accounts into units of current purchasing power by applying the retail price index in a series of calculation.
Current liabilities Short term debt mainly comprising of trade creditors and bank overdraft.

Database A structured file of basic data usually computerised that enables it to be used for a wide variety of applications.
Debenture A legal document securing loan finance. May be a fixed, or a floating charge on the assets of the business.
Debit One side of a double entry book-keeping system, usually the left. Abbreviation Dr.
Debtor A business or individual that owes another business money for goods or services supplied.
Debtor turnover The average time period for the settlement of outstanding invoices.
Deferred credit An accounting method for spreading out the receipt of income, such as government grants, over several accounting periods.
Deferred tax The difference between the financial profit and taxable profit that may become payable at a later date.
Deferred revenue expenditure Revenue expenditure that is capitalised.
Depreciation A calculation that spreads the cost of an asset over its useful life.
Deprival value A value measurement based on the net loss to a business if an asset is taken away.
De-stocking The planned reduction of stock levels to improve the cash flow.
Direct expense Costs that are directly related to production but are not in the direct material or direct labour category.
Direct labour Employees whose labour is directly related to production.
Direct materials Raw materials and sub-assemblies directly used in production.
Disaggregation The term used to describe the published division of sales profits and selected data on a geographical and product basis.
Disclosure An emotive term often substituted for reporting.
Distributions This describes what is done with the part of all of the profit after tax. It may be recorded as dividends by a company and drawings by a sole trader or partnership.
Dividends An amount paid by limited companies to their shareholders.
Dividend cover Often called the pay out ratio because it represents the amount that is paid out in dividends in relation to the company's earnings that are attributable to the ordinary shareholders.
Dividend yield An investors' ratio that represents the gross dividend paid to investors as a percentage of the market price of its ordinary shares.
Double entry A book-keeping principle where every transaction is recorded with a corresponding debit and credit entry.

Earnings per share (EPS) Profit after tax divided by the number of shares in issue.
Earnings yield Calculated by dividing the earnings per share by the share price. It is the reciprocal of the P/E ratio and represents the return on investment. (ROI)
Economic value Expected future earnings from an asset or group of assets. Also called present value and future utility.
Efficiency ratios A set of ratios used to assess specific aspects of business performance.
Employee accounts Accounts prepared specifically for employees. Distinguish from employment report.
Employee ratios A set of ratios that use the number of employees or aggregate employee remuneration as a basis for the calculations.
Employment report A report about employees included in the published accounts. Distinguish from employee accounts.

Employee shares A class of shareholding often representing a form of incentive payment to employees that does not significantly affect the company's cash flow.
Entity An accounting concept that assumes a business is completely separate from its owners.
Equity interests The amount belonging to the owners of the business.
Equity method of accounting When an investment in a company is shown in the consolidated balance sheet at the cost of the investment with some adjustments.
Exempt private company A privileged category of private company abolished by the 1967 Companies Act.
Exposure draft (ED) A discussion document issued by the Accounting Standards Committee for comment as part of the process of producing an accounting standard.
External reporting Reporting to people outside the business. Mainly creditors, the public and the government. Sometimes used for reporting to shareholders.
Extraordinary general meeting (EGM) A general meeting of a company called by-the directors or by more than 10% of the voting share capital holders which is not the annual general meeting (AGM).
Extraordinary items (extraordinary gains/profits or losses) Significant items of income, expenditure or profit that arise from events outside the normal trading activities of the business.

Final accounts The accounts drawn up at the end of an accounting period. Usually refers to the profit and loss account and balance sheet at the end of the financial year.
Finance leases A lease arranged to last of the entire useful life of the asset. Distinguish from operating leases.
Financial gearing Relationship of debt to equity.
Financial lease A lease arrange to last for the whole useful life of an asset.
Financial ratios A set of ratios that attempt to measure a business's ability to meet its short term debt and assess its financial structure.
Financial year A year based on the financial accounting period. Usual year endings are: 31st March or 31st December.
Franked Income The receipt of dividend payments from a UK company by a UK company.
Franked payments Payments of dividends by a UK company to UK residents or companies.
Funds statement A statement that shows where a business got its funds from and how they were used during the accounting period.
Future prospects statement Proposals that published accounts should give more detail about the future prospects of the company.
Future utility A value measurement based on the future discounted net earnings of an asset or group of assets.

Gearing adjustment An inflation accounting adjustment related to the level of long term debt held by a business.
General ledger A grouping of accounts not related to trade purchases or sales. Sometimes called the nominal ledger.
Going concern An accounting concept that assumes that a business has a continuing existence.
Going concern value A method of valuing a business on a going concern assumption. Usually calculated by estimating future profits or net cash flows for a number of years into the future.
Goodwill An intangible asset representing the difference between the going concern value and asset value of a business.
Gross margin Gross profit as a percentage of sales.
Gross profit Sales less cost of sales. Calculated in the trading account.
Group accounts The adding together of the subsidiary companies' accounts into consolidated financial statements.
Guarantee company A limited company where members do not subscribe the initial capital, they guarantee funds will be available if the company is wound up.

Hardware The tangible parts of a computer system including the central processing unit, input/output devices and backing storage.
Hidden gearing Financial arrangements that do not affect the debt equity relationship. For example leaving assets instead of purchasing them.
Highlights of the year statement A quick reference statement containing selected data about a company's annual accounts.
Hire purchase A method of financing the acquisition of assets where title does not pass until the option to purchase is paid.

Hiring A form of bailment for the short term use of assets. Title does not pass.
Historic cost Exchange value at a past point in time.
Historical summaries Published statements included in the annual accounts that provide a five to ten year summary of profits, sales and other selected data.
Holding gain The gain arising from holding stock during a period of rising prices. The gain may be realised or unrealised.
Horizontal integration Amalgamation of companies that reduces competition.
Hyde proposals A set of interim proposals for inflation accounting in the UK during 1977.

Imputation system An aspect of corporation tax that allows the recipients of dividends to receive the full amount plus a tax credit equal to the standard rate of income tax. See also franked income and franked payments.
In house indices An index constructed by a business for management purposes and inflation accounting.
Income flows The measurement of the flow of income through a business based on accounting conventions.
Income statement A presentation of the profit/loss calculation.
Indexation Relates to calculations that usally apply a form of price index to historic cost figures.
Indirect expense Costs not directly related to production.
Inflation A general rise in prices or conversely a fall in the general purchasing power of money. Distinguish from relative price rises which are a function of resource allocation.
Inflation accounting A system of accounting that makes adjustments for the effect of rising prices.
Intangible assets Assets that cannot be easily quantified or valued and therefore rarely appear in the accounts.
Interest An amount payable or receivable usually calculated on a percentage of money owed to or by a business.
Interim accounts Accounts drawn up for a time period less than the usual annual accounting period. The most common interim accounts are the six monthly accounts required for listed companies.
Internal audit An independent appraisal activity within an organisation for the review of operations as a service to management.
Internal check An auditing term for a system of organising work so that no one member of staff has control over a complete set of transactions.
Internal control A broad auditing term that describes the complete system of organisation and record keeping in a business from the viewpoint of reliability of records and prevention of fraud.
Internal control letter An important audit letter bringing to the directors' attention significant internal control weaknesses that exist in the business.
Internal reporting Reporting to people inside the business, mainly to management, employees and employee represenatives.
International accounting standard (IAS) Accounting standards issued by an international accounting standards committee (IASC) with the objective of harmonising accounting practice in different countries. Not binding on UK accounting practice, they only have a persuasive influence.
Inventories Usually combines stock and work in progress. The closing inventory is entered in the balance sheet and opening and closing inventories in the income calculation.
Investor ratios A set of ratios that attempt to assess the future performance of a business mainly based on market expectations.
Invoice A document stating amount due for payment for goods and/or services rendered together with the terms of payment.

Leasing A method of acquiring the use of assets where title does not pass.
Ledger A grouping of accounts: for example a sales ledger would include all the sales accounts. The ledger may be in a book or a computer file.
Lessee A business or individual that acquires the use of an asset through leasing arrangements.
Lessor An individual or business that leases an asset or assets to other individuals or businesses.
Letter of representation A statement written and signed by the directors providing details about the company's assets and liabilities required by the statutory auditors.
Leverage Refer to operational leverage.
Liabilites What a business owes. They are broadly divided in the balance sheet into short term (current liabilities) and long term (capital).
Limited company May be public or private. Shareholders liability is limited to investment.
Limited partnership A partnership where one

or more of the partners liability is limited to their capital input. At least one partner must have unlimited liability.
Liquidation value The value of a business calculated by deducting total debt from the estimated net realiseable value of all the assets.
Liquidity A general term used to describe the short term cash position of a business. See liquidity ratios.
Liquidity ratios The main ratios take the relationship of current assets, or part of the current assets, to current liabilities.
Listed company A public company quoted on the Stock Exchange. Also called a quoted company.
Loan capital Long term debt such as debentures.

Macro-economic The study of large scale activity such as National Income and Expenditure.
Mainstream corporation tax (MCT) The balance of corporation tax payable after ACT and deferred tax calculations.
Manufacturing account An account that totals the cost of manufacturing for an accounting period.
Manufacturing period A notional profit usually based on the costs of manufacture.
Margin Usually used to describe a percentage level of profit which can be a gross or net margin. Also distinguish between margin and mark-up.
Mark-up A percentage calculation using the cost price as the denominator whereas the margin calculations use the selling price as the denominator. Mainly used by retailers.
Market capitalisation The number of ordinary shares in issue multiplied by the market value per share.
Matching A concept that requires costs and revenues to be matched in discrete accounting periods.
Materiality A concept that allows accounting rules to be relaxed because the amount involved is considered insignificant and not material to the accounts.
Micro-economic The study of small scale activity such as single business units.
Minimum lending rate (MLR) A guideline for the general level of interest rates in the UK based on the average discount rate for treasury bills.
Minority interest. The portion of a subsidiary company that the holding company does not own.
Monetary adjustments The adjustment of cash or debt to allow for the change in the general purchasing power of money.
Monetary items A general term used in inflation accounting when referring to cash, cash equivalents and debt that are likely to be affected by a change in the general purchasing power of money.
Monetary working capital adjustment (MWCA) An inflation accounting adjustment to monetary items that makes an allowance for a change in the general purchasing power of money.

Negative interest rate Refers to a rate of interest that is below the rate of inflation and therefore does not compensate for the loss in the general purchasing power of money.
Negotiated disclosure A form of reporting arising from the legal rights of trade unions to demand informaiton for collective bargaining.
Net assets Current assets minus current liabilities plus fixed assets. Same value as capital employed.
Net liquid funds Cash and cash equivalents. Such as short term investments less bank overdraft and other short term borrowings.
Net margin Net profit before tax and interest as a percentage of sales.
Net profit/loss Gross profit less expenses. Can be net profit before tax or after tax. Note also the adjustments for extraordinary items and minority interests.
Net realiseable value Sales value of an asset less the costs of disposal.
Netting off A common method of reducing (sometimes concealing) the detail in published accounts. Cost and revenues or movements of funds are netted off against each other and only the balancing figure is shown.
Nominal ledger A grouping of accounts not related to trade purchases or sales. Some times called the General ledger.
Nominal value Usually refers to the legal value of a share. Distinguish from market value.
Objectivity A concept that accounts should be based on facts that can be objectively measured, recorded and audited.
Off balance sheet finance Acquiring the use of assets and finance that does not appear on the balance sheet.
Operating gains Sales value less current replacement cost of goods sold.

Operating leases When the lease period is for a period shorter than the asset's life and lease payments are based on the assumption of re-leasing the asset.
Operating ratios A wide range of ratios that are used to assess business performance.
Operational leverage The level of fixed costs in relation to total costs of expected levels of output. Often illustrated with a break even chart.
Optimal capital structure A debt equity mix where the average cost of capital is minimised.
Ordinary shares A class of share capital representing the ultimate power in a company. This power may be exercised at the Annual General Meeting (AGM) but this rarely occurs.
Overheads Costs that are not directly attributable to a specific product or service and tend to be fixed or semi-fixed in nature.
Overtrading When the growth in sales is not safely financed from internally generated funds and/or secured manageable loans.

Par value Refers to the legal value of a share. Often called nominal value. Distinguish from market value.
Participating preference shares Class rights attached to certain preference shares that allows the holders to participate in the benefit arising from high profits.
Partnership Two or more people engaged in business together without forming a company.
Payroll An accounting system that records and analyses the different parts of wages such as tax and national insurance payments.
Preference shares A class of share capital that has preferential treatment for the payment of dividends and return of capital in the event of liquidation.
Prepayments Amounts that have been paid in advance at the end of an accounting period.
Present value Expected future earnings from an asset or group of assets. Also called future utility and economic value.
Price/Earnings ratio An important investor ratio that is the number of years earnings represented by the share price.
Prime cost Total direct costs incurred in manufacture.
Prior year adjustment These are material accounting adjustments necessary to accounts from earlier periods arising from changes in accounting policies or correction of fundamental errors.
Private company A registered company with legal limitations on the sale of its shares and the maximum number of members.
Private ledger A grouping of confidential accounts.
Proprietary company A private limited company with some legal privileges.
Profit Total revenue minus total cost.
Provision A sum set aside in the accounts to meet a specific contingency. This is not necessarily represented by cash.
Public corporation A corporation created by a public Act of Parliament.
Published accounts The accounts of companies that are sent to shareholders and filed with the Register of Companies.

Qualified audit report A statement by the statutory auditor that can range from saying that an opinion cannot be formed due to the inadequacy of the underlying records to a technical qualification based on non-compliance with an accounting standard.
Quoted company A public company with Stock Exchange quotation. Also called a listed company.
Quoted investments Holdings of shares that are listed on the Stock Exchange and can usually be quickly converted into cash. Distinguish from shareholdings in subsidiary and associate companies where they are not quickly convertible into cash.

Ratios The relationship between two or more figures that enable the effects of scale to be removed.
Realiseable value A measurement of value based on the sales value less costs of disposal.
Realisation An accounting concept that should prevent accountants entering revenue in the accounts until it has been realised, usually invoiced.
Realised profits (realised gains) The difference between the selling price when sold and the replacement one.
Redeemable The term used to describe preference shares or debentures that have a specified redemption date(s) when the principal is due for repayment by the company.
Replacement cost A measurement of value based on the cost of replacement.
Retail price index (RPI) A very important general index calculated on average

household expenditure. Often used to represent the general purchasing power of money and living standards.
Retained profit Net profit after tax less appropriations. Can be retained profit c/fwd or b/fwd, be certain of the difference.
Reserves Amounts of 'book profit' retained in a business for specific or general purposes. It is not necessarily represented by cash.
Retentions It is the portion of the after tax profit that is not distributed.
Return on capital employed Profit before tax, interest, extraordinary items and minority interests divided by average capital employed.
Return on investment The earnings an investor receives on the investment, usually called earnings yield. Distinguish from return on capital employed.
Revenue expenditure Where the benefit is consumed during one accounting period. Also see capital expenditure.
Revenue reserves Amounts of profit retained for general use in the business. No legal restrictions on their use for distribution.

Sandlands Report The report of a government committee of enquiry (1974) on inflation accounting that advocated a system of current cost accounting.
Secret reserves Reserves that do not appear in the balance sheet.
Share capital The issued share capital represents the ownership of the company. Distinguish between authorised and issued share capital.
Share premium The difference between the sales value and nominal value of an ordinary share.
Simplified financial statements Written for the non-financial reader with an option to receive the full set of published accounts.
Software A computer programme. Also see hardware.
Sole trader A person engaged in business on his/her own.
Sources and applications of funds A statement recording the movement of funds through a business over an accounting period.
Specific indices A very wide range of indices mostly using the wholesale price index as a base and grouped according to the Standard Industrial Classified. Two main types used for inflation accounting: asset specific and industry specific.
Statements of Standard Accounting Practice (SSAP) See accounting standard.
Statutory audit A legal requirement that the accounts of limited companies should have an annual audit by approved auditors.
Statutory company A company created by a special Act of Parliament.
Stewardship reporting Reporting to the owners.
Stock Exchange Commission A regulatory body in the USA for investor protection.
Stock Exchange Council A self governing regulatory body in the UK for investor protection.
Stock relief A calculation based on the increased costs for replacing stock that provides some relief from the tax burden.
Stock turnover The average length of time that stock remains in the stores.
Subsidiary company A company that is controlled by another company through share ownership and the board of directors.
Supplementary statements Statements included in annual reports that are not legally required and usually not audited.
Surplus The same as profit.

Take over bid When one company attempts to buy a controlling interest in another company.
Tax and price index (TPI) A general index supposed to show the combined effect of changes in prices and taxes on the average UK household.
Taxation An amount payable to the government calculated on income, profits or sales.
Tax avoidance This is a legal game played between accountants/lawyers and the inland Revenue and is the arrangement of affairs in such a way as to reduce tax liability. Sometimes called tax planning. Distinguish from tax evasion.
Tax evasion The falsification of accounts that understates revenue or overstates costs so as to reduce the impact of taxation. This is illegal.
Test pack An audit tool comprising of a set of test data that is passed through the system to test system reliability.
Timing differences This usually refers to the difference between the financial and taxable profit due to the timing differences arising from depreciation and capital allowances.
Total gains concept The total gains (or losses)

made by a business during an accounting period divided into realised, unrealised, holding and operating gains.
Trade creditors Trade suppliers that provide a business with goods and/or services on credit.
Trade debtors Customers who have received goods on credit.
Trial balance A listing of all the debit and credit balances in a book-keeping system.
True and fair view An important legal requirement for published company accounts to give a true and fair view of the underlying records and the state of the business.
Turnover The total income received by a business during an accounting period. Not necessarily the same as sales because there may be other sources of income.

Unincorporated association An organisation without a separate legal identity.
Unlimited company An organisation with a separate legal identity but members do not have limited liability.
Unlisted security Shares that do not have a stock exchange quotation.
Unrealised profit (unrealised gains) The difference between the current sales value and current replacement cost of goods not sold.

Valuation model The basis for measuring value. The most well known is the historic cost valuation model.
Value added tax A form of sales tax collected on an added value basis by businesses where the final user bears the tax burden.
Value to the business A value concept explained in the Sandilands report as an alternative to historic cost.
Verification An audit function that is to ensure that the recorded assets and liabilities actually exist and details such as valuation are correct.
Vertical balance sheet A balance sheet layout where assets are usually listed above liabilities instead of the traditional layout of liabilities on the left and assets on the right. (The reverse in the USA).
Vertical integration Amalgamation of companies to secure supplies and/or distribution and benefit from the economies of scale.
Vouching An audit technique that examines documentary evidence to support the authenticity of transactions.

Work in progress Partly finished goods passing through the manufacturing process.
Working capital Current assets minus current liabilities. Also called net current assets.
Working capital cycle The amount of time it takes for cash to pass through the working capital of the business from stock and back to cash.

Two further books by Paul Norkett that will enable the non-accountant who needs to understand accountancy to do just that.

Accountancy for Non-Accountants: Financial Accounting

— Enables the reader to understand and interpret published accounts.

— Gives broad coverage with emphasis on the profit and loss accounts and the balance sheet.

— Clean, simple style.

— Glossary of accounting terminology plus readers' guide for quick reference.

— Explains accountancy jargon.

Accountancy for Non-Accountants: Management Accounting

— Assumes no specialist accounting knowledge.

— Discusses the principle of planning and control.

— Explains the techniques of tactical and strategic decision making.